The European Football Championship

Millennium: Journal of International Studies
The London School of Economics
and Political Science
Houghton Street
London   WC2A 2AE
E-mail: Millennium@lse.ac.uk
Web site: http://www.e-millennium.ac

Football Research in an Enlarged Europe

Series Editors:
Albrecht Sonntag, Professor and Director of the EU-Asia Institute at the ESSCA School of Management, France
David Ranc, Assistant Professor at the EU-Asia Institute at the ESSCA School of Management, France

Titles include:

Football Research in an Enlarged Europe
Series Standing Order ISBN 978-1-137-37972-6 Hardback
978-1-137-37973-3 Paperback
(*outside North America only*)

You can receive future titles in this series as they are published by placing a standing order. Please contact your bookseller or, in case of difficulty, write to us at the address below with your name and address, the title of the series and the ISBN quoted above.

Customer Services Department, Macmillan Distribution Ltd, Houndmills, Basingstoke, Hampshire RG21 6XS, England

The European Football Championship

Mega-Event and Vanity Fair

Edited by

Başak Alpan
Middle East Technical University, Turkey

Alexandra Schwell
University of Vienna, Austria

Albrecht Sonntag
ESSCA School of Management, France

First published 2015 by
PALGRAVE MACMILLAN

Palgrave Macmillan in the UK is an imprint of Macmillan Publishers Limited,
registered in England, company number 785998, of Houndmills, Basingstoke,
Hampshire RG21 6XS.

Palgrave Macmillan in the US is a division of St Martin's Press LLC,
175 Fifth Avenue, New York, NY 10010.

Palgrave Macmillan is the global academic imprint of the above companies
and has companies and representatives throughout the world.

Palgrave® and Macmillan® are registered trademarks in the United States,
the United Kingdom, Europe and other countries.

ISBN 978–1–137–45505–5

This book is printed on paper suitable for recycling and made from fully
managed and sustained forest sources. Logging, pulping and manufacturing
processes are expected to conform to the environmental regulations of the
country of origin.

A catalogue record for this book is available from the British Library.

A catalog record for this book is available from the Library of Congress.

Contents

vi *Contents*

Preface

Albrecht Sonntag

> *Vanity Fair, where you light on the strangest contrasts laughable and tearful: where you may be gentle and pathetic, or savage and cynical with perfect propriety...*
>
> William Makepeace Thackeray,
> *Vanity Fair*, Chapter XVII

In the middle of the 19th century, William Makepeace Thackeray published a long serialised novel in the satirical magazine *Punch*, which he named *Vanity Fair*. He borrowed his title from John Bunyan's allegory *The Pilgrim's Progress* (1678), where 'Vanity Fair' is one of the stations on the journey of redemption towards the 'Celestial City'. It may be assumed that Thackeray chose this title because it allowed him to provide a snappy résumé of his vision of the human condition while at the same time positioning himself as a detached and sarcastic observer of the human species, made up of individuals frantically running around in their absurd search for self-esteem and pride.

What would he say today on watching an event like the European football championship? Would he observe, as in Thackeray's famous novel, a 'vain, wicked, foolish place, full of all sorts of humbugs and falsenesses and pretensions' or would he be inclined to show leniency in his judgement? Would he point out, with the biting irony that characterised his writing, the excessive proportions of this mega-event? Would he see nothing but a great bustling fair of stereotypes, a carnival of emotions shamelessly unleashed in public, a festival of the permanently noisy display of imaginary loyalties, to use his words, a 'Vanity Fair of performances, representations, and identities'?

Or would he detect, behind the Babylonian confusion, the joyful celebration of an extraordinary game and the simple pleasure of the masses in finding themselves, for once, united by shared passion?

Thackeray never knew modern football. He died aged fifty-two in December 1863 in London. By coincidence, at the other end of town, eleven representatives of pioneering football clubs and schools were about to come to an agreement on the rules of this new game which they had set out to codify a few weeks earlier. If he had attended one of their meetings at the Freemasons' Tavern in Covent Garden, could he only have imagined what kind of 'vanity fair' this new sport would produce over a century later?

It is perfectly possible, though, that the Victorian novelist, had he been miraculously 'beamed' to the Poland of 2012, would not have felt out of place. After all, he certainly was, together with the London society of his time and his famous contemporaries Charles Dickens, Charlotte Brontë and Lewis Carroll, an enthusiastic visitor to the Great Exhibition of 1851, the first ever 'World Fair'. A genuine mega-event *avant la lettre*, this was hosted in the spectacular 'Crystal Palace', which received its nickname in the satirical pages of *Punch*, where Thackeray had just published his novel. One may therefore assume that the great writer would readily engage in addressing parallels between the 'Great Exhibition' of 1851 and the great European football exhibition of 2012. Both can be perceived as great opportunities for the host nations to showcase their achievements and indulge in a good dose of self-celebration – a 'Vanity Fair' in the crudest sense of the word. He would no doubt be impressed by the number of travellers converging on the host cities from all over the continent. True, he might be intrigued by the fact that the centre of interest of this huge fair was only a ball game, and a rather simple one at that. But then again, would it not only be logical that the industrial machines and inventions of the 19th century were finally replaced as the object of worship by something even more trivial or 'vain'? As a matter of fact, it would only strengthen his point about the inherent stupidity of mankind, a vision that left him, in his own words, 'more melancholy than mirthful'.

It is striking to see the extent to which the great literary works of the 19th and early 20th centuries provide us with keys for the understanding of contemporary society. If these novels and their characters still have something to say about the society we are living in, it is not only because their authors had outstanding skills of psychological empathy with their protagonists, but also because the psycho-social programming of the human mind, its desires, fears and aspirations, do not seem to have changed that much since the days of Thackeray. Large social groups still have the same hunger for collective pride, which is still mainly satisfied through identification with the nation-state. They still have the same need for the 'social self-love' that Emile Durkheim considered inseparable from the very existence of nation-states; they still have the same urge to claim their community's singularity that Isaiah Berlin identified as one of the most irrepressible drives of modern history.

This book brings together seven different accounts of visitors to the 'Vanity Fair of European Football' that took place in Poland and Ukraine in the summer of 2012. What they have in common, despite their different national origins and their respective focuses of interest, is the impression of witnessing a period of transition and uncertainty. A period in which feelings of belonging are still framed by the stronghold of national identity, but where loyalties and identifications, as well as dominant ideologies, are permanently negotiated and even publicly debated. A moment in time in which representations of self and Other are increasingly fluid, but where 'blind spots' stubbornly persist. It is a phase in which collective stereotypes, self-perceptions and 'vanities' are considerably weakened by large-scale phenomena like migration, cultural globalisation and supranational integration.

The 'Vanity Fair of European Football' thus reveals itself as an ideal laboratory for the social scientist, where individuals and groups converge to redefine themselves and interact with each other, where, as Thackeray said, 'the strangest contrasts laughable and tearful' are laid out before the eyes of the researcher.

Contributors

Başak Alpan is an Assistant Professor and a Lecturer in European Politics and Political Sociology at the Department of Political Science and Public Administration, at the Middle East Technical University, Ankara, Turkey. She holds a PhD from the University of Birmingham, UK, with her research on the Turkish discourses on 'Europe'. She conducts research and writes extensively on European integration, discourse theory, post-structuralism, Turkish-EU Relations and football and identity. She currently works as a researcher in an FP7 project, titled, 'FREE-Football Research in an Enlarged Europe', which aims at contributing to a better understanding of football as a highly relevant social and cultural phenomenon in contemporary Europe.

Michał Buchowski is a Professor in the Department of Ethnology and Cultural Anthropology at the Adam Mickiewicz University in Poznań and holds the Chair of Comparative Central European Studies at the European University Viadrina in Frankfurt (Oder). His scientific interest lies in anthropological theories and Central European postsocialist cultural and social transformations. Michal has published over a hundred articles as well as books, among which are *English Reluctant Capitalists, The Rational Other* and *Rethinking Transformation* (in Polish). He has served as the President of the European Association of Social Anthropologists and is currently chairing the World Council of Anthropological Associations.

Małgorzata Kowalska is a PhD Researcher in the Department of Ethnology and Cultural Anthropology at the Adam Mickiewicz University, where she works for the FREE project. She conducts ethnographic fieldwork in Poznań and writes her thesis at the European University Viadrina in Frankfurt (Oder). Her PhD thesis revolves around the topic of mega-events as promotional vehicles for competing cities and as triggers of social change. Before her PhD, Malgorzata worked for several years in public relations and marketing in companies in Ireland and Poland, where she developed her interest in the anthropology of political economies in general.

Yağmur Nuhrat was born and raised in Istanbul. She completed her undergraduate studies in sociology at Bogaziçi University after which she moved to Providence, Rhode Island, to enrol at Brown University's graduate program in anthropology. Upon completing her MA thesis in 2008 on the subject of receiving migration in Istanbul, she went on to study the concept of fairness and fair play in football in Turkey. In 2013 she earned her PhD in this field at Brown. She currently resides in Istanbul, teaching part-time at Sabanci University and working at an independent social research company, SAM Research and Consulting.

Alexandra Schwell is an Assistant Professor in the Department of European Ethnology, University of Vienna. She obtained her PhD in Comparative Cultural and Social Anthropology in 2007 from the European University Viadrina in Frankfurt (Oder). Research interests include border studies, Eastern Europe, anthropology of security and the state, football, and European integration. Furthermore, she is also a part of the FREE project, where she leads the Work Package, 'The Anthropology of European Football: Fusions and Fissions'. Alexandra has published several journal articles on Europeanisation, borders, and security discourses and practices.

Özgehan Şenyuva teaches at the Department of International Relations at the Middle East Technical University, Ankara, Turkey. He holds a PhD in political science from the Centre for the Study of Political Change at the Università Degli Studi di Siena, which focuses on Turkish public opinion and the EU. He previously worked for the FP6 research project, 'Integrated and United? A Quest for Citizenship in an Ever Closer Europe'. Özgehan has extensive knowledge of quantitative research methodologies and measurement and, within the FREE resarch project, he coordinates the collection and processing of comparative cross-national data on public opinion about European football.

Albrecht Sonntag is a Professor and the Director of the Centre for European Integration at ESSCA School of Management, Angers, France. His recent research focuses on issues of identity construction such as collective memory, political symbolism and political emotions. He is currently the project coordinator of the FP-7 project, 'FREE-Football Research in an Enlarged Europe'. Among many, he is the author of a book on the impact of football in contemporary identity-construction processes, *Les identités du football européen*, which was awarded the prize for the best football book 2008 by the French Union of Professional Football Clubs.

Nina Szogs studied European Ethnology, Conflict Studies and Russian Philology at Marburg, Giessen and Kazan Universities. After graduation, she worked for an international human rights organisation in Berlin. Subsequently she started her PhD research on football fan identities, migration and mobility at Vienna University as part of the FREE project. Her doctoral thesis focuses on fan identities and migration, which aims at understanding the consequences of an increasing mobility within Europe and the ties of transnational fan networks. In particular, she looks into the impact that exclusion and inclusion patterns within the everyday lives of Galatasaray and Fenerbahçe fans in Vienna.

1
Introduction

Negotiating Europeanness: the Euro 2012 Championship and Spectator Narratives in an Enlarged European Perspective

Başak Alpan and Alexandra Schwell

Football and the constitution, performance and negotiation of identities

In June 2012 teams and supporters from all over Europe and beyond gathered in Poland and Ukraine to attend the UEFA European Football Championship. Sixteen national teams, including the hosts, qualified for what was to be the first European championship to take place in post-socialist Europe. While some football-crazy countries such as Turkey did not qualify, the media in the countries that did soon bowed their heads in sorrow: would Poland and Ukraine be capable of organising such a challenging event? And, more importantly, would they be able to ensure that visitors could survive the trip to the 'Wild East'? Not only international observers, but also local populations, put the host countries under scrutiny. The critics questioned the huge public spending and the effect this had on the weakest members of society.

Such critical anticipations have become a recurrent feature of football mega-events. Each of them, depending on the international perception of the host, is different in the expectations, fears and warnings that it raises. For instance, the main narrative that underpinned the 2010 FIFA World Cup in South Africa was the expectation that the World Cup would be a catalyst for 'bringing the nation together' (Bolsmann, 2014; Ottosen et al., 2011). Indeed, after the end of the apartheid regime and the transition to multi-party politics in 1994, the 2010 World Cup gave a message of reconciliation, nationhood, and unity. At the same time, there were repeated warnings about security risks and (somewhat condescending) concerns about the young state's capacity to be up to the organisational and logistical challenge of such an event.

Four years later, the fears and warnings raised by the 2014 FIFA World Cup in Brazil focused on the social protest movements against the costs of the event (and, more generally, against budgetary priorities of the government and widespread corruption) that had occurred during the 2013 Confederations Cup. Depending on ideological attitudes, some were concerned that the tournament might be seriously disturbed if not put to a halt altogether by the protesters, while others feared that the event would be well organised, but only at the costs of police brutality that would cast a lasting shadow on what was supposed to be a celebration of the host country.

As for Euro 2012, according to Yatsyk, the event was initially represented as a de-bordering project aimed at demonstrating the opportunities for co-hosting a mega-event by an EU member state (Poland) and its neighbour eager to move closer to the European normative order (Ukraine). In early 2012, however, the sharpening of the normative and value-driven issues in EU–Ukraine relations (in particular, the debate on the liberation of Iulia Timoshenko) led to the portrayal of Ukraine as a country drifting away from European standards and governed by a corrupt and undemocratic regime, which fortified the symbolic and political contrast between Ukraine and Poland (Yatsyk, 2014).

What these football mega-events, beyond the country-specific risks, apprehensions and warnings, all have in common is that they bring to light questions of longing and belonging, of loyalties and rivalries, of identity and alterity, issues that in everyday life often go unquestioned and tend to operate in the background. During a tournament, there is no diplomatic courtesy or polite behaviour. The concept of 'may the best team win!' does not exist. It is either black or white, unconditionally and wholeheartedly. If your team is not playing tonight, or if it has – God forbid – dropped out altogether, then you are again faced with the dilemma: who to support?

Football is a sport highly charged with emotions and because it is a social arena where various social forces culminate and are negotiated it has for a long time attracted scholarly attention from various fields and disciplines. This volume mainly stems from an attempt to delve into football as a realm of constructing and negotiating identities. In this respect, we aim to problematise three main phenomena:

1. The relationship between national football and national identity formation.
2. Europeanisation and transnationalisation of football and football identities.
3. The transcendence of borders of the European Union by the European football space, which renders 'Europe' a fruitful laboratory to attest practices/modalities of Orientalism within Europe itself (that is, 'intra-European Orientalism').

The notion of Orientalism was originally developed by Edward Said (1979). Orientalism refers to a set of practices, narratives, discourses and imaginaries which the West constructs about the Orient with the primary aim to define its own 'self' against this 'Other'. According to Said, the Orient has thus helped to define Europe (or the West) as its contrasting image, idea, personality, experience (Said, 1979). However, the relations between the West and the Orientalised are much more complex. Gerd Baumann explains that 'Orientalism is thus not a simple binary opposition of "us = good" and "them = bad", but a very shrewd mirrored reversal of "what is good in us is [still] bad in them, but what got twisted in us [still] remains straight in them"' (Baumann, 2004, p. 20). As will be argued by Schwell in Chapter 2, Orientalising practices aptly describe the relationships between various social groups, for example between nation-states in Europe, but also within societies.

Thus, *The European Football Championship: Mega Event and Vanity Fair* pays special attention to the ways in which football appears as an identificatory and transformatory tool. Central to this understanding is, not surprisingly, the concept of 'identity'. The authors in this volume refer to identities as endless, relational, and contingent phenomena that are constantly under construction, where different subjects are grouped together under two diametrically opposed entities: an *Other*, which confronts a *Self*. This points to the incomplete, open and negotiable character of every identity (Laclau and Mouffe, 1985, p. 104). According to Stuart Hall, the concept of 'identity' does not, as in the past, specify a stable core of the 'Self' which develops to completion and endures social and historical changes. Modern times, Hall argues, brought about a fragmentation of identity, and at times a split identity, which is embodied in various, even contrasting, practices (Hall, 1996, pp. 5–6). Football identities are no exception.

What is in question here are not objective realities, but instead performances, subjectivities and discursive constructions in determining who is in versus who is out and who is perceived as a football supporter – in both male and female cases. Football supporters create their identities in a performance of the Self – a kind of 'doing football fandom'. In a Foucauldian sense, discursive construction constitutes the football supporter as a subject (Foucault, 1982). We contend that, even in a postmodern world, football supporter identities are not fluid and entirely open to negotiations. Similar to what Judith Butler has argued in regard to gender, identity categories become socially fixed and are reproduced and incorporated, they become part of the actor's own bodily experience (Butler, 1991). This is exactly what the contributions by Schwell, Szogs, as well as Buchowski and Kowalska debate in this volume. Drawing upon ethnographic fieldwork in Poland and Germany, the authors aim to capture how an international and extensively regulated event such as Euro 2012 constitutes football subjects and emerges as a performance. An actor-centred and praxeological focus on the 'doing' of football identities allows us to perceive identities as the focal point of various influences. Identities are negotiable and open for interpretation by the actors themselves, who use them to construct their strategies of action. In this respect, the main question that the authors discuss is how football identities are constituted, performed, and negotiated.

The marketplace of fan identities

Football identities are subject to both top-down and bottom-up influences. On the one hand clubs and national teams make offers for identification and provide an important framework for experiences but, on the other hand and more importantly, fans organise and construct their fan identities from below. Fans actively use, reframe, interpret and subvert signs, symbols, language and images of self and other. By creating their own social systems, fans also invent rituals and traditions. It is the football identities from below which invigorate the game and fill it with life beyond the restricted and increasingly restrictive space of the stadium. While already existing cultural identities are reflected and negotiated, 'football is also an important site at which new cultural identities are created, and existing ones are reproduced and potentially transformed' (Feixa and Juris, 2000, p. 206). This does not take place in an isolated manner, but is instead facilitated by new media, such as the Internet and social networks, through complex networks, ties and connections. Across national boundaries, particularly in Europe, fan friendship communities have a long and remarkably stable history. The mental maps of football fandom are not restricted to local and national rivalries but run transversal and cross, sometimes also unexpectedly, national boundaries.

Without any doubt, loyalties can shift. The marketplace of fan identities, where one can choose the various aspects of his/her fan identity, is not entirely liberalised. The decision to support a team (and thus reject another) is strongly influenced by factors that must be included in the analysis. Those factors are socio-cultural and historical, as well as political and involving class identities.

Shifting and reconstructed identities do not exist in an ideational vacuum. Similar to how a *bricolage* is not forged from scratch but rather draws upon and chooses from pre-existing components, a football fan identity draws upon cognitive patterns that shape his/her images of Self and Other (Lévi-Strauss, 1966). Using Evans-Pritchard's research on the Nuer's social organisation, Baumann argues that the logic of segmentation in the organisation of identity, alterity and coalition-building leads to a structure which 'resembles that of a football league, or rather, the football fans, for while clubs do not usually merge or split up, fans do' (Baumann, 2004, p. 22). Supporters from two separate villages might be bitter enemies, but they might easily unite on a higher level, for example when their local selection plays the neighbouring district's champion. Likewise, support for the national team in international tournaments can temporarily unite fans by suspending lower-level rivalries. In agreement with Baumann we go beyond the very formalistic model of Evans-Pritchard and contend that football supporters' everyday lives and loyalties are much more complex.

While traditional research on football has already extensively elaborated on national fan loyalties, it is important to pay attention to the largely under-researched realm of shifting loyalties. In the case of a national team not participating or dropping out early, most spectators will choose another team to support, even if it is only temporary. This highly contextual identification process does not happen independently. Personal experiences, historical and socio-cultural narratives, media representations, and corresponding stereotypes and prejudices all create and legitimatise loyalties and denegation. In their contribution to this volume, Alpan and Şenyuva (Chapter 4) show how national stereotypes, concerning the Euro 2008 and Euro 2012 championships in Turkey, were placed into the newspaper commentaries. The Self–Other nexus also plays a significant role within this contextual identification process. While the use of national stereotypes is considered normal and acceptable for Turkish newspapers, it created negative reactions and resentment when other European newspapers used similar discourses about Turkey.

Shifting loyalties are also likely to appear within the context of migration, be it in the form of migrant footballers, as is thoroughly scrutinized by Sonntag and Nuhrat in their respective chapters in this volume (5 and 6), or cultural integration of migrants to the host country's culture. The intensification of multi-directional migratory movements and shifting citizenship affiliations also lead to the iteration and reiteration of football identities.

National identities in the wake of transnationalisation and globalisation of football

In recent years transnationalisation of football identities and transnational identification at supporter and spectator levels have increased dramatically. Thanks to satellite technology, growing intensity of transnational events such as European championships and World Cups, increased global mobility of football players and fans, and global marketing of teams, football may be referred to as the 'global game' (Giulianotti, 1999; Giulianotti and Robertson, 2004). Football is indeed an excellent tool for understanding the unfolding of globalisation processes in the final decades of the 20th century and the beginning of the 21st century because the markers of the latter, such as increasing mobility, transnational communication, formal and informal networks, exchange of information, all have a direct impact on how football events are exercised and represented. Last decade the journal *Global Networks* dedicated a special issue to sport and globalisation, with many of the contributions dealing explicitly with football and transnationalism (Giulianotti and Robertson, 2007). The ongoing internationalisation of teams that were previously perceived as being firmly anchored in a local or regional environment is a recent phenomenon related to commercialisation and (neo-)liberalisation, which is often dated back to the famous 1995 Bosman ruling of the European Court of Justice but actually started before. To the surprise of all those who predicted the end of supporters' identification with club teams composed of transnational 'mercenaries', it appears that such transnationals can easily be localised, naturalised and perceived ethnocentrically as being part of 'us'. As David Ranc has very convincingly demonstrated, nationality is definitely not a decisive identity marker (Ranc, 2012). In other words: the alien may become 'ours' at the very moment he wears our team's jersey.

Just like globalisation has not erased differences and cleavages across the globe, football has not assumed a cosmopolitan meaning for all of its fans and followers. In an attempt to look beyond the rim of the local and national teacup and describe football in terms of cosmopolitanism – a topic which is currently high on the agenda of social sciences in general (Hannerz, 1990; Beck and Sznaider, 2010; Glick Schiller, 2010; Rapport and Wardle, 2010; Soysal, 2010) – one runs the risk of ignoring the fact that many 'ordinary people' hardly experience cosmopolitanism in their everyday life. We contend that people are socialised into their respective football identities in a way that reflects and is determined by their social and cultural environment. A fan's identity fits neatly into, is reproduced by, and in turn reproduces culture as, in Raymond Williams' (1963) famous words, 'a whole way of life'.

While the literature on transnationalisation and globalisation of football identities draws heavily upon the ways in which football adapts to globalisation's mechanisms of production, experience and consumption, the ongoing significance and prevalence of national identity in a transnational football context, to some extent, still maintains the national nexus of football identities. In this respect, the literature has thoroughly scrutinised the emergence of football as a marker for national identity at international tournaments. International football events, such as the Football World Cup and the European Football Championship, are often framed as a matter of national identity by social scientists and the media, in the footsteps of Eric Hobsbawm's famous and oft-quoted statement: 'The imagined community of millions seems more real as a team of eleven named people. The individual, even the one who only cheers, becomes a symbol of his nation himself' (Hobsbawm, 1990, p. 4). According to Bernstein, international tournaments provide an opportunity for people to experience the elusive sense of national identity and belonging to their 'imagined community'. He contends, 'such events also serve as occasions for national "flag-waving", and thus offer a perfect opportunity for the public fanning of nationalist sentiments' (Bernstein, 2007, p. 653). These popular expressions of nationalism become important because, as von der Lippe notes, national identity is defined by 'how a citizenry sees and thinks about themselves in relation to others' (von der Lippe, 2002, p. 374).

Even in cases where international tournaments receive traditionally moderate attraction (such as in the case of England), there is an intense expression of national sentiment. The traditional English Saint George's flag is an excellent illustration of this point. While in 1966, when England won the World Cup on its home soil, the Union Flag was still very present in Wembley and in the streets, it has now been massively replaced by the Saint George's cross, which for decades had been associated to nationalist fringe-groups of the far right. According to Jeremy Paxman, the first greeting cards adorned with a Saint George's cross made their appearance only in 1995. At Euro 1996, hosted by England, a large number of spectators had their faces painted with the red cross. In 1997 the *Sun* asked their readers to cut out a Saint George's cross from the paper and stick it to a window pane in their house, and at the 1998 World Cup in France, it had replaced the Union Jack almost entirely (Paxman, 1999, p. 21). In only two months in the summer of 2002, between the World Cup, the Queen's Jubilee and the Wimbledon tournament, the major supplier of Saint George's flags realised a turnover of 6 million pounds sterling (Waser, 2002). This prompted observer Nick Hornby to publicly express his thanks to football for having allowed the English to re-appropriate their symbol, which 'had hitherto been more commonly seen stretched over the beer belly of a National Front voter walking a pit bull than fluttering from the window of a family hatchback' (Hornby, 2002). In the *Guardian*, Jonathan Glancey even went so far as to paraphrase the famous quote by Winston Churchill commenting on the landing of the Allied troops in Normandy in 1944: 'Never in the field of English history, or at least not since the Crusades or Agincourt, have so many red-cross flags been waved by so many for so many' (Glancey, 2002).

Anthony King also sees the Saint George's flags as a symptom for a 'new' English national identity. According to him, Euro 2004 emerged as an event where the English people mobilised themselves around the concept of a new localised national identity with the devolution of political power and the consequential fragmentation of British identity (King, 2006, p. 255).

Jacqueline Abell focuses on the internal and external attribution of British and Scottish stereotypes. She argues that the representation of a collective English national identity (as expressed through national football) and 'their' stereotypes of the Scottish legitimise the assertion of a shared Scottish national identity, the maximisation of differences between the national groups, and the justification for anti-English sentiment (Abell, 2011). Richard Weight similarly recalls how after defeating Germany in two wars, England's World Cup victory against West Germany 'mutually reinforced war and football in the English mind' in 'us vs. them' narratives (Weight, 2002, p. 461).

The link between football and national identity is also significant in terms of immigrants' cultural adjustments to the host country, and the role that football plays in national identity (re-)construction. According to Giulianotti and Robertson, football constitutes a particularly potent domain in which locality and cultural identification are intensively produced across a shifting global terrain. In this respect, sports teams provide migrant social groups with strong symbols of cultural identity that may connect to other, lived dimensions of personal biography or collective memory, most notably those associated with nationality and ethnicity (Giulianotti and Robertson, 2006, p. 194). Gregg Bocketti focused on migration and immigrant communities in Brazil and the Italian immigrants in São Paulo specifically in the early 20th century. He argues that, through football, Italians obtained agency in negotiating the process by which they became Brazilian and found a means to preserve a sense of discrete ethnicity within São Paulo's multi-ethnic community (Bocketti, 2008, p. 275). Likewise, Giulianotti and Robertson, through the term, 'glocalisation', focus on the North American-based supporters of the Scottish football teams Celtic and Rangers. They argue that forms of popular cultural identification, such as those associated with football, can enable migrant groups to develop symbolic and institutional responses to their routine experiences of relativisation within new cultural contexts and a highly potent sense of differentiation from the host societies (Giulianotti and Robertson, 2006, p. 194).

While numerous authors detect indicators for an ongoing 'glocalisation' (Giulianotti and Robertson, 2004; Lechner, 2007) of football identities, we argue that it is tempting, but not sufficient, to construct ideal types of a local and a global culture engaging in a constructive interplay, creating a 'glocal' football identity hybrid. Not only does such a perspective tend to idealise, essentialise and simplify the very complex processes and practices of constructing the Self and the Other, but it misses an important frame of reference for identity processes related not only, but also to football: Europe. A European football space is undoubtedly created through the mobility of both fans and players and the cross-cutting national and regional borders of identification.

What has 'Europe' got to do with it? The Europeanisation of football identities

So far, most research in this field focuses on how football is instrumentalised or becomes a tool and carrier for national identity. Yet the question of whether perception patterns and increasing mobility of both players and fans within Europe undergo changes through transnational football encounters, and whether this may enable individuals to develop a certain reflexive understanding of Europeanness, generally remains unexplored. Europe plays an important role for football identities, both as place and space because, following Michel de Certeau, 'space is a practiced place' (de Certeau 1988, p. 117). There are many ways to 'think Europe', but no matter how you look at it Europe is a relevant category to order, categorise and 'think' the social world and to locate self and other. Likewise, the Europes of the European Union, the Eurovision Song Contest and the Champions League are not identical. Each relates to differing spatial and geopolitical frameworks, and each triggers respective emotions and imaginations (see Bolin, 2006). Adding a European perspective does not imply a clear-cut definition of what Europe is. Throughout history the very concept of 'Europe' has proved very resistant to concise definitions, which is why it has very often been grossly defined in negation: Europe is not Asia, is not the Islamic world, is not the US, and so on. This volume does not aim at providing yet another definition of what Europe is. It simply aims to look at the practices, actions and ways of interpreting the social world of football fans in Europe. This drive to 'think Europe' in terms of identities has intensified drastically during the past two decades.

Now that European integration is – albeit contested – reality, the social and political questions that once remained in the background have once again centralised. The 'no' votes in the referenda on the Constitutional Treaty in France and the Netherlands, and for the Lisbon Treaty in Ireland, suggest that national publics have become increasingly concerned with the challenges to national identity and sovereignty. Meanwhile the economic crisis brings to the fore questions about the nature of and the feelings attached to the European project. After the demise of the Cold War, a new need to explain the drastic transformations of the social structure and new social and political identities emerged. This became the main issue within the analytical agendas of critical theory, post-Marxism, post-structuralism, postmodernism, and so forth. European studies also shifted its focus to this new academic 'demand', and consequently a myriad of studies aiming to reconceptualise an identity-based politics flourished.

After the treaties of Maastricht (1991) and Amsterdam (1997) were signed, the EU reached a degree of integration where identification with 'Europe' went beyond hitherto known forms of intergovernmental cooperation. The newly emerging forms of identification within Europe now involved a new conception of 'identity' as well as novel or extended practices of politics. New studies trying to understand 'Europe' as a layer of identity (for example, Maier and Risse, 2003; Diez Medrano and Gutiérrez, 2001; Hülsse, 1999, Jiménez et al., 2004), a public sphere (for example, Bärenreuter, 2005), a possibility for multicultural citizenship (for example, Lavdas, 2001), a political geography (for example, Agnew, 2001; Kuus, 2004; Moisio, 2002; Smith, 2002), and a metaphor (for example, Drulak, 2006; Musolff, 2000) could be explored along those lines. According to this perspective, in a democratic society, political practices are not consistent with 'defending the rights of preconstituted identities, but rather in constituting those identities themselves in a precarious and always vulnerable field' (Mouffe, 2000, p. 148). In addition, anthropological studies have studied Europeanisation extensively from various angles with regard to identities, institutions, imaginations and boundary-drawing (Goddard et al., 1996; Bellier and Wilson, 2000; Shore, 2000; Demossier, 2009). Within those studies, 'Europe' is taken as performative, mobile, hybrid, partial and fluid.

Starting in the late 1990s, European-focused research that delved into identities also overlapped with what is dubbed in the literature as 'the Europeanisation turn' in European Studies (for the most outstanding examples of Europeanisation literature, see Cowles et al., 2001; Featherstone and Radaelli, 2003; Schimmelfennig and Sedelmeier, 2005). At the broadest level, the process of Europeanisation is the creation/construction of distinct European institutions, policies, behaviour, discourses and social aggregations at the domestic level due to the impact of the 'European level'. Alpan and Diez contend that especially within the context of the recent enlargement rounds of 2004 and 2007 and the Turkish EU accession, the term has been reconceptualised as a bottom-up process, covering different aspects of society and politics (Alpan and Diez, 2014). Thus, the recent literature variations distinguish between different modalities of Europeanisation, such as policy Europeanisation, where the adoption of the *acquis* in concrete policies and domestic law is at the centre; political Europeanisation, where the transformation of the political process is at stake (for example, through the adoption of particular decision-making structures as a response to EU requirements, or more broadly through pluralisation); societal Europeanisation, which in the course of the integration process encompasses re-articulations of identities and interests; and discursive Europeanisation, which captures the degree to which other EU member states and actors within these states are referred to in public debates (see Diez et al., 2005 for a detailed account of this differentiation).

While traditional accounts focus on a narrow understanding of Europeanisation as the effects of the EU institutions and its policies on its member states, we broaden our view. Europeanisation takes place in many different areas; and football is one 'site' where we can study the large 'field' of Europeanisation. Already in 1997, anthropologists Borneman and Fowler stated that:

Like the EU itself, soccer is an institutionalised system of aggressive yet cooperative competition among global, national, and local entities. As such, it is the quintessential European pursuit and is fast becoming an archetypal example of Europeanisation (Borneman and Fowler 1997, p. 508).

When considering the Europeanisation of football, academics frequently focused on the repercussions of football laws and policies at the national level within the European Union (García, 2009, 2011; Parish, 2003; Holt, 2007; Ranc and Sonntag, 2011). The most powerful and extensive study in this area is titled 'The Transformation of European Football: Towards the Europeanisation of the National Game'. In this volume, the editors, Niemann, García and Grant explore domestic football in various European countries and the level of engagement that the nations have with the EU governance and the European project (Niemann et al., 2011).

Another significant edited volume in this field, initially published as special issue of *Soccer and Society*, is Wolfram Manzenreiter's and Georg Spitaler's 'multidisciplinary reading of Euro 2008'. Their analysis of how political and economic processes of Europeanisation paved the way for transformations of transnational football consumption cautiously highlights 'the opalescence and opaqueness of a progress in which football has transgressed its traditional boundaries and expanded into new realms of public space and public sphere' (Manzenreiter and Spitaler, 2011, p. 2).

In line with Diez et al.'s categorisation, football scholars have also exemplified societal Europeanisation, which focuses on identity shifts and alignments. For instance, Armstrong and Mitchell focus on football in Malta and how the image of an egalitarian football space in Europe brings back the national fears of a post-colonial island living on the fringe of Europe (Armstrong and Mitchell, 2008, p. 6). On a different note, Brand and Niemann question whether there are changes at the level of supporters' and spectators' perceptions, and their identities in Europe (Brand and Niemann, 2013).

This volume intends to add football to the above list of issues that deal with European identity, and to delve into the question of whether football could emerge as a pan-European identity marker. Similar to the one posed by Sonntag at an earlier endeavour, the main question emerges: could people's perceptions or fan behaviour at the European Football Championship, which can also be witnessed very clearly at events such as the Eurovision Song Contest, be considered as something distinctly European (Sonntag, 2007)? But then again, what is European?

In 2012, it was particularly important that the European Championship took place in two countries, both of which had belonged to the state-socialist sphere of influence until 1989. Poland and Ukraine 'returned to Europe' after the fall of communism, undergoing a strict political and economic transformation with strong repercussions for the socio-cultural field.

Poland and Ukraine diverged in their respective pathways. Both countries, albeit to differing degrees, have been subject to a paternalistic and orientalising view from the Western European media and public perception. The famous 'Polish plumber' (see Johnson, 2011) and the 'Ukrainian forced prostitute' are but two of a variety of images that illuminate the 'West's' fantasies about the 'East'. This adds another dimension to the picture that already included stereotypes, fears and asymmetries (Said, 1979; see also Burgess 1997; Berdahl et al., 2000).

At the time of this writing, in spring 2014, three major events are taking place. First, Ukraine is in turmoil. None of the observers would have foreseen the Maidan revolution or the violent creation of the Donetsk People's Republic. Football fans and hooligans from rival clubs unite under the banner of Ukrainian nationalism (see for instance Historia Vivens, 2014; Lukov, 2014). The gap is widening between what is perceived as Western and what is perceived as Eastern in public discourse. Second, Conchita Wurst, a bearded Austrian drag queen, wins the Eurovision Song Contest and divides Europe into liberal democrats and conservative homophobes – a divide which interestingly, and contrary to many statements, crisscrosses West, Central and East European societies. Finally, many European countries see a dramatic increase in votes for right-wing populist and far-right positions in the 2014 European parliamentary elections. The project of Europe is likely facing its most serious crisis. Football may seem to be a minor site within this larger field of Europeanisation, yet, like a burning glass it gathers social forces and makes them appear before our eyes like a kind of magnifier.

Euro 2012, as described in this volume, is not only about football. Euro 2012 is fraught with many different layers of meaning. Its story does not consist of one single narrative, but instead it is told and re-told differently in different places. Euro 2012, both as a symbol and as a very tangible social and economic reality, acquires different meanings for different groups and various actors appropriate it differently. The aim of this book is to tell some of these stories.

The structure of this book

Following this introduction, Alexandra Schwell's chapter delves into the meaning of 'football' as it had been depicted in the European football championship. She pays particular attention to the dichotomous division of Europe into West and East and its reflections in the relations of power in European football. According to Schwell, East-European football still is a blind spot on the mental map of West-European fans. With Euro 2012 organised in Poland and Ukraine these mental images are increasingly brought to the forefront. Drawing upon an analysis of media discourse in Western Europe and field research conducted in Poland, her chapter 'Offside. Or Not Quite: Euro 2012 as a Focal Point of Identity and Alterity' analyses how the West constructs images of Self and Other with regard to a perceptive 'European football space'.

A similar anthropological perspective is employed by Nina Szogs in her account, 'Loyalty Jungle – Flexible Football Fan Identities in the Framework of Euro 2012'. By drawing upon ethnographic fieldwork in Poland, Germany and Austria, Szogs seeks to show how an international and extensively regulated event such as Euro 2012 is approached in individual and sometimes subversive ways. The key questions she asks are how people adapt this European event to their local requirements and what kind of meaning they allot to it in the process, and finally, what the local interpretation of the championship by the spectators looks like.

The fourth chapter, co-authored by Başak Alpan and Özgehan Şenyuva, also focuses on the portrait of Self and Other with respect to football. In their article titled, 'Does Qualifying Really Qualify? Comparing the Representations of Euro 2008 and Euro 2012 in the Turkish Media', Alpan and Şenyuva examine the Turkish national identity negotiations in two different periods through a qualitative analysis of the country's media. Football relations between Turkey and Europe can be seen as ideal objects of analysis towards understanding the European complex in the formation (and perpetual re-formation) of

Turkish national identity. In terms of football, the chapter departs from this close link between the formation of Turkish national identity and the 'encounter with Europe'. It aims to understand whether the existence or non-existence of the Turkish national football team on the field feeds into the identifications and narratives of Turkish football spectators, through the lens of the media.

The fifth chapter by Albrecht Sonntag, 'Up to Expectations? Perceptions of Ethnic Diversity in the French and German National Teams', compares the public perception of the ethnic composition in both France and Germany's national squads. Both teams include a significant number of players with migrant background, and in both countries this has become a major issue of public debate and political implications, as was visible again at Euro 2012. The chapter highlights differences and similarities in perception and expectations towards these players and in the social roles that are ascribed to them by the public. In Sonntag's analysis football appears not only as a carrier of stereotypes, but also as a mediator of perceptions, capable of moving, putting into perspective, and sometimes even returning stereotypes. It helps updating perceptions – even the most selective ones – that we have of ourselves, and it unfolds the ways in which nations coexist, look at each other and meet with each other. It, finally, reveals significant, often unconscious, aspects of the difficult transformation of national identities – shaken, weakened and undermined by the accumulated effects of the globalisation process – that European society experiences today.

In her chapter, 'Mediating Turkishness through Language in Transnational Football', Yağmur Nuhrat aims to identify the nuances of identity negotiations for the European footballers of Turkish descent and foreground football as a social arena where Turkishness is formed. By investigating the experience of migrant footballers (such as in the case of Mesut Özil in particular who scored a goal for Germany against Turkey in the qualifiers to Euro 2012) and the discourses circulated concerning them, Nuhrat argues that these everyday negotiations through national teams bear importance in terms of conceptualising shifts in the nation-state's definition of itself and its citizens in terms of claims, loyalty and origins.

Michał Buchowski and Małgorzata Kowalska develop an anthropological perspective with the aim of understanding an oppositional interpretation of the European championship, in the host city

Poznań. While the city authorities presented the event as a kind of joyful carnival, many citizens and activists perceived it as an unnecessary expenditure that came at the cost of society's weakest members. Buchowski and Kowalska focus on the nationwide demonstration 'Bread, Not Games' that took place in Poznań. By analysing the protest they aim to gain further insights into ethnographic writing and doing anthropology.

The volume is concluded by a brief afterword by Albrecht Sonntag which attempts to put into perspective the different observations made at the Vanity Fair of European Football, and the manner in which this event provides a stage for the negotiation of performances, representations and identities.

References

Abell, J. (2011) '"They Seem To Think 'We're Better than You'"': Framing Football Support as a Matter of "National Identity" in Scotland and England', *British Journal of Social Psychology*, Vol. 50, Issue 2, pp. 246–64.

Agnew, J. (2001) 'How Many Europes? The European Union, Eastward Enlargement and Uneven Development', *European Urban and Regional Studies*, Vol. 8, Issue 1, pp. 29–38.

Alpan, B. and T. Diez (2014) 'The Devil is in the Domestic? European Integration Studies and Limits of Europeanisation in Turkey', *Balkan and Near Eastern Studies*, Vol. 16, Issue 1, pp. 1–10.

Armstrong. G. and J. P. Mitchell (2008) *Global and Local Football: Politics and Europeanisation on the Fringes of the EU* (London: Routledge).

Bakić-Hayden, M. (1995) 'Nesting Orientalisms: the Case of Former Yugoslavia', *Slavic Review*, Vol. 54, Issue 4, pp. 917–31.

Bärenreuter, C. (2005) 'Researching the European Public Sphere and its Political Functions: a Proposal', in T. Nesbit and J. Steinberg (eds), *Freedom, Justice, and Identity* (Vienna: IWM Junior Visiting Fellows' Conferences), p. 18.

Baumann, G. (2004) 'Grammars of Identity/Alterity: a Structural Approach', in G. Baumann and A. Gingrich (eds), *Grammars of Identity/Alterity: a Structural Approach* (New York and Oxford: Berghahn), pp. 18–50.

Beck, U. and N. Sznaider, N. (2010) 'Unpacking Cosmopolitanism for the Social Sciences: A Research Agenda', *British Journal of Sociology*, Vol. 61, Issue 1, pp. 381–403.

Bellier, I. and T. M. Wilson (eds) (2000) *An Anthropology of the European Union. Building, Imagining and Experiencing the New Europe* (Oxford and New York: Berg).

Berdahl, D., M. Bunzl and M. Lampland (eds) (2000) *Altering States: Ethnographies of Transition in Eastern Europe and the Former Soviet Union* (Ann Arbor: University of Michigan Press).

Bernstein, A. (2007) '"Running Nowhere": National Identity and Media Coverage of the Israeli Football Team's Attempt to Qualify for EURO 2000', *Israel Affairs*, Vol. 13, Issue 3, pp. 653–64.

Bocketti, G. P. (2008) 'Italian Immigrants, Brazilian Football, and the Dilemma of National Identity', *Journal of Latin American Studies*, Vol. 40, pp. 275–302.

Bolin, G. (2006) 'Visions of Europe: Cultural Technologies of Nation-states'. *International Journal of Cultural Studies*, Vol. 9, Issue 2, pp. 189–206.

Bolsmann, C. (2014) 'The 2010 World Cup in South Africa. A Continental Spectacle?', in S. Rinke and K. Schiller (eds), *The FIFA World Cup 1930–2010. Politics, Commerce, Spectacle and Identities* (Göttingen: Wallstein), pp. 372–88.

Borneman, J., and N. Fowler (1997) 'Europeanization', *Annual Review of Anthropology*, Vol. 26, pp. 487–514.

Buchowski, M. (2006) 'The Specter of Orientalism in Europe: From Exotic Other to Stigmatized Brother', *Anthropological Quarterly*, Vol. 79, Issue 3, pp. 463–82.

Burgess, A. (1997) *Divided Europe: The New Domination of the East* (London and Chicago: Pluto Press).

Butler, J. (1991) *Gender Trouble: Feminism and the Subversion of Identity* (New York: Routledge).

de Certeau, M. (1988) *The Practice of Everyday Life* (Berkeley and London: University of California Press).

Cowles, M., J. Caporaso and T. Risse (eds) (2001) *Transforming Europe: Europeanization and Domestic Change* (Ithaca and London: Cornell University Press).

Demossier, M. (ed.) (2009) *The European Puzzle: The Political Structuring of Cultural Identities at a Time of Transition* (New York and Oxford: Berghahn Books).

Diez, T., A. Agnantopoulos and A. Kaliber (2005) 'File: Turkey, Europeanization and Civil Society – Introduction', *South European Society and Politics*, Vol. 10, Issue 1, pp. 1–15.

Diez Medrano, J. and P. Gutiérrez (2001) 'Nested Identities: National and European Identity in Spain', *Ethnic and Racial Studies*, Vol. 24, Issue 5, pp. 753–78.

Drulak, P. (2006) 'Motion, Container and Equilibrium: Metaphors in the Discourse about European Integration', *European Journal of International Relations*, Vol. 12, Issue 4, pp. 499–531.

Featherstone, K. and C. M. Radaelli (2003) *The Politics of Europeanization* (Oxford: Oxford University Press).

Feixa, C., and J. S. Juris (2000) 'Football Cultures', *Social Anthropology*, Vol. 8, Issue 2, pp. 203–11.

Foucault, M. (1982) 'The Subject and Power', in H. L. Dreyfuss and P. Rabinow (eds), *Michel Foucault: Beyond Structuralism and Hermeneutics* (New York: Harvester Press), pp. 208–26.

García, B. (2011): 'The Influence of the EU on the Governance of Football', in H. Gammelsæter and B. Senaux (eds), *The Organisation and Governance of Top Football Across Europe* (London: Routledge), pp. 32–45.

Gingrich, A. (1998) 'Frontier Myths of Orientalism: The Muslim World in Public and Popular Cultures of Central Europe', in B. Baskar and B. Brumen (eds) *MESS: Mediterranean Ethnological Summer School Piran/Pirano Slovenia 1996* (Ljubljana: Inštitut za multikulturne raziskave), pp. 99–127.

Giulianotti, R. (1999) *Football: A Sociology of the Global Game* (Cambridge: Polity).

Giulianotti, R. and R. Robertson (2004) 'The Globalization of Football: A Study in the Glocalization of the "Serious Life"', *British Journal of Sociology*, Vol. 55, Issue 4, pp. 545–68.

Giulianotti, R. and R. Robertson (2006) 'Glocalization, Globalization and Migration: The Case of Scottish Football Supporters in North America', *International Sociology*, Vol. 21, Issue 2, pp. 171–98.

Giulianotti, R., and R. Robertson (2007) 'Recovering the Social: Globalization, Football and Transnationalism', *Global Networks*, Vol. 7, Issue 2, pp. 144–86.

Glancey, J. (2002) 'By George!', *The Guardian*, 20 June 2002.

Glick Schiller, N. (2010) 'Old Baggage and Missing Luggage: a Commentary on Beck and Sznaider's "Unpacking Cosmopolitanism for the Social Sciences: a Research Agenda"', *British Journal of Sociology*, Vol. 61, Issue 1, pp. 413–20.

Goddard, V. A., J. R. Llobera and C. Shore (eds) (1996) *The Anthropology of Europe: Identity and Boundaries in Conflict* (Oxford and Washington DC.: Berg).

Hall, S. (1996) 'Introduction: Who Needs "Identity"', in S. Hall, and P. D. U. Gay (eds), *Question of Cultural Identity* (London: Sage), pp. 1–17.

Hannerz, U. (1990) 'Cosmopolitans and Locals in World Culture'. *Theory, Culture & Society*, Vol. 7, Issue 2, pp. 237–51.

Historia Vivens (2013), 'Unity is power! Ultras of Ukraine united to protect the Euromaidan …', at: www.historiavivens.eu/2/unity_is_power_ultras_of_ukraine_united_to_protect_the_euromaidan_1032900.html (accessed 10 September 2014).

Hobsbawm, E. J. (1990) *Nations and Nationalism since 1780: Programme, Myth, Reality* (Cambridge: Cambridge University Press).

Hornby, N. (2002) 'We Are The World', *The New Yorker*, 15 July 2002.

Hülsse, R. (1999) 'The Discursive Construction of Identity and Difference – Turkey as Europe's Other?', Discussion paper presented at the ECPR Joint Sessions of Workshops, Mannheim, 26–31 March 1999.

Jiménez, A. M. R., J. J. Gorniak, A. Kosic, P. Kiss and M. Kandulla (2004) 'European and National Identities in EU's Old and New Member States: Ethnic, Civic, Instrumental and Symbolic Components', *European Integration Online Papers (EIOP)*, Vol. 8, Issue 11.

Johnson, J. K. (2011) 'The Curious Tale of the Polish Plumber: Rebranding Nations for New Social and Political Situations', *Advertising & Society Review*, Vol. 12, Issue 1.

King, A. (2006). 'Nationalism and Sport', in G. Delanty and K. Kumar (eds), *The Sage Handbook of Nations and Nationalism* (London: Sage), pp. 249–59.

Kürti, L. and P. Skalník (eds.) (2009) *Postsocialist Europe. Anthropological Perspectives from Home* (New York and Oxford: Berghahn).

Kuus, M. (2004) 'Europe's Eastern Expansion and the Reinscription of Otherness in East-Central Europe'. *Progress in Human Geography*, Vol. 28, Issue 4, pp. 472–89.

Laclau, E. and C. Mouffe (1985) *Hegemony and Socialist Strategy: Towards a Radical Democratic Politics* (London and New York: Verso).

Lavdas, K. A. (2001) 'Republican Europe and Multicultural Citizenship', *Politics*, Vol. 21, Issue 1, pp. 1–10.

Lechner, F. J. (2007) 'Imagined Communities in the Global Game: Soccer and the Development of Dutch National Identity', *Global Networks*, Vol. 7, Issue 2, pp. 193–229.

Lévi-Strauss, C. (1966) *The Savage Mind* (Chicago: University of Chicago Press).

Lukov, Y. (2014) 'Ultras United: Football Fans Rally for Ukraine's Sake', BBC News 24, May 2014, at: www.bbc.com/news/world-europe-27540360 (accessed 10 September 2014).

Maier, M. L. and T. Risse (eds) (2003) 'Europeanisation, Collective Identities and Public Discourses, Project', final report (Florence: Robert Schuman Centre for Advanced Studies, European University Institute).

Manzenreiter, W. and Spitaler, G. (eds) (2011) *Governance, Citizenship and the New European Football Championships – The European Spectacle?* (London: Routledge).

Moisio, S. (2002) 'EU Eligibility, Central Europe, and the Invention of Applicant State Narrative', *Geopolitics*, Vol. 7, Issue 3, pp. 89–116.

Mouffe, C. (2000) 'Politics and Passions: The Stakes of Democracy', *Ethical Perspectives*, Vol. 7, Issue 2–3, pp. 146–50.

Musolff, A. (2000) *Mirror-Images of Europe: Metaphors in the Public Debate about Europe in Britain and Germany* (Munich: Iudicium).

Ottosen, R., N. Hyde-Clarke and T. Miller (2011) 'Framing the Football Fan as Consumer: a Content Analysis of the Coverage of Supporters in *The Star* during the 2010 World Cup', paper presented at the IAMCR conference, Kadir Has University, Istanbul, Turkey, 13–17 July 2011.

Paxman, J. (1999) *The English. The Portrait of a People* (London: Penguin).

Ranc, D. (2012) *Foreign Players and Football Supporters. The Old Firm, Arsenal, Paris Saint-Germain* (Manchester: Manchester University Press).

Rapport, N. and H. Wardle (2010) 'A Cosmopolitan Anthropology', *Social Anthropology*, Vol. 18, Issue 4, pp. 381–470.

Said, E. (1979) *Orientalism* (New York: Vintage).

Schimmelfennig, F. and U. Sedelmaier (2005) *The Europeanization of Central and Eastern Europe* (Ithaca: Cornell University Press).

Shore, C. (2000) *Building Europe. The Cultural Politics of European Integration* (London and New York: Routledge).

Smith, A. (2002) 'Imagining Geographies of the "New Europe": Geo-Economic Power and the New European Architecture of Integration', *Political Geography*, Vol. 21, Issue 5, pp. 647–70.

Sonntag, A. (2007) 'Sweat, Tears and…Fun!: Reflections on Spectator Behaviour at the Football World Cup 2006', in Bettina Kratzmüller et al. (eds), *Sport and the Construction of Identities* (Vienna: Turia & Kant), pp. 790–98.

Soysal, N. Y. (2010) 'Unpacking Cosmopolitanism: An Insider–Outsider's Reading', *British Journal of Sociology*, Vol. 61, Issue 1, pp. 405–11.

Todorova, M. (1997) *Imagining the Balkans* (Oxford: Oxford University Press).

von der Lippe, G. (2002) 'Media Image: Sport, Gender and National Identities in Five European Countries', *International Review for the Sociology of Sport*, Vol. 37, Issue 3–4, pp. 371–96.

Waser, G. (2002) 'Royalisten und Hooligans', *Neue Zürcher Zeitung*, 28 August 2002.

Weight R. (2002) *Patriots: National Identity in Britain (1940–2000)* (Basingstoke: Macmillan).

Williams, R. (1963) *Culture and Society 1780–1950* (Harmondsworth and New York: Penguin).

Wolff, L. (1994) *Inventing Eastern Europe: The Map of Civilization on the Mind of the Enlightenment* (Stanford: Stanford University Press).

Yatsyk, A. (2014) 'Making Borderland Identity: The Case of the European Football Championship 2012 in Lviv', lecture given at the Seminar Series, the Centre for Urban History of East Central Europe, Lviv, Ukraine, 23 June 2014.

2
Offside. Or Not Quite

Euro 2012 as a Focal Point of Identity and Alterity

Alexandra Schwell

Introduction: Old and new asymmetries

Over ten years after the accession of eight post-socialist countries to the European Union, differences still persist. Many authors have argued (for a recent account see Epstein and Jacoby, 2014) and recent events, such as in Ukraine, have vividly proven that Europeanisation is not the smooth and homogeneous modernisation process everyone would like to embrace.[1] The Western members are no ideal types to which new members and candidate countries have to catch up. Each new member or candidate is facing different challenges due to post-socialist and other socio-cultural legacies and political trajectories. The economic crisis and the evolving discussion concerning European internal solidarity have created new cartographies of debt and changed public perception of Europe's periphery. It appears that in place of the old East–West asymmetry a new North–South divide, both in economic and in cultural terms, is opening up (cf. Eder, 2006) – and it has already reached football. Panagiotidis shows how both German and Greek media emphasised sentiments and cultural stereotypes during the Germany vs. Greece Euro 2012 quarterfinal, thereby exacerbating an already existing asymmetry (Panagiotidis, 2012). The North–South divide has not substituted but complemented the 'traditional' East–West asymmetry. Ten years after accession, asymmetries do not proliferate in the guise of diametrically opposed political systems or national economies. Instead asymmetries persist particularly within the micro practices of everyday life – and particularly within the micro practices of ignorance and stereotyping.[2] I will argue that these are explanatory frames, which rely on traditional narratives the West produces about the East, and likewise about itself. Thereby they inform practices of explaining and making sense of social realities.

This chapter will take a close look at how football is used as a vehicle for 'selfing/othering' under the influence of the East–West divide, that is, locating the 'self' by linking it to an 'other' in a reciprocal relationship. Mega-sports events, such as World Cups or European Championships, provide great opportunities for research. This is because states of exception within the 'ordinary' event cycle of football supporters reach out beyond their usual audience to include so-called event fans who normally would not care for football. It can be argued that it is these 'irregular' supporters who account for the myths that are created with regard to football mega-events (cf. Barthes, 1972). An example would be Germany's 2006 'summer fairy tale' (cf. Sonntag, 2007).

This chapter draws upon ethnographic field research that was conducted in Poznań during Euro 2012. My account is a rather impressionistic tale; hence data is neither exhaustive nor overly systematic.[3] It aims at taking the meaning of the expression 'social event' literally and asks what we can see when we look at football as being embedded in its social, political, economic, cultural and historical context. In the following, I will provide two ethnographically informed readings of Euro 2012 in Poznań. I focus on the way various actors stage the self and the other with regard to who and what is Eastern and Western. My examples will elaborate on 1) the way Eastern Europe is othered by both Western visitors and the media; and 2) the celebration of loyalties and national stereotypes and the negotiation of the respective images and self-positioning on a map of Europeanness. I will draw upon Baumann's 'Grammars of Identity/Alterity' for an analysis of the various and distinct ways of selfing and othering: the grammars of orientalisation, segmentation and encompassment (Baumann, 2004). Using Baumann's concept will enable me to take a look at social forces, power structures and the negotiation of cultural symbols through the looking glass of football.

Carnival and shifting loyalties/rivalries

World Cups and European Championships are reminiscent of carnival (Giulianotti, 1995; Pearson, 2012; Sonntag, 2014). We find colourful costumes, boisterous chants and lots of alcohol. Carnival is performative: the costumes, dresses, funny hats and face painting allow for identity experimentation. In carnival we can display loyalties and aversions much more openly than would normally be acceptable. One could ask: is there another moment when it is appropriate to celebrate wholeheartedly, to yell blunt stereotypes, to engage in name-calling – both positive and negative – or uncontrolled weeping?

According to Bakhtin, carnival is the season of a seemingly unruly state of exception; power hierarchies are turned upside down, and authorities are ridiculed (Morris, 2009; see Gurjewitsch, 1999, for a critique). It is a time characterised by ambivalence and social inversion. Nevertheless, 'carnivalesque' sports events take place according to specific rituals, which ensure all participants of a common share, and which define the boundaries of the acceptable. These boundaries are not strict and unchangeable, but dynamic. Free and Hughson contend: 'The carnivalesque dissolution of established social boundaries may *police* them through implicit knowledge, later made explicit for the doubtful, that those boundaries are *im*permeable' (Free and Hughson, 2003, p. 143 [emphasis in original]). We know from both carnival and ritual theory that the state of exception, or the liminal phase, as wild and exciting as it may be, has the effect of confirming and reproducing the normal state of affairs, the general world order (van Gennep, 1961; Turner, 2001 [1964]). Social hierarchies can paradoxically be confirmed by their inversion.

Ritual celebration of one's own nation is important for many fans, even for those who in their everyday life would reject such an outright praise of the nation. In a quantitative analysis of German students, sport sociologist Michael Mutz (2012) found that those who watched the German team's matches during Euro 2012 experienced a strong increase in German patriotism, and a moderate increase in nationalism.[4] The German black, red and gold plastic flower chain, or the Austrian red-white-red scarf, and songs that are jointly sung, all create a feeling of belonging – if only for 90 minutes. Yet, as Szogs argues in this volume, carnival-like events such as World Cups and

Euros inform practices and performances that have an impact on all the actors involved and go beyond the mere restoration and reconfirmation of the status quo ante. We can grasp the dynamics that are linked to football-carnival and its practical impact when we direct our attention not only towards the most obvious loyalties, such as national affiliations, but also towards recognising that both loyalties and rivalries can shift.

While a large amount of research has focused on club and national team supporters (including such diverse authors as Bromberger, 1995; Armstrong and Giulianotti, 1997; van Houtum and van Dam, 2002; Lechner, 2007), little has been done regarding the question of what happens when one's own team is not in play, or worse, does not even participate in the tournament (any more). Which loyalties, rejections and affections are created is a most illuminating field of research for cultural anthropologists. Who roots for whom, but also how social groups celebrate, are not merely individual and autonomous decisions. As Şenyuva and Alpan show in this volume, media representation and narratives play an important role, along with commercial interests. These aspects determine, to a large degree, the way football is interpreted and experienced by various actors. Stadiums and fan zones are highly commercialised spaces. Their form and organisation are not only predefined by FIFA and/or UEFA, but also by multinational corporations sponsoring the event. Viewer participation in the social event comes at the price of accepting their rules. It can be argued that these objects and materialities are 'actants' (Latour, 1993, 2005) that inform and shape supporters' behaviour and their perception of social realities (see Szogs in this volume).

Loyalties, but also rivalries, can shift under specific circumstances while being absolutely non-negotiable in a different context. Secondary or plural fandom does not take place randomly. Support for a distant football club, other than one's 'own' local or national team, neither changes on a daily basis nor is it an individual decision. It follows certain trajectories that are historically and socio-culturally determined, and as such are not subject to an entirely individual choice. A shifting loyalty/rivalry, like any identification, can be considered a strategy of action, conceived and employed by football fans according to their respective cultural tool-kit (Swidler, 1986). It is a practice of distinction and negotiation of identities in a specific social field (Bourdieu, 1984).

Affection and rejection in football do not only depend on success or failure. St Pauli's popularity reaches far beyond Hamburg's city limits, but it is certainly not based on their football capabilities. Affection and rejection do not have to be related to football. The pitch (both practically and virtually) can serve as a proxy for non-sports-related differences, which can acquire highly political meaning. Examples can be seen in the Balkans (Nielsen, 2009) or in Egypt (Montague, 2013), to name but a few (cf. Boniface, 1998).

Football loyalties and rivalries point towards salient or subconscious processes of identification and negotiations of self and other. Affection and rejection are thus meaningful practices of identity/alterity. But how are identity and alterity practised, and how do actors use both concepts to produce meaning? My analysis will draw upon Baumann's 'Grammars of Identity/Alterity'. He delves into concepts developed by Said, Evans-Pritchard and Dumont to distil, discuss and analytically extend on three distinct ways of selfing and othering: the grammars of orientalisation, segmentation and encompassment. In his own words:

> Orientalizing creates self and other as negative mirror images of each other; segmentation defines self and other according to a sliding scale of inclusions/exclusions; encompassment defines the other by an act of hierarchical subsumption. (Baumann, 2004, p. 47)

Being rather unsatisfied with their binary and thus simplistic structure, Baumann engages in a 'ternary challenge'. He argues that these three grammars, each in their own way, are in fact ternary, not binary. They always involve a third person or social group to which the two groups in the equation can relate. In the case of the segmentary grammar, football supporters may be rivals on a local level but, on a higher league level, they may unite against a common enemy from another region or country. Baumann himself uses this football example to illustrate his argument (Baumann, 2004, p. 22). Encompassment of one social group implicitly excludes another group: if members of group A are like 'us', even unwillingly, then they are by definition not like group B, who automatically stands in opposition to both of 'us'. The Orientalising grammar can include a third actor, when, for example, first-generation migrants point their fingers at late-comers who, they argue, fulfil all the stereotypes attached to migrants by the dominant society, simultaneously disclaiming any relationship whatsoever. In order to evade this ascription, Orientalising is done by the Orientalised.

I will trace the 'ternary challenge' in the various ways I encountered the 'making of the other' during my fieldwork and in media discourse. Thus, the three grammars help illuminate and understand the various and complex processes of selfing and othering around and beyond the football pitch with particular attention to the East–West divide. The first analytical section will focus on how the imagination of the Eastern Other serves as an explanatory frame of reference for Western media coverage and informs reciprocal perception during Euro 2012.

Dangerous, yet tempting: Eastern Europe as the Western Other

Edward Said (1979) coined the notion of 'Orientalism' as a critical category. Orientalism is a set of discursive practices of intellectuals through which the West structured, managed and even produced an imagined Orient in various ways. Said himself famously defined Orientalism as follows:

> Orientalism can be discussed and analyzed as the corporate institution for dealing with the Orient – dealing with it by making statements about it, authorizing views of it, describing it, by teaching it, settling it, ruling over it: in short, Orientalism as a Western style for dominating, restructuring, and having authority over the Orient. (Said, 1979, p. 3)

This last point is particularly important for Said because it limits the scope of the interpretive framework available to Westerners, thus limiting the Orient's agency:

> Moreover, so authoritative a position did Orientalism have that I believe no one writing, thinking, or acting on the Orient could do so without taking account of the limitations on thought and action imposed by Orientalism. In brief, because of Orientalism the Orient was not (and is not) a free subject of thought or action.

> This is not to say that Orientalism unilaterally determines what can be said about the Orient, but that it is the whole network of interests inevitably brought to bear on (and therefore always involved in) any occasion when that peculiar entity 'the Orient' is in question. (Said, 1979, p. 3)

He concludes by emphasising both the objective and the consequence of Orientalism: 'European culture gained in strength and identity by setting itself off against the Orient as a sort of surrogate and even underground self' (Said, 1979, p. 3).

Said inspired a sequel of works on Eastern Europe and the Balkans as an imagined semi-Orient and internal European Other that also depart from his original concept and account for regional varieties and particularities (Bakić-Hayden and Hayden, 1992; Wolff, 1994; Bakić-Hayden, 1995; Moisio, 2002; Kuus, 2004; Kürti and Skalník, 2009). Created by intellectuals in the West, the Western image of Eastern Europe, like Said's account of the Oriental image, does not need a dialogue. It instead relies on a representation whose first and foremost aim is to establish a cultural and civilisational distance in order to emphasise its own progressiveness.

Scholars, such as Larry Wolff (1994), identified the invention of the East as the result of an intellectual history that began in the 18th century. Western intellectuals, such as Voltaire, needed a backward other to emphasise the progresses of Enlightenment. A Western public discourse, that refuses to abolish its mental Iron Curtain, still does not notice 'Eastern' visions of locating the self and the other in Europe and 'Eastern' attempts to seek out differences within the imagined East (Kundera, 1984; Kuus, 2004). Similarly to Said's Orientalism, the discourse about the East proves so powerful and authoritative that any account of the East almost automatically entails a referential framework. This produces an imaginative geography that is difficult to escape. Symbolic geography, which ignores perceptions and practices within the region, is an important feature of Easternness, much like Orientalism. At the same time, Western accounts tend to become incorporated into the self-image, in a kind of self-orientalisation.

The dichotomous division of Europe into West and East can also be seen in the relations of power in European football. The image of the cultural 'football East' derives its power from more general and widespread imaginations of the barbarian, uncivilised and backward

East. Not only are the most successful teams found in the Western part of the continent, but this reality, generated by economic factors, is assisted by a plethora of general 'Orientalising' images about Eastern countries. Those areas usually include insufficient sport arena infrastructure, intrinsic corruption, hooliganism and so on.

Judging from parts of the Western media discourse, it seemed that Euro 2012 had opened up the door to a part of the continent that large parts of the West apparently had not actually taken note of before. Suddenly all the stereotypes and prejudices were on the plate again, but this time the East talked back.

' ... you could end up coming back in a coffin'

Jokes about Polish thieves and burglars are well known, particularly, but not exclusively, in Poland's adjacent Western neighbouring countries. Jokes such as 'come to Poland, your car is already there' regained currency in the run-up to Euro 2012. Davies (1982) argues that jokes drawing upon ethnicity and nationality serve to draw moral boundaries and strengthen existing hierarchies and stereotypes. They can be seen as an expression of underlying anxieties of a seemingly different threatening other – one who is believed to cross our borders and do harm (see also Johnson, 2011). Such anxieties were expressed in newspaper and magazine articles, on blog posts and TV programmes all over Europe. One in particular gained widespread publicity.

On 28 May 2012 the BBC broadcasted a documentary entitled 'Stadiums of Hate', which triggered a fierce controversy. The BBC announced: 'With just days to go before the kick-off of the Euro 2012 championships, *Panorama* reveals shocking new evidence of racist violence and anti-Semitism at the heart of Polish and Ukrainian football and asks whether tournament organiser UEFA should have chosen both nations to host the prestigious event' (BBC, 2012a). During the documentary, former English captain Sol Campbell uttered the now already famous words: 'Stay at home, watch it on TV. Don't even risk it ... because you could end up coming back in a coffin' (BBC News, 2012). The BBC subsequently was accused of using highly selective and one-sided material in its documentary. Several people who had been interviewed protested heavily against the way they appeared on screen, such as the executive director of the Jewish

Community Centre of Kraków (Eastern approaches blog, 2012). Even worse, the BBC redrew the map of Europe and mistakenly exchanged Austria for the Czech Republic. Many observers noted this, including blogger Peter Gentle:

> Unless there have been huge changes in borders and peoples around Europe, in secret, that only the BBC knows about, then Austria does not border Poland. Meanwhile, the Czech Republic has slipped south, and borders with a large country which appears to be Yugoslavia. (Gentle, 2012)

For Poland and Ukraine the documentary was, as he put it, 'a PR car crash' (Gentle, 2012). Prime Minister Tusk, the Foreign Office, and the Ministry of Internal Affairs all publicly responded to the BBC (Ministerstwo Spraw Wewnętrznych, 2012a; TheNews.pl, 2012). TV discussions, which involved government officials, academics, and anti-racism activists, proceeded (Stowarzyszenie NIGDY WIĘCEJ, 2012a) and local activists took up the fight. A Polish flag was hung from King Zygmunt's Column in front of the Warsaw Castle, a very prominent site, saying 'BBC Welcome to Real Poland'. In front of Warsaw's fan zone, young women wearing 'Bad Boy Campbell' T-shirts asked supporters to throw postcards with greetings to the BBC into two paper coffins (Kontakt 24, 2012; TVN Warszawa, 2012). A petition asking the BBC to 'Apologise for the bias presented in "Euro 2012: Stadiums of Hate"' (Change.org, 2012), however, managed to mobilise only 599 signatories. Creative Western football fans who dared to visit Euro 2012 came to the defence of the host countries by opposing the dominant media narrative (see, for example, O'Neill, 2012). The BBC issued a brief statement arguing that '*Panorama* believes it was in the public interest to highlight the behaviour of some Polish and Ukrainian football supporters ahead of the championships' (BBC, 2012b). The BBC editors defiantly defended the programme's educatory mission: 'It's certainly much harder right now for Poland and Ukraine to look the other way when such things happen' (Giles, 2012).

Racist incidents did indeed occur during Euro 2012, seemingly proving the BBC right. UEFA even wrote a letter to the mayors of the Polish and Ukrainian host cities and also to Poland's sports minister, Joanna Mucha

[...] to ask that all effective and necessary measures – including an increased police presence – be implemented to prevent any display of discriminatory or racist behaviour at such public sessions. UEFA has also requested that the authorities ensure that any person found to be engaging in racist behaviour be immediately ejected from the stadium and its vicinity, and that criminal proceedings be launched against such individuals. [...] UEFA is nevertheless confident that the local authorities will deal adequately with the issue. (UEFA, 2012)

Neither UEFA, nor most news sources, mentioned the nationality of the fans in question. That leaves the reader to implicitly assume that the perpetrators were of Polish or Ukrainian descent. In fact, Spanish and Russian fans committed the related incident that preceded the letter (FARE Network, 2012). Ultimately, it was found that travelling supporters from Croatia, Spain, Germany and Russia committed all the major instances of racism that UEFA fined during Euro 2012. From the point of view of UEFA, however, it seems that Eastern European hosts still cannot fully be trusted in this respect and need a 'gentle reminder'. This in turn points toward the fact that to Western observers violent football fans are not the only problem, but that they are part of a larger issue that reaches deeper into the society. This is precisely why stories about seemingly deviant groups, as lurid as they may be, also have a significance that goes beyond the depiction of a violent group of outcasts. They serve as symptoms and representations of the wrong in a society as a whole.

More than 20 years after the transition to democracy, social actions and events are still framed in terms of civilisation vs. backwardness dichotomies and a lagging modernisation narrative. Journalists embarked on 'expeditions' to the Wild East and reported as if they had discovered unexplored land, where no civilised man's foot had ever stepped (see, for example, Sundermeyer, 2012). Also, authors within academia apparently like to generate this kind of pleasant shiver among their audiences. Sport scientist Blecking, for example, draws a direct line from the democratic transformation to Polish football and football hooligans (Blecking, 2013). He contends: 'The transformation to democracy was difficult and was accompanied by corruption and sports defeats. Polish fan cultures until today are a problematic and retarded part of Polish civil society' (Blecking, 2013,

p. 251 [author's translation]). He continues: 'Neotribal regressions on the level of fan cultures mirror the fact that the development of civil society has not kept pace with the rapid economic development' (Blecking, 2013, p. 258). Fan cultures, particularly their violent and aggressive parts, are taken as a symptom for the state of a society as a whole; as opposed to an economic system that has been created according to Western standards.

Let us look at this picture from another angle: would any observer of German football consider taking Borussia Dortmund's recent problems with some of its Ultra groups' fascist tendencies as a symptom of Germany's deficits in coming to terms with its past? Corruption, insider relationships and mismanagement are certainly not specific to Eastern Europe, but can be found in football clubs and associations throughout Europe; both FIFA and UEFA themselves have been repeatedly criticised for their practices in this respect. This is not meant to play down the relevance of negative tendencies in Polish football. In fact, there are strongly committed groups and activists within the country who address these problems. Anti-racist associations such as 'Stowarzyszenie Nigdy Więcej' closely cooperated with the Euro 2012 organisational team (Stowarzyszenie NIGDY WIĘCEJ, 2012b). Framing racism and violence among Polish football supporters solely as a remnant of a socialist past, identifying the relevant actors as stuck in long-gone realities, and being less civilised is far from the point.

From the analytical point of view, clearly an Orientalising grammar is applied: Western media and observers define a standard from where to judge others. UEFA even goes so far as to write a letter to mayors and the sports minister to ask for something that should be self-evident: 'to ask for the full support of the Polish authorities in dealing with these important matters' (UEFA, 2012). Western narratives create a highly biased image of Eastern Europe as one homogenous dangerous, violent, barbaric and uncivilised space. Again, I do not intend to downplay the virulence of racism in football, but by emphasising it as a Polish and Ukrainian problem, it is by definition not (or no longer) a Western problem. The claim that it is considered too dangerous for Westerners to travel there automatically makes Westerners more civilised, non-violent and much more progressive. Westerners draw upon historically transmitted images and imaginations of an East that they invented to present themselves in a favourable light.

The ternary staggering of the Orientalising grammar becomes apparent when we include the host's self-representation. The issue of violence and racism, as described above, can generally be considered a part of a larger discourse on safety and security within the imagination of the wild and barbaric East. There is an increasing body of literature on security issues with regard to sports events (Winter and Klob, 2011; Bennett and Haggerty, 2012; Klauser, 2012; see also the special issue of *Urban Studies* edited by Giulianotti and Klauser, 2011). The Polish organisers anticipated Western fears and anxieties, and the way they meet these concerns can be analysed using the ternary grammar. As one example of the many publications and statements that I encountered, I will refer to one issue of 'EURO echo miasta', a Polish-English newspaper that was distributed for free during Euro 2012. Page 1 already emphasises service and safety:

> The last few months have not been easy for the residents of Poznań. They have had to deal with major road works, enormous traffic jams and multiple changes in tramway timetable. Repairs and renovations seemed endless, and lots of us kept asking the same question – what is it all for? It is for you – football fans. All of it has been done to make you feel safe and comfortable in Poznań. (Idczak, 2012a)

Safety and security are of utmost concern for the self-representation of the host city: The 'fans are watched by over 150 cameras' and the fan zones are 'safe and convenient' (Idczak, 2012a), also trains and locomotives carrying supporters 'provide comfort and safety' (Idczak, 2012b). Carriers 'guarantee that trains will be clean' (Idczak, 2012b). With regard to attractions in the fan zone, EURO echo miasto does not fail to mention: 'And what is really important for many people, the fun will be safe. The site is monitored 24/7 and patrolled by over 300 security guards' (Fertsch, 2012). As for the site of the fan zone, 'Plac Wolności will not only be interesting and safe, but also clean' (Fertsch, 2012).

This emphasis on cleanliness, safety and security accounts for a certain anticipatory obedience on the part of the Polish organisers. You expect our trains to be dirty and our fan zones to be dangerous? Well, then you'll be surprised! Within the grammars of identity/alterity, this can be analysed with reference to the ternary staggering of the Orientalising grammar: those previously Orientalised use a third actor to distinguish themselves from. Yet, in this case the third actor is their own perceptive past. It is the historically produced and delegated image of oneself that originated in the West, and is now successfully imported to the East.[5] Now the challenge is to escape Easternness – for example when the third actor appears with a more self-confident attitude and the Orientalised turn the tables on the West. Jacek Cichocki, then interior minister, during a visit to Poznań, underlined that 'The Poznań fan zone is better situated, provides much more comfortable conditions for fans than similar objects that have been organised during earlier championships in Austria and Switzerland' (Ministerstwo Spraw Wewnętrznych, 2012b [author's translation]).

Poland, and this is the message, is not as bad as the West still seems to believe; on the contrary, it has done its homework and exceeds its Western counterparts. Polish official actors, therefore, do not dismiss the accusation, but they relegate it to the past and to those groups within society who they suspect of being stuck in the past – similar to how first-generation migrants accuse those who arrive at a later stage of confirming hegemonic stereotypes (Baumann, 2004, p. 39), Polish public relations attempt to evade and counter the stereotype by putting the blame on their own historical self, which they believe to have overcome, and on those marginalised social groups who they believe have not yet internalised and adapted to the neoliberal system (cf. Buchowski 2006).

Their efforts will have little impact. The BBC and large parts of the Western media and public will most probably prefer not to alter their stereotypes. They are likely to remain rather untouched, as it is just too tempting to stick to a sensational explanatory frame of reference that has proven to be very functional and selling.

The picture is not complete though: we must not forget that the East is Janus-faced; it is simultaneously dangerous and tempting. There is both a male and a female version of the dangerous East.

The tempting East

First steps into Euro 2012: at the Poznań train station I approach one of the information tables that have been set up for travelling supporters. One of the flyers particularly catches my attention: The flyer reads: 'Cheer for health. 5 rules for a safe and healthy cheering.' The warnings not only include reminders that alcohol is banned in public places and that drugs are illegal in Poland, but also advises travellers to care for their hygiene and warns against unprotected sex: 'Avoid casual sex! In order to avoid a contagion with HIV and other sexually transmitted diseases, please use a condom.' The flyer was produced by Poland's State Sanitary Inspectorate (Główny Inspektorat Sanitarny) in collaboration with several other health agencies, such as the National AIDS Centre and the WHO Europe (field notes, 7 June 2012).

The threat behind the 'casual sex' warning, particularly with regard to nationality or gender, is not defined in more detail, but the context of the flyer gives us some hints as to how to interpret its intention. UEFA, FIFA and local clubs are increasingly trying to 'civilise' football and exclude violent Ultra and hooligan groups, thus turning the match into a family-friendly experience. However, the flyer's target group was most likely the male Western football supporter, travelling with his football mates. Although women are increasingly present at the stadiums, it is still highly improbable that the flyer warns travellers of having sex with female fans. As will be argued below, female fans did not play a significant role in the host's self-representation. Instead, it can be assumed that the threat comes in the disguise of local women.[6] The fact that Euro 2012 takes place in Poland and Ukraine seems to make it necessary to add an explicit reminder. Western men, who would generally be described as the active part and sometimes even as perpetrators, due to gender, are victimised in this specific case.[7] Again, Poland is constituted as the West's 'other' – this time epitomised not by violent and angry male aggression, but by a tempting female that carries the risk of severe contagion.

Generally, healthcare issues are important for mega-sports events, and a survey, focusing on measles conducted after Euro 2012, found that supporters are often accused of being too careless regarding travel health advice (Janiec et al., 2012). During the World Cup 2006 in Germany and Euro 2008 in Austria and Switzerland, campaigns took place that did not only give health advice to supporters and distribute condoms, but included the point of view of female (and male) prostitutes. Many of these campaigns drew attention to the issue of forced prostitution and trafficking in human beings, while some merely insisted on the importance of a respectful business relation (see Kimm and Sauer, 2011). The official Euro 2012 flyer focuses solely on supporters. Kimm and Sauer contend that 'the German campaigns deployed a xenophobic subtext with reference to trafficking networks and prostitutes from "the East", contributing to the ongoing struggle over a more restrictive immigration law' (Kimm and Sauer, 2011, p. 825).

In Poznań's official self-representation, women do not appear as active football fans, but instead, for the city's self-marketing, they are decorative and highly sexualised assets. A look back at 'EURO echo miasta': the front page shows a picture with three blonde girls, only slightly dressed, holding footballs – they do not hold them like football players, but rather like Eve offered the apple in the garden of Eden. The caption reads: 'Football fans from abroad are impressed not only with the city, but also with the beauty of local girls' (EURO echo miasta, 1). While the East always entailed a notion of exoticism, desire and sexual attraction, this fuses with an inherent threat for Western travellers' health safety.

Celebration of loyalties and stereotypes

Until now this chapter has focused on the ways Eastern host countries, and Poland in particular, have been perceived as the Western visitors' and observers' 'significant Other', constantly reproducing images of the 'Cultural East', albeit to varying degrees. The next section will take a look at the host country and its public opinion of fans from abroad. It specifically emphasises the relationship and the negotiation of distance and relatedness, of affection and rejection, and the importance for their self-image.

During Euro 2012, the city of Poznań was host to three national teams: Croatia, Ireland and Italy. Oddly, Poznań thus welcomed teams and fans from three predominantly Catholic countries, making it, as locals jokingly said, a kind of Catholic football capital. My account will include the former two because during my stay in Poznań neither the Italian team nor their fans had arrived yet. Therefore, I will focus exclusively on the way the local population perceived the Croatian and Irish fans. I will argue that mainstream public opinion did not equally perceive of and create a link with football fans from each country. It varied due to the different socio-political, cultural and historical set of relations, their negotiation between self and other, and a specific dialectic of affection and rejection on the map of Europeanness.

Croatian fans

At first glance Croatian and Irish fans could be differentiated by differences in social structure.[8] Following Giulianotti's taxonomy many different spectator identities filled the city of Poznań: supporters, followers, fans and flâneurs (Giulianotti, 2002). Neither side could be described as constituting a truly homogeneous group, yet certain tendencies could be observed.

The Croatian group was dominated by young men in their twenties and thirties. Very few women wearing the Croatian jersey, or any other fan accessories, were seen. For most of the Croatian group, Euro 2012 was not a family event, and it was probably not an event that made a qualitative difference. The Croatian supporters rather resembled Ultra, and sometimes even hooligan, groups. They were reported within a narrative that could be described as the dark side of the Croatian stereotype, which is related to the image of the fierce Balkan. Many authors (Bakić-Hayden and Hayden, 1992; Todorova, 1997; Močnik, 1998; Mungiu-Pippidi, 2003; Mishkova, 2008) have argued that, similarly to the Western representation of Eastern Europe and Russia, the Balkans are depicted as wild, barbaric and fundamentally different from Western civilisation. Yet, as Todorova argues, Balkanism is not simply another version of Orientalism but: 'Unlike orientalism, which is a discourse about an imputed opposition, balkanism is a discourse about an imputed ambiguity' (Todorova, 1997: 17). According to Todorova, there is no feminine version of Balkanism, since 'balkanist discourse is singularly male' unlike the Orient, which is depicted as feminine (Todorova, 1997, p. 15).

Back to the field: my favourite spaghetti bar in Poznań. At the adjacent table there are two Croatian men in their early twenties, flirting with two Polish girls, approximately 18 years old. The Croats, trying to handle the conversation in Polish, while coquetting with their lack in language skills, compliment the girls and make quite straightforward moves. The Croats' performance is that of the hot-blooded Southerner; they cultivate their Latin lover image, which apparently works quite well for the Polish girls (field notes, 8 June 2012).

I observed the Croatian 'Latin lovers' meeting with giggling Polish girls, who apparently felt flattered by their interest, not only at the spaghetti bar, but also at other locations. Many Croatian fans engaged in a masculine heterosexual performance that explicitly emphasised not only badges of masculinity and male football fan culture (cf. Sülzle, 2005), but they also fused it with a specific sexual connotation directed at the Polish women. This self-representation, its narration, and its negotiation could function as a basis for understanding with Polish male football supporters, as notes from the field show:

> It is the Germany vs. Portugal match. We are in 'Stajenka Pegaza', a small pub just outside the bustling city centre. 'Stajenka Pegaza' has a projector and a nice and crowded outside area. My partner, my 3-year old son, and I take a seat at one of the less noisy benches in the back. For the most part, the crowd is rather quiet, and to my surprise not everyone cheers for Portugal; even some Poles seem to prefer the long-hated neighbour Germany to Cristiano Ronaldo. The match already started and a group of three late-coming Croats takes a seat on the bench to our left. They look about, clearly looking out for new acquaintances. We, the couple on their right with a child, are not what they had in mind, so they prefer to ignore us. In front of the Croats sits a group of three Poles who are actively following the match. In order to establish contact, one of the Croats taps the shoulder of the Pole in front of him. Initially, the Poles are quite reluctant; they obviously prefer to watch the match. In a disinterested, yet not unfriendly, way the Poles briefly answer questions and then turn their back on the Croats. But the Croats do not give up so quickly. They use all of their male-drunk ammunition: 'Poland is great, we love Poland. Polish women are great'. This finally works. The Poles answer: 'Yes, you are perfectly right, Polish women are great; they are the most beautiful women in the world'. The Poles eventually return the compliment: 'Polish women do love Croats; if you tell them where you come from, you can have them all!'

After discussing Polish women, the Croats move on to more football-related issues: they use their mobile phones to show pictures of their club, Hajduk Split. After this initial warm-up phase the Poles are much more accessible and interested. I do not see the pictures, but judging from what I hear – talk about flags and other equipment, explanations of the who-is-who in the group – I assume that the images show a male-dominated hero narrative and iconography of an Ultra group. Their offensive self-representation apparently is attractive for like-minded Poles who also bring stereotypes into the conversation and confirm the image of the macho and the Latin lover (field notes, 9 June 2012).

That night, both the Poles and the Croats found a commonality through their staging of sexist attitudes toward women. Each groups' masculinity is performatively reproduced. In Baumann's terms, both groups follow the grammar of segmentation: the Croatian and Polish young men are united in their perception and judgement of Polish women. This is not to say that they would actually behave the way they pretend – talk and action do not necessarily have to coincide. We should consider this story-telling and self-glorification a performance of how life, from the point of view of young male Polish and Croatian football fans, should be like – even though reality might look completely different on both sides. Story-telling is a strategy where we create an image and paint a picture, in order to establish a relationship with a listener. Thus, both sides engage in a role-play that is specific for this type of setting, but could be different in a changing setting (Goffman, 1990 [1959]).

The category of Polish women is subject to a male definition and defined as male property without agency – an indicator of the third grammar, the grammar of encompassment. Baumann himself refers to the gender example: 'Seen from below, woman is the opposite of man. Seen from above, that is, the level of man as defining the generic term, woman is but part of mankind' (Baumann, 2004, p. 25). Women are not actively participating subjects, but rather are made into an object to be appropriated. A fusion on a segmentary level is only temporary. We can imagine that the discursive connection can quickly change when Polish men feel the need to protect the seemingly helpless Polish women against fierce and brutal Balkan men, all triggered by an Orientalist interpretation. In this case, Polish men might quickly side with tabloid media and anti-Croatian public opinion and engage in a Balkanist/Orientalist stereotyping of their former buddies. Selmer and Sülzle (2010, p. 808) show how during Euro 2008, in the Austrian town of Klagenfurt, Croatian and Polish fans 'were portrayed as being a dangerous and predominantly male out-of-control mass – a clear threat to women in particular'.

The Croatian fans' exotic Latin lover macho image is quite attractive for like-minded Poles and parts of the female population. Yet, not everyone was entirely happy with the Croatian performance. Polish newspapers complained and found the Croatian fans' behaviour, particularly their aggressive appearance and their treatment of women, inappropriate. Before the Ireland vs. Croatia match a Polish ethnology student confessed to me that he sincerely hopes that the Croats will win – 'because otherwise they will destroy the city'. He says that Slavs are inclined to support each other, thus shift their loyalty to a group that is perceived to be close and familiar in terms of culture and language. In the specific case of Croatia he expresses his fears that a defeat might unleash the Croats' uncontrollable fury. It goes without saying that there is always an, albeit not openly spoken, reference to the Balkan Wars in such utterings: we have seen what they are capable of, beneath their civilised surface. For this Polish student, the choice to support the Croatian team against Ireland does not stem from a whole-hearted feeling and pan-Slavic solidarity, but from rational considerations that draw upon deeply rooted stereotypes of the Balkan other. Similarly to large parts of the Poznań population, as we will see in the next section, this Polish student's emotional support was with the Irish team.

Unfortunately, a group of Croatian fans confirmed this bad reputation and the Oriental grammar. In Poznań's old town, before the match started, Croatian fans, from the clubs Hajduk Split und Dinamo Zagreb, had already got into a fight with the police and with each other:

> Croatian fans threw chairs, bottles and flares at Polish riot police in the city of Poznań as they clashed ahead of Sunday's Euro 2012 game between Croatia and Ireland. [...] The spokesman said it began after a clash in one of the bars between intoxicated fans of two rival Croatian teams from Zagreb and Split shortly after 5:00 pm (1500 GMT) (Eurosport, 2012).

Croatia won 3:1, which in the eyes of the Polish student most likely saved the Poznań city centre and spared it from becoming entirely devastated.[9]

Irish fans

Both Polish public and media seemed to agree on a rather sceptical perspective regarding the Croatian supporters, but their attitude towards the Irish fans was entirely different. The rejection of the Balkan other emphasised the civilised, restrained and self-controlled self, whereas the Irish other was welcomed with great affection, establishing a type of spiritual kinship. In terms of gender and age, the Irish supporters were much more diverse than the Croats. Most Irish fans were aged between 25 and 50, although there were many outside that range. The vast majority of them were in an outspoken, joyful mood, which created an open and friendly atmosphere. In the sky above Poznań we saw a lot of Ryanair aeroplanes. This led us to conclude that many Irish people had taken advantage of this uncomfortable, yet cheap, way of travelling and used Euro 2012 as an opportunity for a family trip to Poland.

The Irish performance fundamentally differed from the Croatian one. We observed a striking staging of Irishness, a nationalisation of the carnivalesque aspect of football at its best. According to Free, in his account of migrant Irish in Britain, the Irish supporters in Poznań can be described as 'the clichéd image of colorful Irish supporters abroad in appearance, hedonistic behavior and good humored engagement of "locals"' (Free, 2007, p. 488). At this and other championships, while other fan groups stuck to the same three (or so) chants, the Irish supporters would engage in a joyful performance. They sang creative songs, some of which were popular songs that they had rephrased, praising for example 'Trappatoni – once he was Italian, now he is Irish' or 'In Trap we trust!'. On YouTube and other online video portals many videos can be found, adding to the perpetuation and (self-)celebration of the Irish image. Once again, football was not only about football. The Irish fans used their performances as vehicles to transport other messages than ones related to the sport. Euro 2012 became a site for the economic crisis debate, and football, and the carnivalesque possibilities of football support, served as an outlet for rage and dissatisfactions that otherwise would not automatically relate to football.

Both politics and economics entered the scene. Irish fans ironically and comically referred to the economic crisis; for example Irish supporters chanted: 'Merkel thinks we're working!' on Poznań's main square or had themselves photographed with a huge banner 'Angela Merkel thinks we're at work'. The website *TheScore.ie* interviewed the fans who held the banner, and they commented: 'We were going to put [Irish Prime Minister] "Enda Kenny thinks we're at work," but then we said we might as well put the woman who pays the bills on the front of the flag' (TheScore, 2012). Declan Pierce, another fan from Ireland, recalls on the same webpage: 'The atmosphere was

serious craic. The Croatian fans were singing these particularly aggressive heavy chants and we tried to sing back the usual stuff but got
shouted down.'

The importance and relevance of such actions is not confined to
the act itself in the here and now, nor is it intended to. More important is the dissemination via the Internet and social media, which
creates an importance that transcends the original moment. The act
acquires its particular relevance and range when the picture or the
video enters distribution via social media (see McManus, 2015).

The generally positive Irish image and stereotype, their self-
representation, and the media coverage contributed to the Irish myth
that they were indeed everybody's darlings during Euro 2012. In the
case of Poland there is more to that. During my fieldwork, when
I talked to Poles most of them expressed a certain sympathy for
Ireland. There were many who had previously worked in the country. They knew it well and had good memories (see also Dundon
et al., 2007; Krings et al., 2009). Both countries share an underdog
image. Many Poles, in various respects, identify with Ireland, not
only due to personal acquaintance, but they see many common-
alities and perceive of this other strikingly Catholic country at the
other edge of the European Union as their Western counterpart. This
was by far not a one-way-street. As results from my Polish colleagues'
fieldwork show, the Irish supporters also vividly emphasised similarities between the nations and drew comparisons. For instance, they
compared England's role in Irish history to German and Russian
oppressors in Poland, stressing the similar history of oppressions
and uprisings. Many Irish fans seemed to have acquired extensive
knowledge about Polish history and were eager to talk about it with
locals (see, for example, Olkiewicz, 2012). This imagined relationship
has been repeatedly emphasised and honoured. In a pub in Poznań
I found a reference to a famous Polish medieval saying. The original
highlighted Polish-Hungarian friendship:

Polak, Węgier — dwa bratanki, i do szabli, i do szklanki,
oba zuchy, oba żwawi, niech im Pan Bóg błogosławi.
(Pole and Hungarian cousins be, good for fight and good for party.
Both are valiant, both are lively, upon them may God's bless-
ings be.)

The adaptation, which was printed on an Irish flag and hung outside a pub in the Old Town, read:

Irys – Polak, dwa bratanki, i do piłki i do szklanki.
(Irishman and Pole cousins be, good for football and good for party.)

Poznań citizens thanked the Irish, as has been documented by many YouTube videos. One comment makes a concrete reference to Polish–Irish like-mindedness: a user named 'onedirectionholizm' writes: 'Ireland is the second Poland:) WE LOVE YOU, IRISH!' A user who goes under the name of 'georgousgeorge69' is also linguistically over-whelmed – his comment is a reaction to another thank-you-video, which had been produced by Poznań students: 'poland thank you for your hospatility! from now on we are brothers. Signed . . . Ireland' (KontraTV Nowy Wymiar Studenckiej Rzeczywistości, 2012; see also, for example, Linukz, 2012).

The Poznań city council's official blogger, a British Poznań resident named Paul, wrote about the Irish: 'I've really never seen a friendlier, more positively boisterous set of supporters in my life. You'd think they'd won the tournament the way they were at it' (Poznan, 2012). The then mayor of Poznań, Ryszard Grobelny, even flew to Dublin to 'personally thank Irish football fans, also known as the Green Army, for their exceptional behaviour during Euro 2012 [. . .]. "We were delighted with the Irish fans. The atmosphere was great and there was a feeling of something missing when the Irish left", Poznan city spokesman Damean Zalewske [sic] told the Independent' (Kelly, 2012).

To a large degree collective identities depend on comparison, self-ing and othering. It is not always the case that 'we' want to be better than 'they', but comparison can result in outright admiration and the wish to belong. If they are like us, then any public admiration or applause for them will also account for us. The Polish display of loyalty and excitement for the Irish can be described using the grammar of encompassment. As the Poznań colleagues found, both relation and attraction are reciprocal: the Poles felt truly liked by the Irish visitors. The guests seemed to have no prejudices and openly showed their friendship and understanding, for example, when the Irish discredited the above mentioned BBC documentary as 'British bullshitting'. Not only did Poles identify with the Irish, but Irish supporters also drew comparisons regarding Irish and Polish history – particularly regarding the fact that now both had suffered from a British patronising attitude, making Britain a third actor in the equation. The Irish made the Poles like them since 'we like people who like us' and treat us as their peers.

In public opinion, the Croatian fans are related to following the grammars of Orientalisation. They were perceived to behave like they had come to conquer new territories – and the women belonging to it. Attempting to say something nice, Poznań's blogger Paul writes about the Croats:

> When the teams were drawn for Poznań, Croatia was the X factor in so much as noone was really sure how many of their fans would turn up. We shouldn't have doubted them. Although not quite as numerous as the Irish, the Croats have made quite a splash here with their colour, noise and Balkan style. (Poznan, 2012)

Large parts of the Polish, and also Western, public opinion tend to Orientalise/balkanise the Croatian supporters, thereby distancing themselves and appearing more 'Western'. This is in line with Baumann's concept of the ternary staggering of the Orientalising grammar. The Poles, being themselves Orientalised and defined as the Eastern significant other, relativise this image by emphasising the negative characteristics of the Croats. The Croats do not even need to be present in the equation. Emphasising the Irish 'friendly invasion' (Kelly, 2012) and the specific relationship between the Poles and Irish, without even mentioning the Croats, undoubtedly sends a strong message. This is the ternary stage in this othering process: there must be a third actor who is left out.

Conclusion

Just like BBC's *Panorama*, this chapter can easily be accused of being biased and highly selective. It did not elaborate on violent Irish, gentle Croats, balanced media coverage, and many other issues that deserve attention. The goal was not to give an objective account of Euro 2012 in Poznań, but to analyse how a football mega-event is used for practices of affection and rejection, of locating the self and the other, and of 'doing' identity and alterity. Baumann's grammars of identity/alterity prove useful for an analysis of such a complex and multi-layered phenomenon, such as Euro 2012. They allow us to grasp more than one version of reality. Although the reference to grammar and structure might lead us to suspect a strictly structural approach, it allows for agency and a focus on praxeology. Dichotomies serve various purposes: as analytical ideal-types in a Weberian sense, as selling point for the media and as landmarks used by actors for orientation. In all these cases we can conclude that clear-cut dichotomies will not survive practical tests; they are too strict and they do not account for the complexity of real life – they constrain actors.

Football – and football fandom – is a practice that has not been fixed once and for all. All the various actors in this chapter relate to different narratives and images of how football and football supporters should act. To put it bluntly, the Croatian fans represent a wild, sexy and therefore truly masculine football image. The Irish fans 'only' got drunk and were not truly interested in go-go clubs or sexual conquests. Even when they hit on girls, they were reported to behave in a much more 'romantic' and gentle way than the Croats, thus representing the rather family-friendly and modernised version of football. We could continue this list to also include diverse actors, such as those who eagerly opposed Euro 2012 and opted for a more democratic and authentic way of playing, watching and celebrating football (see Buchowski and Kowalska, this volume). These various narratives illuminate the many ways in which concepts such as Europeanisation and Orientalisation operate, how they are appropriated and instrumentalised by actors for their own purposes who either ascribe them to others or consider them a part of their identity. Suffice to say, all these actors, who are somehow – marginally or abundantly – involved in this mega-event, practice different versions of football and contribute to a general discursive concept of what football is. They participate in intersubjective negotiations about the meaning of the game. Each supporter takes his or her share and appropriates it while simultaneously defending it against other versions of reality. All of these practices are informed by historically transmitted perceptions, mediated images and personal experience, thus making football a truly social event.

Notes

1. Europeanisation is more than simply a harmonisation and alignment of institutions, norms and regulations. As Alpan and Schwell argue in the introductory chapter to this volume, Europeanisation relates to questions of identity and alterity, imaginaries, and performative, political, discursive and social practices that are informed by historically transmitted narratives.
2. Even anthropologists sometimes appear not to be immune: I went to Warsaw in 2011 with a group of Viennese European Ethnology students. They later confessed that they had been amazed by the sight of skyscrapers and shops with Western brands, which they had not expected to be found that far in the East. They previously had discussed whether it would be dangerous to wear expensive jeans (see Gozzer, 2012).
3. Fieldwork was carried out in close collaboration with the Poznań branch of the FREE project, Michał Buchowski and Małgorzata Kowalska and their team from the Department of Ethnology and Cultural Anthropology, UAM. I will refer repeatedly to their observations in the course of this chapter. For another detailed ethnography of Euro 2012 see Burszta et al. (2012).
4. His working definition perceives of patriotism as something desirable and of nationalism as harmful. This relationship, obviously, is subject to ongoing debates, yet suffice to say that football, and the emotions released in football, tend to strengthen and/or weaken existing affections and rejections.
5. Hierarchies, of course, characterise the image of the West about the East as well. The ternary model of the Orientalising grammar can be fruitfully applied to the way the West differentiates between Poland and Ukraine. As space is limited, it would lead too far to elaborate more deeply on this topic. Suffice to mention that while both are on the same page with regard to hooligans and racism, Poland by many observers is perceived as one of 'us' in both cultural and economic terms in contrast to crime-ridden and undemocratic Ukraine; see, for example, 'EURO in the Ukraine: A Guest of the Mafia's' (Bidder and Eichhofer, 2012) and about Poland: 'Next Door Wonder' (Follath and Puhl, 2012).
6. Local women served rather as decorative accessories, which is a striking difference to what Selmer and Sülzle (2010, p. 805) observed for Euro 2008 in Austria, where women were explicitly mentioned as 'new' fans, albeit in a highly sexualised way. Yet, they mention that popular media representation portends that women become fans out of different (and rather not football-related) reasons such as sexual attraction to football players. Generally, large parts of football research have been accused of neglecting gender issues (Free and Hughson, 2003).
7. Prior to the 2006 World Cup in Germany, politicians, churches and civil society warned against the import of tens of thousands of forced prostitutes from Eastern Europe. Some cities planned to put up special

boxes that should be used for 'business'. In the end, these much discussed 'Verrichtungsboxen' were not installed. See, for example, Moos (2005).

8. It is important to stress that I have not conducted any quantitative surveys, nor do I rely on numbers or other seemingly objective variables. My account draws upon both my own and my Poznań colleagues' observations and the way Euro 2012 was covered in local, national and international media.

9. Studies found that football and violence, both domestic and other, correlate positively: '...studies have suggested that testosterone levels increase in individuals when watching football matches, a chemical associated with an upsurge in aggression' (Kirby et al., 2013, p. 5). The study found that 'although incidents *increased* when the team won or drew (26 per cent), this finding intensified when the England team lost and exited the competition (38 percent) (Kirby et al., 2013, p. 12). The authors conclude: 'Although it is difficult to say the tournament is a causal factor, the prestigious tournament does concentrate the risk factors into a short and volatile period, thereby intensifying the concepts of masculinity, rivalry, and aggression' (Kirby et al., 2013, p. 13).

References

Armstrong, G. and R. Giulianotti (eds) (1997) *Entering the Field. New Perspectives on World Football* (Oxford: Berg).

Bakić-Hayden, M. (1995) 'Nesting Orientalisms: The Case of Former Yugoslavia', *Slavic Review*, Vol. 54, Issue 4, pp. 917–31.

Bakić-Hayden, M. and R. M. Hayden (1992) 'Orientalist Variations on the Theme "Balkans": Symbolic Geography in Recent Yugoslav Cultural Politics', *Slavic Review*, Vol. 51, Issue 1, pp. 1–15.

Barthes, R. (1972) *Mythologies* (New York: The Noonday Press).

Baumann. G. (2004) 'Grammars of Identity/Alterity: A Structural Approach', in G. Baumann and A. Gingrich (eds), *Grammars of Identity/Alterity: A Structural Approach* (New York and Oxford: Berghahn), pp. 18–50.

BBC (2012a) 'Euro 2012: Stadiums of Hate', BBC One Panorama, 28 May 2012, at: www.bbc.co.uk/programmes/b01jk4vr, accessed 10 March 2014.

BBC (2012b) 'Statement regarding Panorama – Euro 2012: Stadiums of Hate', BBC Media Centre, 30 May 2012, at: www.bbc.co.uk/mediacentre/statements/panorama-euro.html, accessed 11 February 2014.

BBC News (2012) 'Sol Campbell warns fans to stay away from Euro 2012', 28 May 2012, at: www.bbc.co.uk/news/uk-18192375, accessed 23 January 2014.

Bennett, C. J. and K. Haggerty (eds) (2012) *Security Games. Surveillance and Control at Mega-Events* (New York: Routledge).

Bidder, B. and A. Eichhofer (2012) 'Fußball-EM in der Ukraine: Zu Gast bei der Mafia', *Spiegel Online* (12 April 2012), at: www.spiegel.de/reise/staedte/0,1518,826787,00.html, accessed 10 March 2014.

Blecking, D. (2013) 'Auf der Suche nach Erfolgen: Der polnische Fußball zwischen Tradition und Transformation', *Ost-West. Europäische Perspektiven*, Vol. 14, Issue 4, pp. 251–58.

Boniface, P. (1998) 'Football as a Factor (and a Reflection) of International Politics', *The International Spectator*, Vol. 33, Issue 4, pp. 87–98.

Bourdieu, P. (1984) *Distinction. A Social Critique of the Judgement of Taste* (Cambridge, MA: Harvard University Press).

Bromberger, C. (1995) *Le match de football. Ethnologie d'une passion partisane à Marseille, Naples et Turin* (Paris: Editions de la Maison des Sciences de l'Homme).

Buchowski, M. (2006) 'The Specter of Orientalism in Europe: From Exotic Other to Stigmatized Brother', *Anthropological Quarterly*, Vol. 79, Issue 3, pp. 463–482.

Burszta, W. J., M. Czubaj, J. Drozda, et al. (eds) (2012) *Stadion – Miasto – Kultura. EURO 2012 i przemiany kultury polskiej. "Święto" – rok 2012* (Warszawa: Instytut Badań Przestrzeni Publicznej).

Change.org (2012) 'Apologise for the Bias Presented in "Euro 2012: Stadiums of Hate"'. Petition by Aleksandra Pecyna, Birmingham, United Kingdom, Change.org, at: www.change.org/petitions/bbc-apologise-for-the-bias-presented-in-euro-2012-stadiums-of-hate-2, accessed 11 February 2014.

Davies, C. (1982) 'Ethnic Jokes, Moral Values and Social Boundaries', *The British Journal of Sociology*, Vol. 33, Issue 3, pp. 383–403.

Dundon, T., M.-A. González-Pérez and T. McDonough (2007) 'Bitten by the Celtic Tiger: Immigrant Workers and Industrial Relations in the New "Glocalized" Ireland', *Economic and Industrial Democracy*, Vol. 28, Issue 4, pp. 501–22.

Eastern approaches blog (2012) 'Euro 2012 Is Overshadowed by Accusations of Racism and Anti-Semitism', *The Economist*, 6 June 2012, at: www. economist.com/blogs/easternapproaches/2012/06/ugly-spectre, accessed 11 February 2014.

Eder, K. (2006) 'Europe's Borders: The Narrative Construction of the Boundaries of Europe', *European Journal of Social Theory*, Vol. 9, Issue 2, pp. 255–71.

Epstein, R. A. and W. Jacoby (2014) 'Eastern Enlargement Ten Years On: Transcending the East–West Divide?', *JCMS: Journal of Common Market Studies*, Vol. 52, Issue 1, pp. 1–16.

Eurosport (2012) 'Croatia Fans Held after Poznań fighting', *Eurosport.Com*, 11 June 2012, at: http://asia.eurosport.com/football/euro-2012/2012/fans-held-after-fighting_sto3306861/story.shtml, accessed 11 February 2014.

FARE Network (2012) 'UEFA Announce Investigations into Two Racism Incidents', 12 June 2012, at: www.farenet.org/news/uefa-announce-investigations-into-two-racism-incidents, accessed 10 March 2014.

Fertsch, K. (2012) 'Plac Wolności is the biggest Fan Zone', *EURO echo miasta* (10–11 June 2012), Nr 42 (675), Poznań, p. 6.

Follath, E. and J. Puhl (2012) 'Das Wunder von nebenan', *Der Spiegel*, 21/2012, pp. 76–83.

Free, M. (2007) 'Tales from the Fifth Green Field: The Psychodynamics of Migration, Masculinity and National Identity amongst Republic of Ireland Soccer Supporters in England', *Sport in Society*, Vol. 10, Issue 3, pp. 476–94.

Free, M. and J. Hughson (2003) 'Settling Accounts with Hooligans: Gender Blindness in Football Supporter Subculture Research', *Men and Masculinities*, Vol. 6, Issue 2, pp. 136–55.

Gentle, P. (2012) 'Euro 2012 Blog – Stadiums of Hate, or Sensationalist Journalism?', *TheNews.pl*, 30 May 2012, at: www.thenews.pl/1/214/Artykul/101074,Euro-2012-Blog-%E2%80%93-stadiums-of-hate-or-sensationalist-journalism, accessed 6 March 2014.

Giles, T. (2012) '"Stadiums of Hate": Legitimate and Fair', BBC News – The Editors, 8 June 2012, www.bbc.co.uk/blogs/theeditors/2012/06/stadiums_of_hate_legitimate_an.html, accessed 6 March 2014.

Giulianotti, R. (1995) 'Football and the Politics of Carnival: An Ethnographic Study of Scottish Fans in Sweden', *International Review for the Sociology of Sport*, Vol. 30, Issue 2, pp. 191–220.

Giulianotti, R. (2002) 'Supporters, Followers, Fans, and Flaneurs: A Taxonomy of Spectator Identities in Football', *Journal of Sport and Social Issues*, Vol. 26, Issue 1, pp. 25–46.

Giulianotti, R. and F. Klauser (eds) (2011) 'Special Issue: Security and Surveillance at Sport Mega Events', *Urban Studies*, Vol. 48, Issue 15.

Goffman, E. (1990 [1959]) *The Presentation of Self in Everyday Life* (Harmondsworth: Penguin).

Gozzer, L. (2012) 'Feldimpressionen aus Warschau. Ethnographische Annäherungen an Selbst- und Fremdbilder', in A. Schwell and J. Wietschorke (eds), *Orts-Erkundungen. Der Stadt auf der Spur* (Wien: Verlag des Instituts für Europäische Ethnologie), pp. 52–64.

Gurjewitsch, A. (1999) 'Bachtin und seine Theorie des Karnevals', in J. Bremmer and H. Roodenburg (ed.), *Kulturgeschichte des Humors. Von der Antike bis heute* (Darmstadt: Primus-Verlag), pp. 57–63.

Idczak, M. (2012a) 'Poznań Welcomes Euro 2012 Fans', *EURO echo miasta* (10–11 June 2012), Nr 42 (675), Poznań, p. 1.

Idczak, M. (2012b) 'Additional Trains Going to Euro', *EURO echo miasta* (10–11 June 2012), Nr 42 (675), Poznań, p. 3.

Janiec, J., A. Zielicka-Hardy, A. Polkowska, et al. (2012) 'Did Public Health Travel Advice Reach EURO 2012 Football Fans? A Social Network Survey', *Euro Surveillance*, Vol. 17, Issue 31, pp. 1–3.

Johnson, J. K. (2011) 'The Curious Tale of the Polish Plumber: Rebranding Nations for New Social and Political Situations', *Advertising & Society Review*, Vol. 12, Issue 1.

Kelly, D. (2012) 'Polish Mayor Thanks Irish for Good UEFA Camaraderie', *Irish Central*, 18 July 2012, at: www.irishcentral.com/sports/polish-mayor-thanks-irish-for-good-uefa-camaraderie-162854976-237516621.html, accessed 6 March 2014.

Kimm, S. and B. Sauer (2011) 'Discourses on Forced Prostitution, Trafficking in Women and Football: A Comparison of Anti-Trafficking Campaigns during the World Cup 2006 and the European Championship 2008', *Soccer & Society*, Vol. 11, Issue 6, pp. 815–28.

Kirby, S., B. Francis and R. O'Flaherty (2013) 'Can the FIFA World Cup Football (Soccer) Tournament Be Associated with an Increase in Domestic Abuse?', *Journal of Research in Crime and Delinquency*, published online before print, 22 July 2013.

Klauser, F. R. (2012) 'Interpretative Flexibility of the Event-City: Security, Branding and Urban Entrepreneurialism at the European Football Championships 2008', *International Journal of Urban and Regional Research*, Vol. 36, Issue 5, pp. 1039–52.

Kontakt 24 (2012) 'Trumny z pozdrowieniami dla BBC', *Kontakt 24* (1 July 2012), at: http://kontakt24.tvn24.pl/temat,trumny-z-pozdrowieniami-dla-bbc,50257.html?categoryId=496, accessed 6 March 2014.

KontraTV Nowy Wymiar Studenckiej Rzeczywistości (2012) 'Thank you, Ireland!', at: www.youtube.com/watch?v=yw9IwVOeNd4, accessed 10 March 2014.

Krings, T., E. Moriarty, J. Salamonska, et al. (2009) 'Migration and Recession: Polish Migrants in Post-Celtic Tiger Ireland', *Sociological Research Online*, Vol. 14, Issue 2, p. 9.

Kundera M. (1984) 'The Tragedy of Central Europe', *New York Review of Books*, Vol. 31, Issue 7, pp. 33–8.

Kürti, L. and P. Skalník (eds) (2009) *Postsocialist Europe. Anthropological Perspectives from Home* (New York and Oxford: Berghahn).

Kuus, M. (2004) 'Europe's Eastern Expansion and the Reinscription of Otherness in East-Central Europe', *Progress in Human Geography*, Vol. 28, Issue 4, pp. 472–89.

Latour, B. (1993) *We Have Never Been Modern* (Cambridge, MA: Harvard University Press).

Latour, B. (2005) *Reassembling the Social. An Introduction to Actor-Network-Theory* (Oxford: Oxford University Press).

Lechner, F. J. (2007) 'Imagined Communities in the Global Game: Soccer and the Development of Dutch National Identity', *Global Networks*, Vol. 7, Issue 2, pp. 193–229.

Linukz (2012) 'Euro 2012: Poznan Thanks the Irish!', YouTube, 18 June 2012, at: www.youtube.com/watch?v=9ctuT1d6HUI, accessed 6 March 2014.

McManus, J. (2015) 'Building a Turkish Fan Community: Facebook, Schengen and Easyjet', in A. Schwell, N. Szogs, M. Kowalska and M. Buchowski (eds), *New Ethnographies of Football in Europe: People, Passions, Politics* (Basingstoke: Palgrave Macmillan).

Ministerstwo Spraw Wewnętrznych (2012a) 'Sprostowanie dotyczące materiału BBC', press release 29 May 2012, Warszawa, at: www.msw.gov.pl/pl/aktualnosci/9847,Sprostowanie-dotyczace-materialu-BBC.html [English version: www.msw.gov.pl/download/1/14735/ResponsetotheBBCreport.pdf], accessed 6 March 2014.

Ministerstwo Spraw Wewnętrznych (2012b) 'Szef MSW z wizytą w Poznaniu', press release 16 May 2012, Warszawa, at: www.msw.gov.pl/pl/aktualnosci/9673,Szef-MSW-z-wizyta-w-Poznaniu.html, accessed 6 March 2014.

Mishkova, D. (2008) 'Symbolic Geographies and Visions of Identity', *European Journal of Social Theory*, Vol. 11, Issue 2, pp. 237–56.

Močnik, R. (1998) 'Balkan Orientalisms', in B. Baskar and B. Brumen (eds), *MESS: Mediterranean Ethnological Summer School Piran/Pirano Slovenia 1996* (Ljubljana: Inštitut za multikulturne raziskave), pp. 129–58.

Moisio, S. (2002) 'EU Eligibility, Central Europe, and the Invention of Applicant State Narrative', *Geopolitics*, Vol. 7, Issue 3, pp. 89–116.

Montague, J. (2013) *Ultras: How Egyptian Football Fans Toppled a Dictator* (London: deCoubertin Short Books).

Moos, A. (2005) 'Sex in the Box', *Die Zeit* (8 July 2005), at: www.zeit.de/2005/28/Verrichtungsboxen, accessed 6 March 2014.

Morris, P. (ed.) (2009) *The Bakhtin Reader. Selected Writings of Bakhtin, Medvedev and Volshinov* (London: Arnold).

Mungiu-Pippidi, A. (2003) 'Of Dark Sides and Twilight Zones: Enlarging to the Balkans', *East European Politics and Societies*, Vol. 17, Issue 1, pp. 83–90.

Mutz, M. (2012) 'Patrioten für drei Wochen. Nationale Identifikation und die Fußballeuropameisterschaft 2012', *Berliner Journal für Soziologie*, Vol. 22, Issue 4, pp. 517–38.

Nielsen, C. A. (2009) 'The Goalposts of Transition: Football as a Metaphor for Serbia's Long Journey to the Rule of Law', *Nationalities Papers*, Vol. 38, Issue 1, pp. 87–103.

O'Neill, B. (2012) 'England's Football Fans Have Proven that They Are Far More Racially Enlightened than the BBC', *The Telegraph*, 20 June 2012, at: http://blogs.telegraph.co.uk/news/brendanoneill2/100166543/englands-football-fans-have-proven-that-they-are-far-more-racially-enlightened-than-the-bbc, accessed 6 March 2014.

Olkiewicz, J. (2012) 'Z piątego stadionu: Irlandczycy. Co za naród...[From the 5th stadium: Irishmen. What a nation...]', *Weszło!* (12 June 2012), at: www.weszlo.com/2012/06/12/z-piatego-stadionu-irlandczycy-co-za-naroda, accessed 9 September 2014.

Panagiotidis, J. (2012) 'Die Krise ist kein Fußballspiel: Bemerkungen zu einem medial inszenierten Konflikt', *Südosteuropa. Zeitschrift für Politik und Gesellschaft*, Vol. 60, Issue 3, pp. 433–54.

Pearson, G. (2012) *An Ethnography of English Football Fans: Cans, Cops and Carnivals* (Manchester: Manchester University Press).

Poznan (2012) 'Poznan – Come and Enjoy', with Paul (Blog): Agony and Ecstasy! 18 June 2012, at: www.poznan.pl/comeandenjoy/en/2012/06/18/agony-and-ecstasy. www.poznan.pl/comeandenjoy/en/2012/06/14/poznans-rocking, accessed 9 September 2014.

Said, E. (1979) *Orientalism* (New York: Vintage).

Selmer, N. and A. Sülzle (2010) '(En-)gendering the European Football Family: The Changing Discourse on Women and Gender at EURO 2008', *Soccer & Society*, Vol. 11, Issue 6, pp. 803–14.

Sonntag, A. (2007) 'Sommernachtsträume. Eine skeptische Bilanz der Fußballweltmeisterschaften in Frankreich 1998 und Deutschland 2006', in Deutsch-Französisches Institut (ed.), *Frankreich Jahrbuch 2006*. *Politik und Kommunikation* (Wiesbaden: VS Verlag für Sozialwissenschaften), pp. 257–78.

Sonntag, A. (2014) 'Regards différenciés et stéréotypes sur un Brésil en mode carnaval', *Le Monde*, 28 June 2014), at: www.lemonde.fr/coupe-du-monde/article/2014/06/28/regards-differencies-et-stereotypes-sur-un-bresil-en-mode-carnaval_4447159_1616627.html, accessed 15 August 2014.

Stowarzyszenie NIGDY WIĘCEJ (2012a) 'Dyskusja o reportażu BBC Stadiony nienawiści', udział – R. Pankowski z NIGDY WIĘCEJ, 5 June 2012, YouTube, at: www.youtube.com/watch?v=Gd0Z-xLSlfs, accessed 10 March 2014.

Stowarzyszenie NIGDY WIĘCEJ (2012b) 'EURO 2012 bez rasizmu', Stowarzyszenie NIGDY WIĘCEJ, 14 January 2009, at: www.nigdywiecej.org/index.php?option=com_content&task=view&id=359, accessed 9 September 2014.

Sülzle, A. (2005) 'Fußball als Schutzraum für Männlichkeit? Ethnographische Anmerkungen zum Spielraum für Geschlechter im Stadion, in A. Hagel, N. Selmer and A. Sülzle (eds), *Gender Kicks. Texte zu Fußball und Geschlecht*) (Frankfurt: Koordinationsstelle Fan-Projekte bei der Deutschen Sportjugend), pp. 37–52.

Sundermeyer, O. (2012) *Tor zum Osten. Besuch in einer wilden Fussballwelt* (Göttingen: Verlag Die Werkstatt).

Swidler, A. (1986) 'Culture in Action: Symbols and Strategies', *American Sociological Review*, Vol. 51, pp. 273–86.

TheNews.pl (2012) 'Foreign Ministry Challenges BBC over "Stadiums of Hate" documentary', *TheNews.pl*, 30 May 2012, at: www.thenews.pl/1/10/Artykul/101082,Foreign-Ministry-challenges-BBC-over-%E2%80%9CStadiums-of-Hate%E2%80%9D-documentary, accessed 6 March 2014.

TheScore (2012) 'Trap's Army: an Oral History of How Ireland's Fans Stole European Hearts', *TheScore.ie*, at: www.thescore.ie/euro-2012-ireland-fans-oral-history-photos-videos-stories-fields-athenry-ice-cream-casillas-suits-505932-Jul2012, accessed 6 March 2014.

Todorova, M. (1997) *Imagining the Balkans* (Oxford: Oxford University Press).

Turner, V. W. (2001 [1964]) 'Betwixt and Between. The Liminal Period in *Rites de Passage*', in A. C. Lehman and J. E. Myers (eds), *Magic, Witchcraft, and Religion. An Anthropological Study of the Supernatural* (Mountain View: Mayfield), pp. 46–55.

TVN Warszawa (2012) 'Trumny pełne pozdrowień dla BBC', *TVN Warszawa Wiadomości* (1 July 2012), at: http://tvnwarszawa.tvn24.pl/informacje,news, trumny-pelne-pozdrowien-dla-bbc,50249.html, accessed 6 March 2014.

UEFA (2012) 'UEFA Steps up Vigilance at Training Grounds, at: www.uefa.org/about-uefa/news/newsid=1814806.html, accessed 22 January 2014.

van Gennep, A. (1961) *The Rites of Passage* (Chicago: University of Chicago Press).

van Houtum, H. and F. van Dam (2002) 'Topophilia or Topoporno? Patriotic Place Attachment in International Football Derbies', *HAGAR, International Social Science Review*, Vol. 3, Issue 2, pp. 231–48.

Winter, I. C. and B. Klob (2011) *Fußball und Sicherheit in Österreich* (Frankfurt: Verlag für Polizeiwissenschaft).

Wolff, L. (1994) *Inventing Eastern Europe: The Map of Civilisation on the Mind of the Enlightenment* (Stanford: Stanford University Press).

3
Loyalty Jungle
Flexible Football Fan Identities in the Framework of Euro 2012

Nina Szogs

Introduction

Fans throughout Europe have developed many diverse ways to celebrate major football events. Audiences watch matches at various locations, such as their favourite pub, their home, in public open-air venues or sometimes even in the stadium. They meet with friends, family, colleagues, fellow football supporters and event fans for many different reasons. These reasons include patriotism, an interest in football, the party and community feeling, and peer pressure. Following media and public discourse during the 2012 UEFA European Football Championship (further referred to as Euro 2012) one might have been tempted to believe that every single person in Europe, and possibly also beyond, was following the football matches, eager to participate in a collective European, or even global, event.

Actively taking part requires having a team to support. Football, due to its fundamental design of binary opposition, systematically invites the spectator – even if his/her team is not involved – to take sides and express partisanship in order to enjoy the thrill of the game and respond to his/her individual and collective 'quest for excitement' (Elias and Dunning, 1986). One may of course always pretend to be a neutral observer, appreciating each match on the basis of the technical skills and tactical know-how displayed by both teams. But it is the emotional involvement of the spectator, his/her 'passionate partisanship' (Bromberger, 1995, pp. 105–11), even if temporary and secondary, that fully deploys the dramatic potential of this game (Sonntag, 2008a, pp. 77–104).

The question then arises: what do you do when your own national team did not qualify or was eliminated at an early stage, but the rest of Europe still has cup fever? How can you be part of it when you have no 'own' team to cheer for?

Since there is always a team you can identify with on some level, having no team to support rarely occurs. Football fan identities, loyalties and rivalries are central to football fan culture. However, football fandom in a globalised world is subject to changes of perception, identity performances and loyalty concepts. Zygmunt Bauman (2000) and Stuart Hall (1996a) – amongst others – have taught us that identities are fluid, plural, competing and processual constructs. Consequently, fan identities are as flexible and processual as identities are elsewhere. I argue that in a globalised world all football affiliations, even on a national level, *can* shift. I am not implying that they must do so, but that there is a possibility for negotiation. This kind of flexibility especially applies to the construction of loyalties to national teams during major tournaments like Euros and World Cups. Loyalties and affiliations to national teams are multilayered constructs that can shift, for example when it is important to identify with a competing (collective) identity.

At the same time, national categories strongly influence identification processes during mega-sports events. Group affiliations and collective identities, such as national collective identities, are seen as 'constructed' (Eisenstadt and Giesen, 1995), 'imagined communities' (Anderson, 1983), and powerful entities that have a great impact on identification. Elga Castro-Ramos points out:

> Modern sports have been constantly linked to the nation-state; both because its structure has been a base for the development of massive sports (urbanization, mass transportation) and because sports have served to validate and enhance national identity. This latter has been especially true for international athletic competitions, such as the Olympic Games, the World Cup and others. (Castro-Ramos, 2008, p. 697)

During Euro 2012 loyalty constructs were flexible and multi-layered while being negotiated in a framework of national attributions. My analysis will first discuss and expand different concepts of loyalty and identification practices. Using the example of travelling with an international group, I will show how flexible and interchangeable national loyalties can become. I will then discuss how loyalty constructs are nevertheless bound to certain variables. In the underlying case, it particularly applies to space and objects that narrow down the chances of flexibility in choosing one's loyalty, and diminish the chance of subversion of dominant discourses. I will conclude that loyalties, in the framework of European or international sports competitions, are not necessarily limited to one's national affiliation and are therefore negotiable and can shift. Meanwhile, global companies make use of this flexible national loyalty to achieve branding goals. However, these negotiations are not detached from, but deeply entangled with, socio-cultural discourses.

To underline my arguments, I will refer to ethnographic fieldwork that I conducted during the months of June and July at Euro 2012 in the Polish cities Słubice, Poznań and Warsaw, in the German cities Frankfurt (Oder), and Berlin, and in the Austrian city Vienna. Similar to Mike Weed's ethnographic research in England during the 2002 FIFA World Cup (2006, 2007), I have been using an ethnographic approach to observe spectators in pubs. I have also been attending matches at diversely sized open-air public viewing facilities and official UEFA fan zones. I partly collected the qualitative data while participating in a summer school programme[1] on football in Frankfurt (Oder) in Germany (see Szogs, 2012).

I use the term 'public viewing' for various ways of watching football in public. The 2006 FIFA World Cup in Germany triggered a large research interest in the incredible success of public viewings during major sports events in Europe (Schulke, 2010, pp. 64–5). The success of public viewings as an open space for all kinds of party-oriented fans and spectators was already very visible at the 2002 FIFA World Cup in South Korea and Japan (Selmer and Sülzle, p. 804). As a matter of fact, the first World Cup to be shown on giant screens in city centres was France 1998, where the invention of massive public viewing was an unanticipated side-effect of the 'ticket nightmare', produced by a whole series of converging factors (accessibility of the host country, emergence of budget airlines, relatively small stadia, large-scale fraud by international travel operators) and resulting in a 'huge disparity between the supply and demand of available tickets both for the domestic and foreign public' (Sonntag, 2014, p. 321; see also Augé, 1998).

The majority of this analysis will focus on my participant observation at the Hyundai Fan Park Berlin in Germany when Germany was playing Greece (22 June 2012). All these instances were mediated experiences.

Plural and flexible loyalty constructs

During my fieldwork I observed fans dressing up in national colours, chanting loudly and joyfully, and singing the national anthem enthusiastically before matches. It was an impressive performance of national affiliations and doing nationalism during Euro 2012. At times people were singing the national anthem twice (once a capella), for example when Polish fans in Warsaw were waiting in the official UEFA fan zone to watch the match against Czech Republic (16 June 2012). Euro 2012 again showed how powerful national categories in international sports competitions remain. Anthony King writes that although both local affiliations and identities connected to European processes are becoming more and more important among (club) football fans, national belongings do not just disappear and, on another level, might still be as important as ever (2000, pp. 437–8).

For Euro 2012 I argue that aspects such as competing group identities, political affiliations, player preferences, family background and so on can become more important to identify with than citizenship. Having more than one team to cheer for is a common practice among many football fans, especially in countries that are less successful in football competitions. Fans must deal with the fact that the national team, likewise with clubs in the Champions League and Europa League, very often do not qualify. As a result, other national teams and clubs become the centre of attention. For some fans, football might still be 'a deep water port [that] offers the traditional fan anchorage in the past, present and anticipated future' (Porat, 2010, p. 288), but for many other fans it has long gone beyond that. Fan identities, like all identities, are '[. . .] never unified and, in late modern times, increasingly fragmented and fractured; never singular but multiply constructed across different, often intersecting and antagonistic, discourses, practices and positions' (Hall, 1996b, p. 4)

As Schwell has already pointed out in the preceding chapter of this volume, Gerd Baumann's 'grammars of identity and alterity' are very useful to the discussion of loyalties in football fan culture. They comprise the categories of orientalising, segmentation and encompassment. These grammars explain how individuals and groups *self themselves* and *other others*. For the underlying case, the relevant grammar is segmentation. Referring to Evans-Pritchard's work on the Nuer, Baumann explains that fusions and fissions are flexible constructs that depend on context. For example, on one level someone may be your enemy and on a higher level they can become your ally. Gerd Baumann uses a football example (2004, p. 22) to illustrate what he is referring to: on a local level two different fan groups cheer for two different, maybe antagonistic, teams. On a regional level and then a national level, it is possible that these different fan groups are supporting the same team. In this case, who is friend and who is foe can alter. Considering Euro 2012, it means that 'people can selve themselves and can other others according to context' (p. 23). When analysing historical, socio-cultural, political, and economic factors that influence the construction of loyalties, the phenomenon becomes even more relevant. Those shifting loyalties then reveal insights in historically grown enmities, allegiances and social changes. When Poland played Russia on 12 June 2012, I observed Polish students enthusiastically chanting, 'Yeah, we didn't lose against Russia!' after achieving only a draw. This most likely highlighted a long and challenging relationship between Russia and Poland (Dmowski, 2015).

Baumann's football example, though, is too simplistic for today's complex world of European football and European identification. Local loyalties can be more important than national ones. Being a Bayern Munich fan, at times, is more important than a victory of a national team. In terms of the internationally famous European clubs, like Barça or Chelsea, a transnational or trans-European fan community may ignore national borders. In his study on Manchester United fans, Anthony King argues that in a Europeanised world of football '"post-national" identity is likely to consist not of a monolithic supranationalism but of shifting cultural identities' (King, 2003, p. 420). According to King, fans identify with various and sometimes competing identities. Identification processes are far more complex and loyalty bonds are formed depending on a range of contexts. Similarly, Albrecht Sonntag discusses that club football 'has taken ever more postmodern traits', but he considers national teams as a 'bastion of modernity and its traditions' (Sonntag, 2008b, p. 266). While I agree with Sonntag that club football has become increasingly detached from national categories, in the next section I will argue that national loyalties, besides serving as 'bastion of modernity', can also be negotiated.

Plural and flexible loyalties – a conceptual expansion

In interviews that I conducted during Euro 2012, in all three countries, fans discussed many different reasons why they cheered for a specific country's team, other than the one whose citizenship they hold. Mentioning only a few examples these reasons included: 'I have travelled there a lot', 'my parents were born in that country', 'I do not really care about that team, but I do not want the other team to win', 'I like their underdog image', 'I prefer their way of playing'. During larger championships historical and socio-cultural contexts play an important role in identification processes. This applies especially, but not exclusively, to the case when one's 'own' national team is not involved in the tournament (any more).

Various football researchers have discussed concepts of plural loyalties and secondary fandom. In his research on Bayer Leverkusen fans, Cornel Sandvoss identifies four different categories that generate plural loyalties in football fandom: 'migration and family links, distant mediated encounters, textual activity and membership to fan networks and travel and cosmopolitan consciousness' (Sandvoss, 2012, p. 86). Hans Kristian Hognestad uses the term 'polygamy' to describe how fans support more than one club, which he writes is 'also as a result of physical explorations and social networking between football communities' (2012, p. 389). Victoria Schwenzer and Nicole Selmer have worked on multiple identifications in migration and football. They say that a fan can cheer for more than one team to emphasise his or her belonging to both the host society and home country (2010, pp. 402–3). Referring to the 2006 World Cup in Germany and the 2008 Euro in Austria and Switzerland they underline the example of Turkish-German flags, and how people with

Turkish origin living in Germany were showing hybrid identities by displaying hybrid fandom (2010, pp. 407–8).

In most cases these concepts describe relatively constant relations and affiliations to a second, third or fourth team on a club and national level that last for a longer period of time and are part of a fan's everyday life. For the underlying case of this chapter I would therefore like to expand the concepts, as they do not account for the complexity of the phenomenon I observed during Euro 2012. By adding the category 'flexible loyalties' a more spontaneous and temporarily limited way of shifting loyalties becomes part of the concept. I define flexible loyalties as temporarily constructed identifications that customarily result from certain spatial and temporal circumstances. They are exceptional and temporarily limited, based on situations in which people have to, or want to, choose a team to support for a short period of time, sometimes for only one match. The reasons why spectators choose a specific team can be similar to the ones that apply for the concepts above. The difference is they do not outlast the match or tournament. For instance, talking to fans in a Viennese pub, when Spain was playing Portugal (27 June 2012), people were not entirely sure whom they should support because they did not really prefer any of the two teams. After contemplating it for a while player preferences became relevant for this match: they either chose to support Portugal because of Ronaldo's 'fantastic way of playing' or to support Spain, because of Ronaldo's 'tremendous and unbearable arrogance'. Even though they are flexible, these loyalties are not entirely independent from other factors. Flexible loyalties require spontaneously and easily accessible identity *offerings*. This is the reason why space and objects can become powerful actors in these impromptu identification processes. Consequently, these loyalties can be easily (ab)used by organisers and sponsors in order to achieve commercial goals, which I will discuss in the last section. Compared to plural loyalties, flexible loyalties are not necessarily less serious or inferior in their symbolic meaning. The lines between both concepts are blurred, but – as I will argue – flexible loyalties have a more playful, functional and temporal dimension, especially during major tournaments. In the next section, I will show how national affiliations can be switched on impulse when it becomes more important to identify with other layers of belonging.

Flexible loyalties as a practice to create group identity

As I previously mentioned, I was partly conducting my fieldwork while participating in a summer school programme. As participants of the summer school, we watched matches in pubs, restaurants, official UEFA fan zones and other public viewing venues in Poznań, Warsaw, Frankfurt (Oder) and Słubice. The programme participants came from different countries in Europe, the Americas, Asia and Africa. Travelling with an international group to different football public viewing facilities in Germany and Poland during Euro 2012 challenged our own loyalties from one match to the other. Since many of us came from countries that were participating in the tournament and we were all interested in football, we would often watch the matches together. At some point it became common practice to join and support one another for the matches of each respective person's national team. This support also included emotional practices like cheering for his or her team and hugging when their team scored. For the sake of our group identity, we all shifted our loyalties several times depending on the team that was playing. Whom we supported depended not (only) on our passports, but also on the nationality of co-members of the group. Personal sympathies sparked off a group dynamic of supporting the other participants' national team. When Croatia was playing we would support Croatia, and likewise with England, Germany, Poland, Ukraine and all the other European countries from which our participants were drawn. Most of the time, the most important layer to identify with was our group identity. One could argue that this only happened out of politeness and that the 'real' loyalties lay somewhere else. It still would not be contradictory to the previously outlined definition that the multiple layers of identification can be antagonistic. In this given situation, identifying with a unified group identity was crucial. For the summer school's non-European participants – according to UEFA's definition of Europe – shifting one's loyalty was an even more playful and flexible performance. Since they did not have their 'own' national team to support, they could shift more easily. This was because they were not as invested in a nexus of the construction of national affiliations as the UEFA-defined Europeans were.

This brings to mind Tim Crabbe's categorisation (2008, p. 434) of a group of fans that he observed during the 2006 FIFA World Cup in

Germany; a group whom he calls 'England's World Cup party people'. Crabbe differentiates between six different sub-groups that operate in different ways to participate in the championship: 1) the well-organised and rather upper-class 'Corporates'; 2) the 'Barmy Army' who uses synchronised dressing to show unity and separation from other groups; 3) the spontaneous, down-to-earth, unorganised 'Survivalists'; 4) the economically as well as party-oriented 'Grafters'; 5) the 'Shirts', who stick to the rules and are well-prepared; and 6) the 'Internationalists', the category our group would most likely fit in:

> With a love of the beautiful game they travel for the football and don't mind which matches they see. Keeping well away from the mass of England fans the tournament provides an opportunity for staged cultural exchanges. (Crabbe, 2008, p. 434)

Crabbe describes how the 'internationalists' of the English fans mingled with German fans in a German nightclub. Most of them were displaying national colours in different ways. Crabbe emphasises that the chanting and singing of the various nationalities' songs led to a performance of internationalism – a performance that was only possible because of the temporal limit of the World Cup and the longing for a community feeling (ibid.). The temporality that Crabbe mentions also applies to the international group that I was travelling with. At the time of Euro 2012, the composition of our group, the interest in the game, and the wish to be and stay part of the group became decisive factors as to how we shifted our flexible loyalties. This mostly, but not only, applied to matches when our respective national teams were not playing. Nevertheless, our loyalties were still pressed in a framework of nationalities, since most of the time we supported one of the group's national team.

To summarise, if modernity is liquid and light (Bauman, 2000), identities uncertain and plural (Hall, 1996a) and communities are as imagined (Anderson, 1983) as collective identities are constructed (Eisenstadt and Giesen, 1995), then (national) fan loyalties can be, must be and will be liquid, light, uncertain, plural, imagined and constructed as well. Still, in a globalised world, where everything might be possible, there are certain representations, discourses or even just objects that hardly allow us to choose with what or who to identify. As Stuart Hall puts it:

Precisely because identities are constructed within, not outside, discourse, we need to understand them as produced in specific historical and institutional sites within specific discursive formations and practices, by specific enunciative strategies. (Hall, 1996b, p. 4)

In the next section I therefore scrutinise how objects and space can be powerful actors in identity construction. During Euro 2012 it became most obvious in the Berlin Fan Park where official organisers and global companies instrumentalised these actors to enforce a community feeling for commercial motives. Aware of the flexibility of (national) loyalties and its playful aspects, they used fan objects to unify all kinds of people. I will show how the Berlin Fan Park was a place where multiple powerful actors co-determined loyalties and identification processes by using objects to trigger positive emotions and to create group identity within and outside national identification.

The Fan Park in Berlin: experiencing the community feeling

The locations where audiences watched football matches during Euro 2012 are central to the construction of flexible loyalties. Chris Stone writes about places that are relevant to football in everyday life that 'the activity space of football extends into people's homes, workplaces and many spaces in between' (Stone, 2007, p. 181). Euro 2012 also has gone way beyond the stadium and entered our homes and workplaces. People decorated their houses in national colours, but – and this is the major difference to everyday practices – only for the time of the event. Many public viewing facilities, whose very concepts demand cheering and support, were created only for the event period. Therefore my observations do not illustrate football in everyday life, but rather football staged as an exceptional European mega-event, which was extraordinary and limited in time. One might argue that qualification matches are part of a football lover's everyday life and part of the whole Euro and World Cup procedure, but for the event itself non-everyday life rules apply. These rules include dressing in national colours, travelling to different football sites, skipping work to watch football, drinking continuously for several weeks, and so on. Nonetheless, the ritual takes place right in the centre of our lives in public places and interferes with our everyday practices in its temporarily limited and exceptional state.

The official Polish and Ukrainian UEFA fan venues and public viewing locations in other countries were created to give football fans and event lovers an arena to share a social experience, and to provide a platform to the championship's sponsors. Hans-Jürgen Schulke already discussed this for the 2006 FIFA World Cup (2010, pp. 64–5): global companies were using fan zones and fan objects to make their product more attractive and to connect it with a positive party feeling. UEFA and its sponsors are also strongly interested in using these mega-events as 'branding opportunities' (Klauser, 2012, p. 1042). In Vienna, for Euro 2012, public viewings were smaller than in Germany and Poland. In Austria, the largest public viewing locations were meant to accommodate 2000 people (Marits, 2012).

What was most striking during my fieldwork was seeing people from Europe and beyond visiting fan zones and dressing up in national colours. Streets, pubs and public viewing venues were outstandingly colourful. The Hyundai Fan Park in Berlin was one of those fan areas. Spectators did not only chose fan objects to display the affiliation to an already existing community, but the fan objects themselves influenced identification and created community.

In contrast to pubs and smaller public viewing venues, the Berlin Fan Park was an extraordinary location for Euro 2012. This was because it was an event that was worth to be 'retold' not only for the 'shared communal experience', as Weed discusses pub spectating (2007, p. 410), but also because of the event itself regarding its size, media coverage and central location. The Hyundai Fan Park, as it was officially called, was a huge fan zone right in Berlin's city centre. According to the organisers, during certain matches almost half a million visitors gathered to watch Germany play (Hyundai Motor Company, 2012). The Berlin Fan Park was not entirely specific to the city of Berlin, but a commercialised public viewing concept for different cities in Europe. Hyundai, according to the company's Facebook page, as one of the main sponsors of Euro 2012, installed Fan Parks in Madrid, Paris, Berlin, Prague, Dortmund, Turin, Moscow and Heilbronn. The Fan Park was not an official UEFA fan zone like those in the host countries, but official sponsors of the tournament were still involved.

One should be aware of the fact that the Berlin Fan Park was a melting pot comprising various interests of different actors: global players like Hyundai and Coca-Cola, the city of Berlin, local businesses, football fans, event fans, tourists, UEFA and others. I will focus on the interaction of fans and fan objects and the role of global players in this nexus.

The Berlin Fan Park stretched from the Brandenburg Gate, way down the Straße des 17. Juni, and almost reached the Berlin Victory Column. In the Fan Park mostly young adults, probably in their twenties and thirties, gathered. Since it was not an official UEFA fan zone, it was not overwhelmed by the violet corporate design of Euro 2012. This does not imply that there were fewer sponsor advertisements. The Fan Park was after all called the Hyundai Fan Park and another sponsor, Coca-Cola, installed a Fan-Transformer.

I visited the Berlin Fan Park when Germany was playing Greece in the quarter-finals at the end of June 2012. I arrived at Berlin Central Station more than three hours ahead of the match to guarantee I secured a place right in the middle of the venue. A friend of mine agreed to accompany me. Berlin Central Station was only a five-minute walk to the Fan Park. After passing the security guards at the outer and then again at the inner entrance, I could already see hundreds of people standing in front of the Brandenburg Gate, drinking, talking and laughing. The venue was largely blocked with solid barricades, but we experienced the security check as disproportionately careless. Security checked us twice, but only our bags. Because of the experiences at other public viewing events during Euro 2012, I was expecting full body checks, like those I had to undergo in Poznań and Warsaw. Nevertheless, the barricades successfully separated the Fan Park from the everyday happenings in Berlin. Nicole Selmer and Almut Sülzle call the fan areas that successfully captured city centres for football events 'fortresses replete with visitation rights, fences and strict regulations' (2010, p. 805).

In front of the Brandenburg Gate the organisers built a large stage, where between music acts, like Los Colorados, the host executed a so-called football quiz. The quiz not only included football questions, but also questions like 'How many doors does the newest model of the Hyundai range have?'. By answering correctly participants could win a Hyundai. The on-stage sales show with the aim of promoting the Hyundai brand continued until the match started. Everything that happened on that stage was shown on several big screens, which were located throughout the Fan Park. Before, during and after the match the host was leading songs the spectators were supposed to sing. He did so by bellowing the first lines of songs into his microphone and then the crowd would join in. These were not national songs, but common German drinking songs like *'Einer geht noch rein'*, which can be translated not only as the English equivalent 'one for the road', but also as 'one more goal is still feasible'.

In the Berlin Fan Park people gathered to watch football, enjoy the cheerful atmosphere of Euro 2012 and to support the German national team. Carnivalistic associations in its very basic meaning arose, with the exception that all the costumes shared the same three colours: black, red and gold. People dressed up as fans and *played* loyalty. Not only German citizens and football lovers went to the Fan Park, but tourists and event fans also joined in and celebrated in a temporary community. People came together to have a great time and to share a great party experience with fellow event lovers. People were drinking, chanting, singing and having a lot of fun. When Germany scored the crowd exploded, beers flew through the air, and the host again directed the singing of drinking songs. With the help of merchandising products, people were *doing nationalism* as social practice to participate in the collective event. Tim Crabbe writes about the 'performance of identity' during the 2006 FIFA World Cup in Germany:

> Whilst it has long been common for football fans to 'dress up' for matches and even for non-attenders to sport the colours of their national team on matchdays, at the 2006 FIFA World Cup finals, many German fans quite freely embraced the 'party' style throughout the tournament. [...] This performance of identity extended far beyond the conventional constituencies of fandom, with little obvious gender or social class distinctions as men and women, girls and boys embraced the tournament, displayed their allegiance and came together in civic spaces to share a communal engagement with the national teams' performances on giant screens and in local bars. (Crabbe, 2008, p. 431)

In the Berlin 2012 Fan Park, creating a community feeling by using German national colours was the central aspect of the party-based 'performance of identity'. Organisers successfully re-enacted the emotions of the 'Sommermärchen'[2] from 2006 that was, as Schulke writes, especially generated by the creation of public viewing facilities (2010, p. 64). The emotional practices in the Berlin Fan Park were pushed by the show host and triggered collective identity. Referring to Émile Durkheim, both Matthias Mutz (2013, p. 523) and Mike S. Schäfer (2010, p. 124) emphasise the importance of emotional practices in football fan culture to create collective identity. Matthias Junge discusses public viewings as spaces where 'all-inclusivity' ('*All-Inklusivität*') applies, and nationalities, as well as social differences, are evened out by an emotionally constructed collective identity that is created for the specific time of the event or even only for the public viewing (2009, p. 197). Nicole Selmer and Almut Sülzle (2010, p. 811) emphasise that this also applies to gender categories.

Powerful fan objects and the Coca-Cola Fan-Transformer

To put it in a nutshell, the hurdle to participate in the community experience was set quite low. There was no room for smart or sophisticated football talk or showing off with fancy football knowledge because 'the main thing about a fan party is to party along' (Selmer and Sülzle, 2010, p. 807). This points to the importance of fan objects as part of the performance. As a matter of fact, objects became relevant and powerful actors in the Fan Park. I had already observed the diversity of fan products during the 2006 World Cup in Germany, but the marketing experts' imagination in creating fan products in the German national colours ran even wilder for Euro 2012. There were wigs, mohawks, bunny ears, armlets, hats in all possible shapes, flower garlands, jerseys, shirts, flags and all sorts of other things. Additionally, the German flag was painted on cheeks and many other different body parts.

From Bruno Latour we know that objects have agency, because '[...] *any thing* that does modify a state of affairs by making a difference is an actor' (Latour 2005, p. 71 [emphasis in the original]). The Fan Park, the flower garlands, and other merchandising products in the German national colours modified the 'state of affairs'. Latour further writes that this does not mean that objects directly cause certain actions, but they 'might authorise, allow, afford, encourage, permit, suggest, influence, block, render possible, forbid, and so on' (p. 72). Therefore, group identity was not only triggered by shared emotional rituals, but also by flagging similar fan objects. In Mikhail Bakhtin's interpretation of carnivalistic gatherings, these 'costumes' generate equality among the participants. The Fan Park was a carnivalistic event, where, as Bakhtin describes, social hierarchies and rules were temporarily abandoned and replaced by a unity among all participants in a specific, limited time, and place (Bakhtin, 1998, p. 55–9, see also Pearson, 2012). All you needed to do was to display the German national colours somewhere and somehow on your body. By *doing Germany*, you got the ticket to enter the party collective and became a member.

The Coca-Cola Fan-Transformer was one of the most intriguing things I observed during my Euro 2012 field research. The Fan Park visitors could walk through the Coca-Cola Fan-Transformer and helpful hands decorated them with flower garlands, make-up and Coca-Cola merchandising in the German national colours. When people left the Coca-Cola Fan-Transformer they were supposedly transformed into a *Germany fan*. As one of the organisers of the Berlin Fan Park wrote on his homepage: 'Here visitors entered as "totally normal" persons and exited as perfectly decorated fans' (Wohlthat Entertainment, 2012 [author's translation]). I am deliberately using the term *Germany fans* because it was not at all important whether you were a German citizen or not to become a *Germany fan*.

The Coca-Cola Fan-Transformer can be looked at as a microcosm of what happened in the entire Fan Park, in fact, nothing short of a 'rite of passage' according to Victor W. Turner's (1979) use of the term created by Arnold van Gennep in 1909 (van Gennep, 1981, p. 14). Fan objects were an important part of the 'rites of passage'. Putting the flower garland around the neck of a *normal person*, to quote Coca-Cola's description again, is the metamorphosis of him or her into *a perfectly decorated fan* like 'a pupa changing from grub to moth' (Turner, 1979, p. 235). Referring further to Tuner's and van Gennep's terminology, entering the Coca-Cola Fan-Transformer equals the phase of 'separation' from the state he or she formerly belonged to. In the Coca-Cola Fan-Transformer, the 'margin (or limen)', he or she is not a *normal person* anymore, nor is he or she a *perfectly decorated fan* yet. Exiting the Coca-Cola Fan-Transformer he or she has transformed into a new and stable state, the 'aggregation': a *perfectly decorated fan* that is part of the new community. Coca-Cola plays with ritualised symbols of transition that can indeed be compared to baptising rituals. The newborn fan now 'is expected to behave in accordance with certain customary norms' (Turner, 1979, p. 235). In this case – shared emotional practices of cheering for the German team, drinking, singing, and being in a good mood.

Nicole Selmer and Almut Sülzle describe how, during Euro 2008, Carlsberg handed out merchandising products in the company's colours and different national colours. They discuss how the gesture reveals that during 'the football carnival' (Selmer and Sülzle, 2010, p. 810) the diversity of fan products in national colours becomes rather unimportant, as everybody looks the same except for the colours. For our case, their observation is quite helpful since it shows how merchandising products have a unifying character and national categories take a step back. In contrast to what Selmer and Sülzle observe, in the Berlin Fan Park the unification went a step further: people were unified by merchandise in the *same* national colours.

To be more specific, the rites of passage in the Coca-Cola Fan-Transformer created one specific loyalty: the support for the German national team. This is the reason why events like Euro 2012 work perfectly well for non-football lovers, too. When you dress up like a *Germany fan*, you know who to cheer for and how to engage in a shared emotional practice. Even tourists from other countries came to the Fan Park to participate in the ritual and cheer for the German national team in order to be part of a cheerful community. Spatial conditions and objects scarcely allowed any further negotiation of loyalties. If you entered the Fan Park, you were required to wear German merchandise and consequently cheer for Germany. Here, because the loyalty is temporal and depends on place, it is flexible for those fans that do not usually cheer for the German national team. From an agency perspective, on the other hand, loyalty is not flexible, as the dominant Germany discourse in the Fan Park is hardly negotiable.

To sum up, the Coca-Cola Fan-Transformer was not about becoming a football fan, but a *Germany fan*. The goal was not (only) to celebrate Germany, but to trigger positive emotions that again created collective identity. Displaying shared symbols created equality among all members, allowing everyone to participate. Ironically, global companies that work on a supranational level used these national symbols to make their brand more attractive.

Conclusion

I conclude with one final observation that showed how, in the Fan Park festivities, doing nationalism was not just a playful and carnivalistic performance, but how it can also be strongly connected to racist discourses and can attract a nationalist clientele. On our way back home, a group of drunk young men, wearing Germany make-up and merchandise, also entered the *S-Bahn*. They were speaking loudly and one of them made the Nazi salute while saying *'Gute deutsche Jungs'* ('Good German boys'). I was still hoping that I had misunderstood when he started singing *'Wir sind arische Jungs'* ('We are Aryan boys'). His friends were not joining in, but were not stopping him either. On the contrary, one of them added *'Viele Japse hier im Zug'* ('Many Japs on the train') and started laughing.

The episode was a strong reminder that even if Euros and World Cups might comprise a playful performance of nationalities and loyalties for the sake of a community (party) feeling, national affiliations remain potentially dangerous and powerful categories. This is particularly so because 'attempts to question [them] and to lift the veil of latency are usually rejected by pointing to [their] naturalness, sacredness or self-evidence' (Eisenstadt and Giesen, 1995, p. 73). The power of fan objects became even more obvious in this situation. After the trip through the Coca-Cola Fan-Transformer I was also wearing a flower garland in black, red, and gold. I felt happy wearing it during the match, as I was enjoying the party and community feeling. After the confrontation in the *S-Bahn*, the flower garland took on an entirely different meaning. Prior to this episode it represented the celebration of the German national team and the party community in the Fan Park. After the incident, it turned into a nationalistic symbol and I felt entirely uneasy with it and threw it into the next trash bin.

Doing nationalism in joyful and carnivalistic ways during mega-sports events has an influence on the perception and enactment of national affiliation beyond the time of the event. It becomes legitimate to feel like a part of a national collective, since it is connected with good feelings. It is often discussed, also in our summer school programme, whether nationalism is the 'bad' way to perform national identity, patriotism is the 'good' way, and whether patriotism is what the majority of people experienced during Euro 2012. However, the exclusion of people that do not fit the ideology is part of both concepts. It is especially ironic that in the Fan Park displaying national colours was a practice designed to include as many people as possible regardless of their background.

I emphasise that there are different, sometimes subversive, interpretations of these nationalist events. It is not only nationality that serves as a marker of identification. Especially in Germany, where national identity can be a difficult and complex issue, people have their own ways to negotiate their national performance. During my fieldwork, I observed some matches with leftist and anti-national football fans where it is common to watch football without displaying the German national colours. In order to participate, a fundamental condition is the rejection of any *'Deutschtümelei'* ('German chauvinism').

So what did one do during Euro 2012 when one had no team to cheer for? Actually, the situation rarely occurred because national teams offer possibilities of identification at many different levels. Political views, historical conflicts or allegiances, citizenship, economic factors, holidays, player preferences, personal bonds and many additional categories can determine the loyalty to football clubs and to national teams. It's a loyalty jungle out there, and it is nearly impossible to not have a preference as to which team you would like to win or to lose. This loyalty jungle of Euro 2012 was a temporary and complex part of larger globalisation and Europeanisation processes that contribute to a 'liquid modernity' (Bauman, 2000), where national categories are still very powerful, but compete with other layers of loyalty and identification. Public viewings in particular are places where it is required to take sides. In conclusion, loyalties can shift according to different contexts and even plural and competing loyalties are possible as they are part of a fluid and flexible construction.

Fan objects, merchandising products or even large venues like a fan zone or Fan Park are additional and powerful variables that are crucial to the carnivalistic performance of loyalties. They suggest, create, trigger and request certain loyalties. We may conclude that loyalties can be flexible to a certain extent. Their constructions depend on social-cultural and historical contexts, as well as on spatial conditions and objects that can enforce them; for example, in order to create a group identity with the aim of selling a product. The Coca-Cola Fan-Transformer and the other organisers of the Fan Park used and likewise encouraged the flexibility of loyalties to enhance temporarily and limited collective identity performances of *Germany fans* in this specific environment. The goal was to include as many people as possible into the positive party and community feeling for commercial reasons. The instrumentalisation of national loyalties by globally operating companies yields many implications that need yet to be researched. Linking nationalism to commercialisation during mega-sports events reveals how exchangeable nationalities become in commercial campaigns and how easily they can be (ab)used, reinforced and boosted for a purpose as simple as selling more soft drinks and cars.

Notes

1. Viadrina Summer University (2012) 'The Culture of Football: Passion, Power, Politics' hosted by the European University Viadrina Frankfurt (Oder).
2. Literally 'Summer Fairy Tale', a term coined during the 2006 World Cup in order to describe the 'unbelievable', 'too-good-to-be-true' character of the event, during which Germany seemed to discover itself in a different light. The term implicitly refers to Heinrich Heine's critical poem *'Ein Wintermärchen'* (1844), which in turn quoted Shakespeare's play 'A Winter's Tale'. The term 'Summer Fairy Tale' was further popularised and consolidated in collective memory through the highly successful, eponymous documentary film by Sönke Wortmann (2006) that showed the German team's journey across the World Cup from inside. Significantly, the film was released in German cinemas exactly on 3 October 2006, 'German Unity Day' since reunification in 1990. More than four million people watched the film in the cinema, and the television premiere in December attracted an audience of over 10 million viewers.

References

Anderson, B. (1983) *Imagined Communities. Reflections on the Origin and Spread of Nationalism* (London and New York: Verso).

Augé, M. (1998) 'Ein Ethnologe bei der Fußball-WM', *Le Monde diplomatique*, German edition, 14 August 1998, p. 2.

Bakhtin, M. (1998) *Rabelais und seine Welt. Volkskultur als Gegenkultur* (Frankfurt/Main: Suhrkamp).

Bauman, Z. (2000) *Liquid Modernity* (Cambridge and Malden: Polity Press).

Baumann, G. (2004) 'Grammars of Identity/Alterity: A Structural Approach', in G. Baumann and A. Gingrich (eds), *Grammars of Identity/Alterity: A Structural Approach* (New York and Oxford: Berghahn), pp. 18–50.

Bromberger, C. (1995), *Le match de football. Ethnologie d'une passion partisane à Marseille, Naples et Turin, Paris* (Paris: Editions de la Maison des Sciences de l'Homme).

Castro-Ramos, E. (2008) 'Loyalties, Commodity and Fandom: Real Madrid, Barça and Athletic Fans versus "La Furia Roja" during the World Cup', *Sport in Society: Cultures, Commerce, Media, Politics*, Vol. 11, Issue 6, pp. 696–710.

Crabbe, T. (2008) 'Postmodern Community and Future Directions. Fishing for Community: England Fans at the 2006 FIFA World Cup', *Soccer & Society*, Vol. 9, Issue 3, pp. 428–38.

Dmowski, S. (2015) 'Football Sites of Memory in the Eastern Bloc 1945–1991', in W. Pyta and N. Havemann (eds), *European Football and Collective Memory* (Basingstoke: Palgrave Macmillan), pp. 171–84.

Eisenstadt, S. N. and B. Giesen (1995) 'The Construction of Collective Identity', *Archive sociologique européenne*, Vol. 36, Vol. 1, pp. 72–102.

Elias, N. and Dunning, E. (1986) *Quest for Excitement. Sport and Leisure in the Civilizing Process* (Oxford: Basil Blackwell).

Hall, S. (1996a) 'The Question of Cultural Identity', in S. Hall, D. Held, D. Hubert and K. Thompson (eds), *Modernity. An Introduction to Modern Societies* (Malden and Oxford: Blackwell), pp. 596–617.

Hall, S. (1996b) 'Introduction. Who Needs "Identity"?', in S. Hall and P. du Gay (eds), *Questions of Cultural Identity* (London, Thousand Oaks and New Delhi: Sage), pp. 1–17.

Hognestad, H. K. (2012) 'Split Loyalties: Football Is a Community Business', *Soccer & Society*, Vol. 13, Issue 3, pp. 377–91.

Hyundai Motor Company (2012): 'Hyundai Fan Parks Attract Record Numbers', Hyundai, at www.hyundai.com/ng/en/MediaCenter/GlobalNews/DF_WW_GLOBALNEWSVIEW_120621_01.html?Row=47, accessed 9 December 2013.

Junge, M. (2009) 'Die kollektive Erregung des public viewing – oder: die Tragödie der Identifikation und der Sozialität', in R. Hitzler, A. Honer and M. Pfadenhauer (eds), *Posttraditionale Gemeinschaften. Theoretische und ethnographische Erkundungen* (Wiesbaden: VS-Verlag für Sozialwissenschaften), pp. 189–201.

King, A. (2000) 'Football Fandom and Post-national Identity in the New Europe', *British Journal of Sociology*, Vol. 51, Issue 3, pp. 419–42.

King, A. (2003) *The European Ritual. Football in the New Europe* (Aldershot: Ashgate).

Klauser, F. R. (2012) 'Interpretative Flexibility of the Event-City: Security, Branding and Urban Entrepreneurialism at the European Football Championships 2008', *International Journal of Urban and Regional Research*, Vol. 36, Issue 5, pp. 1039–52.

Latour, B. (2005) *Reassembling the Social. An Introduction to Actor-Network-Theory* (Oxford and New York: Oxford University Press).

Marits, M. (2012) 'Fußball-EM: Public Viewing am Pool', *Die Presse* (Austrian daily newspaper), 18 May 2012.

Mutz, M. (2013) 'Patrioten für drei Wochen. Nationale Identifikation und die Fußballeuropameisterschaft 2012', *Berliner Journal für Soziologie*, Vol. 22, Issue 4, pp. 517–38.

Pearson, G. (2012) *An Ethnography of English Football Fans: Cans, Cops and Carnivals* (Manchester: Manchester University Press).

Porat, A. B. (2010) 'Football Fandom: A Bounded Identification', *Soccer & Society*, Vol. 11, Issue 3, pp. 277–90.

Sandvoss, C. (2012) 'Jeux sans frontières? Europeanisation and the Erosion of National Categories in European Club Football Competition', *Politique Europèenne*, No. 36, pp. 77–101.

Schäfer, M. S. (2010) 'Fans und Emotionen', in J. Roose, M. S. Schäfer and T. Schmidt-Lux (eds), *Fans. Soziologische Perspektiven* (Wiesbaden: VS Verlag für Sozialwissenschaften/GWV Fachverlage GmbH Wiesbaden), pp. 109–32.

Schulke, H.-J. (2010) 'Challenging the Stadium. Watching Sport Events in Public', in S. Frank and S. Steets (eds), *Stadium Worlds. Football, Space and the Built Environment* (London and New York: Routledge), pp. 56–73.

Schwenzer, V. and N. Selmer (2010) 'Fans und Migration', in J. Roose, M. S. Schäfer and T. Schmidt-Lux (eds), *Fans. Soziologische Perspektiven* (Wiesbaden: VS Verlag für Sozialwissenschaften/GWV Fachverlage GmbH Wiesbaden), pp. 387–413.

Selmer, N. and A. Sülzle (2010) '(En-)gendering the European Football Family: The Changing Discourse on Women and Gender at EURO 2008', *Soccer & Society*, Vol. 11, Issue 6, pp. 803–14.

Sonntag, A. (2008a) *Les identités du football européen* (Grenoble: Presses Universitaires de Grenoble).

Sonntag, A. (2008b) 'The Unbearable Lightness of Belonging: The World Cup as Producer of Virtual Emotion and Postmodern Sociability', in T. Pavlin, Univerza v Ljubljana, Fakulteta za sport (ed.), *Sport, Nation, Nationalism*, pp. 259–69.

Sonntag, A. (2014), 'France 98 – A Watershed World Cup', in S. Rinke and K. Schiller (eds), *The FIFA World Cup 1930–2010. Politics, Commerce, Spectacle and Identities* (Göttingen: Wallstein), pp. 318–36.

Stone, C. (2007) 'The Role of Football in Everyday Life', *Soccer & Society*, Vol. 8, Issue 2/3, pp. 169–84.

Szogs, N. (2012) 'Too Nice To Be Credible?' *FREE project blog*,at: www.free-project.eu/Blog/post/too-nice-to-be-credible-344.htm2012, accessed 25 September 2013.

Turner, V. W. (1979) 'Betwixt and Between: The Liminal Period in *Rites de Passage*', in W. A. Lessa and E. Z. Vogt (eds), *Reader in Comparative Religion: An Anthropological Approach* (New York et al.: Harper & Row) pp. 234–43.

van Gennep, A. (1981) *Les rites de passage* (Paris: Picard).

Weed, M. (2006) 'The Story of an Ethnography: The Experience of Watching the 2002 World Cup in the Pub', *Soccer & Society*, Vol. 7, Issue 1, pp. 76–95.

Weed, M. (2007) 'The Pub as a Virtual Football Fandom Venue: An Alternative to "Being There"?', *Soccer & Society*, Vol. 8, Issue 2/3, pp. 399–414.

Wohltat Entertainment (2012) 'Hyundai Fan Park zur EM 2012', at: www.wohlthat-entertainment.de/unsere-highlights/fanmeile-berlin-em-2012.html, accessed 9 December 2013.

4
Does Qualifying Really Qualify? Comparing the Representations of Euro 2008 and Euro 2012 in the Turkish Media

Başak Alpan and Özgehan Şenyuva[1]

Introduction

If there is one thing that academia has learnt from football, it is that football indeed emerged as a significant marker of identity. As the chapter by Szogs in this volume convincingly demonstrates, football, due to its fundamental design of binary oppositions, continuously invites the spectator – even if his/her 'own' team is not involved – to take sides and express partisanship. Contrary to conventional wisdom, football does not 'reflect society'. As Sonntag argues, 'what football or rather the collective behaviour patterns football makes visible, can actually reflect is not so much society as such, but collectively shared, mostly unconscious desires and fears which move the individuals that make up society' (Sonntag, 2008, p. 266). Moreover, it provides a wonderful opportunity for delving into the questions of *Self* and *Other*, representation, belonging, exclusion, trans-regional and transnational identifications on the part of the spectators, which is an invaluable field for the media coverage.

Departing from this very idea that football has been, still is, and is most likely to remain, a terrain for expression and representation of identity, this chapter aims to examine the Turkish national identity representations vis-à-vis European identity in two different events, Euro 2008 and Euro 2012, where the Turkish team was able to qualify in the former, but not in the latter. We depart from two theoretical claims: that the practice of representation is crucial in terms of understanding the construction of identities, which are relational and constituted against a series of *Others*; and that *the Other* can be interpreted in radically different ways, which implies an acknowledgement of the fact that constructions of identities can produce varying degrees of Otherness. In our cases, we claim that although the Turkish national identity has predominantly been constructed during Euro 2012 vis-à-vis 'Europeanness', we do not see this as the *radical Other* of Turkish national identity. What is almost consensual in the literature is that a *radical* or *threatening Other* is sine-qua-non for constructing the identity of the *Self*. However, through the debate on football and the national identity relationship at European championships, what we argue instead is that constructions of identities can produce varying degrees of Otherness, which is not necessarily organised around a sharp *radical Other* vs. *Self* dichotomy.

A large theme in the above debate on transformation of identities through football is the notion of 'representation', particularly the manner in which sport operates symbolically to produce ideological versions of collective identities, associated with locality and nationality as well as gender, ethnicity and race (Bernstein and Blain, 2003, pp. 12–17). As will be scrutinised later, according to Hall, language, photography, music as well as turning up at football matches with banners and slogans inscribed with certain symbols could all be thought of as representational systems (Hall, 1997). As De Biasi and Lanfranchi assert, 'in a manner similar to politics and the arts, football continues to create and diffuse tensions in the nation and offers endless possibilities to local pride and chauvinism' (De Biasi and Lanfranchi, 1997, p. 88). While their work is particularly on Italian football, the very same argument can easily be applied to different regional, national and even international cases. In our case, the historical tensions between Turkey and Europe at large constitute the level of analysis.

One key function of media sport texts is, then, ideological: 'to win the consent of the people to a shared image of the nation and identity' (Higson, 1998, p. 356). As Blain and Boyle state, 'the way in which sport is written about becomes a source of information about our beliefs, opinions and attitudes as cultures' (Blain and Boyle, 1998, p. 370). Rowe et al. maintain that popular media representations are best understood – both 'materially and symbolically' – as part of a tripartite structure consisting of media, readers/viewers who are interpreting the world(s) represented or implied, and those who are doing the representing (Rowe et al., 1998, p. 121). Indeed, media have always been a potent agent of providing a sense of belonging, that is, the 'we-feeling' of the community. Similarly, according to Arimoto, media representations of national teams have become resources for people to narrate football and other things in everyday life (Arimoto, 2004, p. 64). Even though there is always the possibility of repetition, reconstitution, appropriation and subversion on the side of the receiver, it seems that the process of representing each national team through a particular stereotype as reflecting nationality is iterated and reiterated every time (Arimoto, 2004, p. 64).

In this respect, transnational football events as spectacular as European championships or World Cups deserve particular attention in terms of scrutinising these identity negotiations on the part of the fans. As Bernstein reminds us, events like the European football championship, now usually referred to as 'Euro', are generally represented as stylised metaphorical wars between nation-states (Bernstein, 2007, p. 657). Bora (2000) refers to the relations between Turkey and Europe through football as ideal objects of analysis towards understanding the European complex in the formation (and perpetual re-formation) of Turkish national identity. Along this vein, Bora and Şenyuva define Turkish football fans' relation with Europe in terms of two important and seemingly contradictory desires: on the one hand, the desire to be accepted and be a part of Europe; while on the other, to take 'revenge' on Europe (Bora and Şenyuva, 2011, p. 39). This contradictory situation coupled with, to use Billig's famous phrase, the 'banal nationalism' that accompanies football, provides a complex link between European football and Turkish national identity (Billig, 1995).

Thus, this contribution pushes forward and develops our understanding of how this *representation* really works. Departing from this close link between the formation of Turkish national identity and 'encounter with Europe' in the field of football, this chapter aims to understand whether the existence or non-existence of the Turkish national football team on the field feeds into the representations and narratives of the media, and assesses the content, style and tone of reports using a qualitative analysis. By this way, we argue, we could detect the identity constructions of Turkish national identity vis-à-vis the 'Europeans' through football. The bulk of the discussion that follows is derived from a subjective reading of the newspaper reporting of Euro 2008 and Euro 2012 by *Hürriyet* and *Fotomaç*. *Hürriyet* ('Liberty'), founded in 1948, is generally recognised as a mainstream, liberal, nationalist and secularist daily newspaper, which could be compared to its German equivalent *Süddeutsche Zeitung* and its French counterpart *Libération* in terms of its circulation and editorial stance. *Fotomaç* ('Photo-Match'), on the other hand, is the most widely read daily sports newspaper, usually criticised for its masculine, speculative and jingoistic discourse. These two newspapers are analysed during two main periods: from early May 2008 (one month before the start of the championship) to the end of July 2008 (one month after the end) in the case of Euro 2008; and from early May 2012 (one month before the start of the championship) until early August 2012 (one month after the end) in the case of Euro 2012. Our aim here is the examination of key themes as put forward by the chosen newspapers, rather than an exhaustive catalogue of media coverage. However, the main methodological inspiration in this regard has been the methodology employed by Garland and Rowe, who aimed to uncover the press coverage of the English team's progress in Euro 1996 (Garland and Rowe, 1999). In this respect, we categorise the press coverage of Euro 2008 and Euro 2012 according to the following themes, which seemed to be recurrent during the analysis: *Turkish national identity* (Turkey's standing vis-à-vis the other nations), *stereotypes* and *Europeanness*. Although these categories are helpful in identifying the general contours of the debate, it should be remembered that these themes are not exhaustive and not mutually exclusive. In line with the general attempt to reflect upon the debates on Euro championships within the selected time intervals, 204 newspaper articles have been singled out and examined.

Theoretical framework

For Hall, 'the practices of representation always implicate the positions from which we speak or write – the position of *enunciation*' (Hall, 1996, p. 210 – *emphasis in the original*). In the same vein, an identity is not an utterly unproblematic and transparent historical fact, but 'is a production which is never complete, always in process, and always constituted within, not outside, representation'

(Hall, 1996, p. 210). That is, in order to have a grasp on identities, we actually need to understand the practice of representation, which is in essence *constitutive* of the identities in question. Thus 'identity is not the immanent quality of a monadic and isolated subject, but [is] a relational and social phenomenon' (Jensen, 1997, pp. 16–17). The construction of meaning in this sense is dependent upon what gets represented, how it is represented and, ultimately, how people conceive of it. Representation is therefore crucial to the process of constructing meaning:

> One soon discovers that meaning is not straightforward or transparent, and does not survive intact the passage through representation. (...) It is therefore never finally fixed. It is always putting off or 'deferring' its rendezvous with Absolute Truth. It is always being negotiated and inflected, to resonate with new situations. It is often contested, and sometimes bitterly fought over. (Hall, 1997, pp. 9–10)

In our case, in order to understand the meanings attached to Euro 2008 and Euro 2012 in the Turkish media, we will investigate the representation of these events, which is indeed the *reality* itself for that particular context and historical juncture. In order to grasp representational systems such as football, we should, according to Hall, be able to understand the context, usage and historical circumstances of meanings (Hall, 1997).

This focus on meanings and representations is the crux of what has come to be dubbed as 'social constructivism' in political science. With its reference to human consciousness and ideational factors, social constructivism 'insists that human agents do not exist independently from their social environment and its collectively shared systems of meanings' (Risse, 2004, p. 160). Thus, social structures and agents are mutually co-determined and constituted. By the same token, we cannot describe the properties of social agents without reference to the social structure in which they are embedded. A possible follow-up to this premise is that any social phenomenon affects the ways in which actors see/define themselves and constitute their discursive and behavioural practices accordingly. This focus on social practices takes 'words, language and communicative utterances seriously' as language is constitutive of the reality (Risse, 2004, p. 164).

The production of meaning is the central practice in the construction of culture, which is mainly about 'shared meanings'. Therefore,
it is important to understand representation, not only to seize the
production of meaning, but also to have an idea how the cultural
realm is shaped. According to Hall, the so-called, 'circuit of culture'
is established by the endless circular interplay between the moments
of representation, identity, production, consumption and regulation
(Hall, 1997, p. 1). That is, in order for us to talk about a culture within
which the participants can build up a shared understanding and
interpret the world in roughly the same way, representation through
language is crucial (Hall, 1997).

These different participants are grouped together under two diametrically opposed entities: an *Other* confronts a *Self*. This goes back
to what we argued above: identity is relational and it is constituted
against an *Other*; and discourses articulating an identity articulate
a *Self* against a series of *Others*. For Herschinger, the identity of a
Self is not only forged via the division of the discursive space and
the relation to an *Other* but also through the creation of a vision
of what the world would look like without being endangered by the
respective *Other* (Herschinger, 2008). In this respect, there is a consensus amongst the anti-essentialist or constructivist interpretations of
identity, which see identity not as a set of pre-social, invariable characteristics of individuals or groups, but rather as an ongoing process
of construction and reproduction of shared understandings about
the Self. What is also almost commonsensical in literature is that a
radical or *threatening Other* is sine-qua-non for constructing the identity of the Self (for major examples of this discussion, see Connolly,
1991; Campbell, 1992; Neumann, 1996). For Campbell, 'the state
needs to articulate threats and *radical Others* to construct its identity,
and hence, there is a drive within the ontology of national identity for turning constructions of difference into Otherness' (quoted
in Hansen, 2008, p. 38). A similar construction has been evident in
the depiction of Europe and Asia and the West and Islam as inherently incompatible and mutually exclusive identities, which have
long formed the basis of the EU–Turkey interaction (Rumelili, 2008,
p. 102).

This being said, *the Other* can be interpreted in radically different
ways, which implies an acknowledgement of the fact that constructions of identities can produce varying degrees of Otherness. This in

turn implies that their construction does not necessarily depend on the identification of a radically threatening *Other*:

> The logic of identity allows for a great deal of variation in self/other relationships. Some of this variation is in the substantive, emotive, and normative content of representational practices. The differences of the other may be represented through various, more or less favourable predicates, metaphors, and binaries, which are often very culturally specific. (Rumelili, 2004, p. 36; see also Hansen, 2006, pp. 38–41)

The EU, argues Wæver, is constituted not against an external, threatening *Other*, but against a temporal Other, the fear of a return to its own violent past (Wæver, 1996). Similarly, exploring significant Others, that is, groups/nations that historically have influenced the construction of 'our' national identity, Triandafyllidou suggests that these *Others* could be 'inspiring' as well as 'threatening' (Triandafyllidou, 2002).

Our research on Euro 2008 and Euro 2012 shows that although the Turkish national identity was predominantly constructed during Euro 2012 vis-à-vis Europeanness, we do not see this as the *radical Other* of Turkish national identity. This is the reason why the practice of representation is crucial in order to fully understand the way in which Turkish national identity was constructed within the course of the Euro tournament. After delving, in the following section, into literature on how the practice of representation works with reference to football and identities, we will devote the fourth section of this chapter to elucidating how 'Europe' shaped the Turkish national identity during Euro 2008 and Euro 2012 through representations and stereotypes.

How representation works

In this section, we will explore various scholarly works to see how the notion of 'representation' comes into play in terms of the football-identity relationship at various settings and contexts. This will provide indications on how representation of the Turkish national identity through football situates within the field of various representations and negotiations in literature.

In his research on the representation of 'Japaneseness' in the media during the 2002 World Cup, Arimoto argues that the 'astonishing physical ability' of the black players during the cup as circulated in the Japanese media was said to be 'challenged by the systematic tactics of the Japanese team' (Arimoto, 2004, p. 64). In this light, Japaneseness was mainly about the 'triumph of systematism' (Arimoto, 2004, p. 64). According to Mandujano, already immersed in the monumental effort of hosting such a massive affair, Japanese governmental, commercial and media circles during the 2002 World Cup had to make efforts to persuade people of the importance of football for the country (Mandujano, 2014). In her interpretative study on the Japanese press coverage of the 2002 World Cup, Mandujano argues that the media used football as a field to openly show and promote historically stained national symbols, sentiments and discourses and encourage the ideological location of Japaneseness in men, whilst condemning success and strength as undesirable traits of Japanese femininity (Mandujano, 2014). This analysis fits well with what we argued above: national identity representations in transnational football events are closely related to particular constructions of national stereotypes and patterns.

In their research on how European football writing stereotyped the characters and pitted the footballers against each other in an unfolding narrative during the European Championship finals held in England in June and July 1996, Crolley et al. focus on the European stereotypes as depicted by the British, Spanish, French and German print media (Crolley et al., 2000). According to this study, 'Englishness' during Euro 96 meant 'warfare' and equalised the qualities demanded of the colonial soldier and the virtues acquired through sport. Within the Spanish press, on the other hand, there were conflicting images of the English as both 'gentlemen' and 'hooligans' (Crolley et. al., 2000, pp. 109–14). Similarly, England's apparent lack of flair is often criticised in French football writing (Crolley et al. quote, for instance, *Le Monde* of 11 June 1996) but 'due acknowledgement is also usually given to the positive side of the English stereotype: England win, apparently, because of their great physical strength, passion, and commitment' (Crolley et. al., 2000, p. 119). Similarly, Garland and Rowe, who aimed to delineate the nature of press coverage of Euro 96 and to place it into a broader socio-political context, found out that the reporting of the championship relied on an offensive 'Little Englandism' and portrayed xenophobic caricatures of England's opponents and a nostalgia to emulate 'bygone glories' of England, both at the pitch and battlefield (Garland and Rowe, 1999, pp. 91–3). Euro 96 has also been the focus of Maguire and Poulton, who argue that the media discourse surrounding the tournament in Britain, characterised by nostalgia and an ethnic assertiveness/defensiveness, can be understood as part of an active construction of 'fantasy group charisma', and that this is based on both 'the invention of traditions' and, at a deeper level, the habitus codes that underpin the 'national character' of European nations (Maguire and Poulton, 1999, p. 18). A similar critical reading was carried out by Garland later on the reporting of the 2002 World Cup by the UK tabloid press (Garland, 2004). According to him, the monocultural and xenophobic understanding of Englishness as depicted by the English press was completely at odds with 'a more diverse and inclusive version that appeared to be evolving amongst England supporters both at home and at the World Cup in Japan' (Garland, 2004, p. 81). The tabloid press, which talked about the 'Swede's' (referring to Sven Göran Eriksson, the then England manager) indulgence with 'our land's bulldog spirit' (*The Sun*, 1 June 2002, pp. 2–3) and represented the Argentinian players as 'cheating foreigners' through a reference to Falklands War rhetoric, believed that 'the English success on the football field had led to a growth, or even a rebirth, of the idea of Englishness and English patriotism' (Garland, 2004, p. 89).

The relation between football and nationalism, as well as the construction, reconstruction and representation of nationalism through football in Turkey are not completely uncharted territories (for good examples, see Kozanoğlu, 1990; Bora and Erdoğan, 1993; Bora, 2013). Especially following the recognition of football as a valid academic research subject starting in the second half of the 1980s, there have been numerous research pieces on the issue. Bora and Şenyuva indicate that while in the earlier years of international competitions strong nationalistic expressions are not strongly apparent, from the 1980s onward the Turkish political scene and football community converged towards overheated nationalistic overtures, particularly towards Europe, which was constructed as *the significant Other*, often as a threatening one (Bora and Şenyuva, 2011, p. 36). As Şenyuva and Tunç demonstrate in their historical analysis of Turkey's entry to UEFA, for Turkish fans, since the establishment of the Turkish

Football Federation within the newly born Republic in 1923, Europe has always been a natural direction, where, despite criticism and tension at times, the sense of belonging is always present (Şenyuva and Tunç, 2013).

Against this backdrop, it is not surprising that the representation of Turkish football encounters with other European teams, both at the national team and club level, with particular reference to nationalist discourses, drew the attention of academics over the last decade. Kösebalaban's analysis of Turkish sports media during the 2002 World Cup, during which Turkey had a historical success in reaching the semi-finals and finishing third, is a very important example (Kösebalaban, 2004). For Kösebalaban,

> Framing of sport encounters with European national teams by both the Islamic and the secular media mirrors a surprising level of patriotism and national zeal. While liberal columnists celebrate Turkey's participation in European games, stressing the European aspect of Turkish national identity (...), the dominant theme in the headlines of both the Islamic and the radical secular media is a characterization of Europe as the other of Turkish national identity. However, radical secularism also marks a sharp internal boundary for Turkish national identity. It forcefully rejects manifestations of Islamic culture as part of national identity, and with respect to sport, it does so by protesting any public display of Islamic symbols by the national team and its athletes. Radical secularism is disturbed to see any displays of cultural diversity, viewing them as a challenge to the imagined homogeneity on which Kemalism is based. (Kösebalaban, 2004, p. 48)

In his extensive analysis, covering the Turkish media for the period of 1990–2002, Gökalp also reaches similar conclusions (Gökalp, 2006). He argues that a heavily exclusive identity is represented through ethnic-nationalist discourses in the Turkish newspapers in reporting and analysing Turkish football encounters with European teams; both at national and club levels,

> [t]he analysis demonstrates that the notion of national identity propagated by many press outlets is based on a conception of Turkish citizenship that is decidedly not multi-cultural. The notion of Turkish nationalism in these media representations is

based on exclusive discourses, thus contributing to a reproduction of essentialist and ethnicist conceptions of Turkish national identity, distinguishing between the 'self' and a variety of 'others', and mobilising old and more novel narratives of 'enmity'. It appears that these mechanisms of 'otherising' play a central role in the maintenance of Turkish national identity under the stress of multiple pressures on established notions of what it means to be 'a Turk'. (Gökalp, 2006, p. 1)

Gökalp continues his research on the nationalistic coverage of football in the Turkish press and in his comparative analysis of Turkish and Greek media together with Panagiotou, arguing that the press both in Turkey and Greece heavily utilise nationalistic discourses with generous usage of war metaphors in their coverage of Turkey–Greece games in the qualifications for the Euro 2008 championship (Gökalp and Panagiotou, 2008).

Past research thus clearly demonstrates strong nationalistic representations within Turkish football press coverage as well as the repetitive pattern of *us* versus *them*, in particular with reference to the encounters with other European teams. However, as Bora and Şenyuva assert, it is possible to claim that the overheated nationalism among Turkish fans is rapidly declining due to several national and international factors. The question remains, however, whether this softening among the fandom is reflected in the press, and whether the participation of Turkish national teams in major international tournaments is an important intervening variable which strongly exacerbates the issue (Bora and Şenyuva, 2011, pp. 49–50). We aim at approaching the issue from this angle by comparing the representations of two tournaments where the Turkish national team was present in one and absent in the other, and claim that 'Europeanness' does not necessarily appear to be the *radical Other of* Turkish national identity. The media coverage of 'Europeanness' at Euro 2012 is a good example of this.

'Stop History, Strike Turkey': Turkish national identity and Europeanness during Euro 2008 and Euro 2012

The UEFA European Championship, originally founded as the 'European Nations' Cup' and today often informally referred to as

'Euro', is clearly the most prestigious continental sports event in the world, attracting an audience that goes largely beyond the borders of Europe. After very humble beginnings, following its launch at the UEFA congress in Copenhagen in 1957 and its first, very modest, final phase in June 1960 in France, the championship increasingly developed and continuously expanded into a spectacular football event, capable of 'challenging the World Cup' (Mittag and Legrand, 2012), especially since its extension to 16 participants at Euro 96. The tournament's next edition, to be held in France in 2016, will see a further increase to 24 participating teams.

Euro 2008 and Euro 2012, on which this chapter focuses, contributed to this impressive development, taking the event to new levels. Between 7 and 29 June, Euro 2008 took place in eight towns in Austria and Switzerland. A total of 31 games were held, of which 16 took place in Austria. Football teams from 12 EU member states, plus Switzerland, Russia, Croatia and Turkey, participated in the tournament. The tournament was eventually won by Spain, defeating Germany 1–0 in the final. Euro 2012 was hosted by Poland and Ukraine, that is, for the first time in post-socialist Europe, between 8 June and 1 July 2012. Thirteen of the participating teams came from EU member states, the three remaining competitors were Russia, Ukraine and Croatia. The competition was won again by Spain, who beat Italy 4–0 in the final at the Olympic Stadium in Kiev, Ukraine (UEFA website, 2013). Turkey had initially contested for the hosting of the event but Greek and Turkish bids were eliminated from the process in 2005.

Both tournaments, the Turkish team's participation notwithstanding, were extensively covered by Turkish media. The analysis of selected newspapers during Euro 2008 and Euro 2012 enables us to identify a certain variety of representations of national identity, which we categorise in the following sub-sections under 'Turkish national identity', 'Stereotypes', and 'Europeanness'.

Turkish national identity

According to Bora, the images, values and metaphors of nationalism, masculinity and militarism feed into and multiply each other, and turn into a symbiotic relationship which facilitates the joint agitation of machismo and militarism and renders their interchangeable use possible. Nowhere does this process operate better than in football (Bora, 2013: 489).

In the analysed media, Turkey's exciting run to the semi-finals in 2008 has often been constructed in a language loaded with references to Turkish victories in the past. Particularly, the use of the term, *'Çılgın Türkler'* ('Crazy Turks') is of importance. The term became popular through the title of a historical novel accounting the heroic deeds of Turkish soldiers during the battles at Gallipoli and the War of Independence that followed the invasion of the Allies in the post-WWI era (Özakman, 2005). In Euro 2008, Turkey played a series of cliff-hanger games, managing to score miraculous last-minute goals. Each of these victories was presented with the use of the expression 'Crazy Turks'. The match reports are full of war metaphors and stories of heroic players with a lot of parallels drawn to the War of Independence. It is, however, important to note that the language used, despite carrying historical militaristic references, is not violent or hateful. The war talk was mainly about heroism and taking a stand, and compared with the football language of the 1980s and 1990s, was very mild and moderate.

The article titled, *'İmparator Yine Seferde'* ('the Emperor is on Military Expedition Again' – 'the Emperor' being the nickname of Fatih Terim, the infamous coach of the Turkish national team between 1993 and 1996 and 2005 and 2009) is a good example of the use of historical references, which in this case refer to the Ottoman expeditions conquering Europe over the centuries (*Hürriyet*, 6 June 2008, p. 13). The irony is that while the headline is historically loaded, the text itself does not include any historical or war references. Historical references are also significant in *Hürriyet*'s later description of the quarter-final that took place between Turkey and Croatia in the historically particularly significant city of Vienna.[2] During this match, Turkey soared in victory through a penalty shoot-out, which is described as yet another last-minute, nail-biter, miracle goal. *Hürriyet* uses the headline, *'Viyana Fatihleri'* ('The Conquerors of Vienna') in its description of the match, demonstrating yet again the use of historical connotations of the 16th-century Vienna Siege (*Hürriyet*, 21 June 2008, p. 32). However, in the coverage of the semi-final against Germany, *Hürriyet* particularly shifts its tone and comes up with the Turkish–German mix cover page headline, *'Kardeşlik Uber Alles'*[3] ('Brotherhood Above All') on the match day (*Hürriyet*, 25 June 2008, front page). The headline is a reference to the first stanza of the German national anthem (based on a poem written in 1841) that was officially banned in 1952 for its ambivalent nationalistic undertones and erroneous, but tenacious, association with the Third Reich, and which remains better known abroad than the new, more consensual, text on 'Unity, Justice and Freedom'. The reference to *'Deutschland über alles'* is also regularly used with satirical intention across European media.

As this example demonstrates, during Euro 2008 the main discourse of the newspapers and the chief editor is built on the historical and social relations with Germany, with special reference to the large community of Turks living in Germany. The same discourse of brotherhood and cultural proximity is even more apparent in 2012 where Turkey was not present. It has frequently been argued that in the tournament, with Turkey missing, Turks would be supporting the team perceived as closest, which is Germany: *'Bizi 150 Milyon Kişi Destekliyor'* ('we have 150 million supporters') (*Hürriyet*, 11 June 2012, p. 30).

More in the line with tabloid rhetoric, *Fotomaç* is more generous in using war-like language than *Hürriyet* in 2008. The game day coverage of Turkey vs. Portugal has the headline, *'Haydi Koçlar Saldırın'* ('Come on Rams, Attack!'), referring to the positive meaning attached to 'ram' in daily Turkish signifying a strong and young man (*Fotomaç*, 7 June 2008, front page). The defeat against Portugal is also emphasised on the front cover page with the headline, *'Analar Ağlıyor'* ('The Mothers are Crying'), which displays the connotations of an alleged armed conflict taking place between Turkey and Portugal (*Fotomaç*, 8 June 2008, front page). *Fotomaç*'s habit of throwing political and social headlines in the face of their readers continues with the Turkish victory against Czech Republic two games later. With reference to Father's Day, the headline reads: *'Bu Zafer "En Büyük Baba" Atatürk'e'* ('This Victory is for Ataturk, the Best Father'), establishing a link with the founder of the secular republic, Mustafa K. Atatürk, and the win by the Turkish national team (*Fotomaç*, 16 June 2008, front page). The nationalistic discourse and the war metaphor are repeated in the following pages. The header compares the Turkish national player, Nihat Kahveci, who scored the decisive goal against the Czechs, to *Ulubatlı Hasan*, a military hero figure who legendarily raised the Ottoman flag on the Byzantine walls during the Ottoman conquest of Constantinople (*Fotomaç*, 16 June 2008, p. 5).

Unsurprisingly, the front page of *Fotomaç* on 20 June 2008, which reports on the quarter-final against Croatia, is covered with symbols and metaphors that refer to historical conquests, with special references being made to the historical siege of Vienna. The cover includes the symbol of the Ottoman army and conveys war rhetoric through images of the Turkish manager and two players 'photoshopped' as *Mehter*[4] players. The headline above reads, '*325 Yıl Sonra Yeniden Viyana Kapılarındayiz, Gazanız Mübarek Olsun*' ('we are at the Gates of Vienna Once Again after 325 Years, Let Your War Be Blessed') (*Fotomaç*, 20 June 2008, front page). The front page is full of further talk of *making history*, *conquest* and *raising the flag*. However, the same war rhetoric is toned down in the follow-up to the victory and the front page of the following day is more euphoric than nationalistic, talking about Turks reaching the 'seventh heaven' (*Fotomaç*, 21 June 2008, front page). Although the second page reminds the reader of the cover of the match day by alluding to the fact that 'the conquest is complete', it is in a much softer tone, avoiding the use of military language (*Fotomaç*, 21 June 2008, p. 2).

Stereotypes

Football matches may sometimes be boring, but media coverage of football can never afford to be so. As Crolley et al. attest, European print media discourse on football does more than cover the game's technicalities; it also shapes its readers' awareness of national identities (Crolley et al., 2000, p. 107). Without any doubt, this is mainly done through stereotypes. The representation of Euro 2008 and Euro 2012 by the Turkish media has been no exception to this. What we could detect is the abundant use of national stereotyping when reporting about other countries in both newspapers. The stereotypes that are used are very generic and simplistic ones, such as *Matadors* for Spain, *Oranges* for the Netherlands and, of course, *Panzers* for Germany. Some other examples include *Russian Roulette* when discussing matches against Russsia. There are countless uses of such simplistic stereotypes; in fact, in both newspapers reviewed, *Hürriyet* and *Fotomaç*, it is more difficult to find articles that do not incorporate uses of *Oranges* or *Matadors* while speaking about the Netherlands and Spain. The use of stereotypes was also highly evident in 2012 when Turkey did not participate in the Cup.

However, while the use of national stereotypes is considered normal and acceptable for Turkish newspapers, strong reaction and resentment is created when other European newspapers incorporate similar clichéd ideas about Turkey. The Swiss media, which have something of a long-standing feud with the Turkish press, are particularly the target for using stereotypes such as döner kebab,[5] and the Turkish victory over the Swiss national team is presented as a form of punishment of this disrespectful act. The front page of *Fotomaç* following the Turkish victory against Switzerland is probably the most violent and offensive in this analysis, as evidenced by the headline, '*Ç...(ikolata) Çocukları*' ('Sons of C...hocolate') making a clear reference to a swear word (*Fotomaç*, 12 June 2008, front page). The headline is accompanied by a very brutal picture, showcasing the heads of Swiss players being sliced by the Turkish manager 'photoshopped' with a Swiss army knife, as reference to the medieval wars. This construction of images is a reaction of revenge to the front cover of the popular daily Swiss newspaper *Blick* on 11 June 2008, where Turkish manager Fatih Terim was caricatured as a döner kebab, which was about to be sliced and served by the Swiss national manager. This overblown reaction and the cry for disrespect are particularly noteworthy, considering the use, by the Turkish press, of national stereotypes in almost its entire tournament coverage. The same *Blick* cover and the reaction towards the use of döner kebab continues on page five of *Fotomaç*, and the fact that the only Swiss goal of the game was realised by two Swiss nationals with Turkish origins leads to a headline '*Evlat Kurşunu*' ('Bullet by Own Son') with slight hints of backstabbing and betrayal (*Fotomaç*, 12 June 2008, p. 5). Interestingly, however, Hakan Yakın, the same Swiss player who scored against Turkey and also scored twice for Switzerland in the match against Portugal, is later praised by *Fotomaç* as *Super Hakan* (*Fotomaç*, 16 June 2008, p. 8). The front page of *Fotomaç* on the day of the semifinal against Germany is also another clear example of stereotyping. The *Fotomaç* headline reads, '*Panzer'in Sonu*' ('The End of the Panzer') accompanied by an image of the Turkish manager Fatih Terim, who is made to appear as a gladiator standing next to a destroyed tank. No doubt, the reader is expected to understand immediately that the tank is meant to symbolise Germany (*Fotomaç*, 25 June 2008).

Europeanness

It would not be an overestimation to claim that, within Turkish politics, 'Europe' as the synonym for modernisation has been the target to be reached, and, indeed, the way itself towards this target starting from the 19th century (Alpan, 2014, p. 68). Since then, the choice for Turkey's European orientation has been associated with an emotional attachment to the idea of being among the 'Europeans'. This attachment acquired a new dimension and has been carried to a more substantive and institutional level with the Helsinki European Council in December 1999 when Turkey was granted formal candidacy status in its application to join the European Union (Alpan, 2014, p. 68). This intense historical preoccupation with 'Europe' and the European integration process also had major effects in the media coverage of football throughout the course of Euro 2008 and Euro 2012. In particular, the mainstream newspaper *Hürriyet* often made references to current European socio-political events when reporting on football. Following the defeat of Turkey against Portugal in the first game of the group stage in 2008, one of the reviews of the game is headed by the title, *'Türklere AB kapısı kapalı'* ('The door to the EU is closed to the Turks') (*Hürriyet*, 9 June 2008, p. 34). The article is mainly about the way in which the result of the game was discussed in newspapers from other major European countries, and emphasis is placed on the political situation between Turkey and the EU, which was also the main topic of discussion in Italian newspapers, who are particularly known to merge themes of football with politics.

The same political references are also present in the 2012 coverage. In particular, the entire Greece vs. Germany game is reported within the context of the ongoing financial crisis and the Greek public reaction to Germany's tough demands of painful structural reforms. Photos of Greek Prime Minister Papandreou and the German Chancellor Merkel appear with the headline, *'O Fotoğrafın Rövanşı'* ('The Revenge of That Photo') (*Hürriyet*, 22 June 2012, p. 28). The photo used is a famous one, where Papandreou was standing in front of Merkel, with his hands crossed during an EU summit, implicitly hinting the 'unequal' relationship between the Greek prime minister and Merkel. The sub-head reads that the Greeks will seek revenge on the Germans for this photo that hints at humiliating the Greeks. All in all, the language of reporting is significantly sympathetic towards Greece, which is portrayed as the unfortunate neighbour who is taking a stand, through the sport of football, for its lost honour and dignity due to its economic problems.

It is highly significant that in 2012 we do not see any questioning of Turkey's Europeanness, and it seems that the journalists and columnists broke their inferiority complex which was clearly apparent in the past decades (Bora and Şenyuva, 2011). The fact that Turkey had not qualified to play in Euro 2012 is very much regretted and discussed, but the debate remains within the borders of the game, that is, lack of young players, lack of quality of Turkish leagues and lack of inclusion of Euro-Turks. The financial dimension of the game is also a major topic of discussion and an extensive report on the economic cost of missing out major tournaments is presented in *Hürriyet* with the headline, '*Avrupa Şampiyonası 200 Milyon Euroluk Tanıtımdan Etti*' ('Euro Championship Bereaved the Advertising worth 200 Million Euros') *(Hürriyet*, 1 July 2012, p. 9), which is covered not on the sports pages but on the Economics pages. Therefore, the language of 'not being there' is not constructed as a litmus test of Turkey's European identity, as it was the case in previous decades, but more in the line of missing out on all the fun and the money.

Conclusion

By comparing the representations of two tournaments where the Turkish national team was present in one and absent in the other, this article made the argument that 'Europeanness' does not necessarily appear to be the *radical Other of* Turkish national identity. The media coverage of 'Europeanness' in Euro 2008 and Euro 2012 is a good example of this. Although media coverage of the Turkish team's entrance into the semi-finals in 2008 is often constructed with loaded language full of references to Turkish (military) victories in the past, this mainly includes references to bravery and strength rather than hatred and violence. On a different note, stereotypes appear to be indispensable to the way in which football is represented in the media during both tournaments. However, while the use of national stereotypes is considered normal and acceptable for Turkish newspapers, when similar ones are used about Turkey by other European newspapers, they are reported with indignation and resentment.

To what extent, however, are such outbursts of indignation and resentment in popular print media – often artificially 'pumped up' by the journalists in order to make them more 'scandalous' or 'sensational' – actually picked up at face value by readers? Media discourse analysis, especially when carried out in a longitudinal perspective like in this chapter, is a useful tool to 'track changes' in discursive habits over time, but it also has its limits. Being exposed to a specific discourse does, obviously, not automatically lead to interiorising it. This is especially the case if the target public of the discourse concerned is, as a large variety of empirical studies have demonstrated, not composed by 'cultural idiots' that can be manipulated at will, but consists of individuals that are perfectly capable of adopting a critical and/or ironical distance towards media discourse.

In the case of stereotyping or war metaphors, for instance, the present discourse analysis would gain from being completed by survey data on how readers actually perceive these – often blatantly sarcastic – practices and to what extent they adopt a posture of shocked indignation, shoulder-shrugging dismissal of stereotypes, or 'tongue-in-cheek' amusement. As punctual analyses of interactive football websites and fan forums have revealed, it turns out that the typical press rhetoric around the political or historical implications of international football matches is either consumed rather critically or ignored altogether (Sonntag, 2013).

As early as in the 1950s Richard Hoggart's seminal work *The Uses of Literacy* warned very convincingly against the elitist assumption that 'the members of the popular classes' are 'conditioned by their reading' (Hoggart, 1957). Introducing the concept of 'oblique attention', Hoggart pointed out that the 'popular aptitude of mockery' allowed working-class readers to absorb press discourse in a very 'nonchalant' manner, never entirely fooled into interiorising it and always capable of making a clear distinction between such discourse and 'real life'.

At the beginning of the 1980s, when football research was still considered a very unusual pastime for 'serious' academics, the great French anthropologist Marc Augé confirmed Hoggart's thesis through his own observations on the terraces of football stadia. He was struck by the 'humour' in the attitude of the supporters, which never entirely disappeared despite the tension of the game, this 'mix of attention, passion, and flippancy' (*'désinvolture'*) that he felt were characteristic of the consumption of the football spectacle (Augé, 1982). It is exactly this seemingly contradictory mix of attitudes that Nick Hornby gave, ten years later, an accomplished literary form.

In his autobiographical novel, *Fever Pitch* (1992), he managed to describe how the discrepancy between, on the one hand, serious and total emotional investment and, on the other hand, a mocking self-consciousness of the grotesque aspects of fandom contributes to the very peculiar pleasure and excitement that football may procure.

Augé's and Hornby's analyses may well be applied to the manner in which the game is 're-enacted' through the consumption of press reports on the following day. As the comments on interactive media websites very clearly show, football journalists are no longer considered experts who 'explain' to their readers what has happened on the pitch, but just one subjective discourse among many, with no supremacy on the views and interpretations of 'ordinary spectators' in any way. The fact that their formulations tend towards semantic exaggeration and emotional provocation is taken for part of a 'game', which one may engage in or not.

In the Turkish case, it is noteworthy to observe that journalists and columnists themselves seem to relativise increasingly their own discourse between 2008 and 2012. This is particularly visible in the issue of 'Europeanness': though omnipresent in both newspapers within the course of both tournaments, is no longer presented through a 'to-be-or-not-to-be' dichotomy. Particularly during Euro 2012, we do not see any questioning of Turkey's 'Europeanness' through football – it seems that the producers of the discourse got rid of their inferiority complex and obsession with 'Europe'. What we witness in terms of construction of identities is not the emergence of a sharp *radical Other-Self* dichotomy, particularly in the eyes of the media. As Bilgin and İnce rightly point out, rather than looking at identities purely in white and black terms by demarcating a sharp distinction line between Self (that is, Turkish national identity) and the Other (that is, European identity), what we need to do is to highlight various shades of grey and grasp the complexity of the relation between Turkishness and Europeanness through football (Bilgin and Ince, 2015).

Notes

1. The authors would like to thank Alexandra Schwell, Pınar Bilgin, Ömer Turan and Albrecht Sonntag for their valuable comments and contributions to the earlier versions of this article.

2. Vienna was besieged by the Ottoman Empire led by Suleiman the Magnificent in 1529. The siege, which was unsuccessful in the end, signalled the pinnacle of the Ottoman Empire's power and the maximum extent of Ottoman expansion in Central Europe. This historical background hints at how highly emotional the topic is on both sides, and how much it stands for an alleged 'clash of civilisations'.
3. This phrase made reference to the first verse of the German national anthem, which had been omitted due to its association with the Third Reich.
4. Ottoman military band.
5. The main reason why the döner kebab metaphor has been found humiliating is probably because it is associated with the Turkish migrants in Europe in a negative and pejorative manner.

References

Non-academic references:

Hürriyet

'İmparator Yine Seferde' ('The Emperor is on Military Expedition Again'), 6 June 2008, p. 13.

'Bizi 150 Milyon Kişi Destekliyor' ('We have 150 million supporters'), 11 June 2012, p. 30.

'Türklere AB kapısı kapalı' ('The door to the EU is closed to the Turks'), 9 June 2008, p. 34.

'Avrupa Şampiyonası 200 Milyon Euroluk Tanitimdan Etti' ('Euro Championship Bereaved the Advertising worth 200 Million Euros'), 1 July 2012, p. 9.

'O Fotoğrafin Rövanşı' ('The Revenge of That Photo'), 22 June 2012, p. 28.

'Viyana Fatihleri' ('The Conquerors of Vienna'), 21 June 2008, p. 32.

'Kardeşlik Uber Alles' ('Brotherhood Above All'), 25 June 2008, front page.

Fotomaç

'Bu Zafer "En Büyük Baba" Atatürk'e' ('This Victory is for Ataturk, the Best Father'), 16 June 2008, front page.

'325 Yıl Sonra Yeniden Viyana Kapılarındayiz, Gazaniz Mübarek Olsun ('We Are at the Gates of Vienna Once Again after 325 Years, Let Your War Be Blessed'), 20 June 2008, front page.

'Haydi Koçlar Saldırın' ('Come on Rams, Attack!'), 7 June 2008, front page.

'Analar Ağlıyor' ('The Mothers are Crying'), 8 June 2008, front page.

'Ç...(ikolata) Çocuklari' ('Sons of C...hocolate'), 12 June 2008, front page.

'Evlat Kurşunu' ('Bullet by Own Son'), 12 June 2008, p. 5.

'Ulubatlı Hasan', 16 June 2008, p. 5.

'Super Hakan', 16 June 2008, p. 8.

'Panzer'in Sonu' ('The End of the Panzer'), 25 June 2008.

Academic sources

Alpan, B. (2014) '"Europe-as-Hegemony" and Discourses in Turkey after 1999: What has Europeanisation Got To Do with It?', *Journal of Balkan and Near Eastern Studies*, Vol. 16, Issue 1, pp. 68–85.

Arimoto, T. (2004) 'Narrating Football: World Cup 2002 and Multi-layered Identifications in Japan', *Inter Asia Cultural Studies*, Vol. 5, Issue 1, pp. 63–76.

Augé, M. (1982) 'Football – De l'histoire sociale à l'anthropologie religieuse', *Le Débat*, No. 19, February 1982, pp. 59–67.

Bernstein, A. (2007) '"Running Nowhere": National Identity and Media Coverage of the Israeli Football Team's Attempt to Qualify for EURO 2000', *Israel Affairs*, Vol. 13, Issue 3, pp. 653–64.

Bernstein, A. and Blain, N. (2003) 'Sport and the Media: the Emergence of a Major Research Field', in A. Bernstein and N. Blain (2003) (eds) *Sport, Media, Culture: Global and Local Dimensions* (London: Frank Cass).

Billig, M. (1995) *Banal Nationalism* (London: Sage Publications).

Blain, N. and Boyle, R. (1998) 'Sport as Real Life: Media Sport and Culture', in A. Briggs and P. Cobley (eds), *The Media: an Introduction* (London: Longman).

Bora, T. (2000) 'Football and Its Audiences: Staging Spontaneous Nationalism', in S. Yasimir et al. (eds), *Civil Society in the Grip of Nationalism* (Istanbul: Egon Verlag).

Bora, T. (2013) 'Futbolda Erkeklik, Militarizm, Milliyetçilik' ('Masculinity, Militarism and Nationalism in Football'), in Y. N. Sümbüloğlu (2013) (ed.), *Erkek Millet Asker Millet (Manly Nation, Military Nation)* (İstanbul: İletişim).

Bora, T. and Erdoğan, N. (1993) 'Dur Tarih, Vur Türkiye' ('Stop History, Strike Turkey') in R. Horak, W. Reiter and T. Bora (eds), *Futbol ve Kültürü* ('Football and Its Culture') (İstanbul: İletişim), pp. 221–40.

Bora, T. and Şenyuva, Ö. (2011) 'Nationalism, Europeanization and Football: Turkish Fandom Transformed?' in G. Robin (ed.), *Football, Europe et Régulations* (Villeneuve d'Ascq: Editions du Septentrion), pp. 35–52.

Campbell, D. (1992) *Writing Security: United States Foreign Policy and the Politics of Identity* (Manchester: Manchester University Press).

Connolly, W. E. (1991) *Identity/Difference: Democratic Negotiations of Political Paradox* (Ithaca: Cornell University Press).

Crolley, L., Hand, D. and Jeutter, R. (2000) 'Playing the Identity Card: Stereotypes in European Football', *Soccer and Society*, Vol. 1, Issue 2, pp. 107–28.

De Biasi, R. and Lanfranchi, P. (1997) 'The Importance of Difference: Football identities in Italy', in G. Armstrong and R. Giulianotti (eds), *Entering the Field: New Perspectives on World Football* (Oxford and New York: Berg), pp. 87–104.

Garland, J. (2004) 'The Same Old Story? Englishness, the Tabloid Press and the 2002 Football World Cup', *Leisure Studies*, Vol. 23, Issue 1, pp. 79–92.

Garland, J. and Rowe, M. (1999) 'War Minus the Shooting? Jingoism, the English Press and Euro 96', *Journal of Sport and Social Issues*, Vol. 23, Issue 1, pp. 80–95.

Gökalp, E. (2006) 'Beware, the Turks are Coming! Reproducing Turkish Nationalism(s) through the Press Coverage of Football Games', *RAMSES*

Series on Europe and the Mediterranean Working Paper, No. 7/06, pp. 1–20, available at: www.sant.ox.ac.uk/esc/ramses/gokalp.pdf (accessed 5 May 2014).

Gökalp, E. and Panagiotou, N. (2008) 'Futbol! Oyun mu, Savaş mı? Türkiye-Yunanistan Futbol Maçlarının İki Ülke Basınındaki Temsili ve Milliyetçilik Söylemi' ('Football: a Game or a War? The Representation of Turkey vs. Greece Football Matches in the Greek and Turkish Media and the Discourse of Nationalism') (Ankara: Ayraç), pp. 229–46.

Hall, S. (1996) 'Cultural Identity and Cinematic Representation', in H. A. Baker, M. Diawara and R. H. Lindeborg (eds), *Black British Cultural Studies: a Reader* (London: University of Chicago Press).

Hall, S. (ed.) (1997) *Representation: Cultural Representations and Signifying Practices* (London: Sage Publications).

Hansen, L. (2006) *Security as Practice: Discourse Analysis and Bosnian War* (London: Routledge).

Herschinger, E. (2008) 'Defining the Global Enemy: Hegemony and Identity Construction in International Terrorism Discourse', paper presented at *the Inaugural World Conference, Ideology and Discourse Analysis (IDA)*, 8–10 September 2008, Roskilde, Denmark.

Higson, A. (1998) 'National Identity and the Media', in A. Briggs and P. Cobley (eds), *The Media: an Introduction* (London: Longman).

Hoggart, R. (1957) *The Uses of Literacy. Aspects of Working Class Life* (London: Chatto and Windus).

Jensen, O. B. (1997) 'Discourse Analysis and Socio-spatial Transformation Processes: a Theoretical Framework for Analysing Spatial Planning', *Working Paper* No. 61, Department of Town and Country Planning, University of Newcastle upon Tyne.

Kozanoğlu, C. (1990) *Türkiye'de Futbol: Bu Maçı Alıcaz!* (İstanbul: İletişim Yayınları).

Kozanoğlu, C. (1999) 'Beyond Edirne: Football and the National Identity Crisis in Turkey', in G. Armstrong and R. Giulianotti (eds), *Football Cultures and Identities* (London: Macmillan Press), pp. 117–25.

Kösebalaban, H. (2004) 'Turkish Media and Sport Coverage: Marking the Boundaries of National Identity', *Critical Middle Eastern Studies*, Vol. 13, Issue 1, pp. 47–64.

Maguire, J. and Poulton, E. K. (1999) 'European Identity Politics in Euro 96: Invented Traditions and National Habitus Codes', *International Review for the Sociology of Sport*, Vol. 34, Issue 1, pp. 17–29.

Mandujano, Y. (2014) 'Japanese Media Ideologies behind the National Football Teams: Representing Japan and Portraying Archetypes of Men and Women?', *Electronic Journal of Contemporary Japanese Studies*, Vol. 14, Issue 1.

Mittag, J. and Legrand, B. (2012) 'Towards a Europeanization of Football? Historical Phases in the Evolution of the UEFA European Football Championship', in W. Manzenreiter and G. Spitaler (eds), *Governance, Citizenship and the New European Football Championships. The European Spectacle* (London: Routledge), pp. 15–28.

Neumann, I. B. (1996) 'Collective Identity Formation: Self and Other in International Relations', *European Journal of International Relations*, Vol. 2, Issue 2, pp. 139–74.

Özakman, T. (2005) *Şu Çılgın Türkler* (İstanbul: Bilgi Yayınevi).

Risse, T. (2004) 'Social Constructivism and European Integration', in A. Wiener and T. Diez (eds), *European Integration Theory* (Oxford: Oxford University Press).

Rowe, D., McKay, J. and Miller, T. (1998) 'Come Together: Sport, Nationalism and the Media Image', in L. Wenner (ed.), *MediaSport* (London: Routledge), pp. 119–33.

Rumelili, B. (2004) 'Constructing Identity and Relating to Difference: Understanding the EU's Mode of Differentiation', *Review of International Studies*, Vol. 30, Issue 1, pp. 27–47.

Rumelili, B. (2008) 'Negotiating Europe: EU-Turkey Relations from an Identity Perspective', *Insight Turkey*, Vol. 10, Issue 1, pp. 97–110.

Şenyuva Ö. and Tunç, S. (2012) 'Turkey and the Europe of Football', paper presented at the FREE conference, *The Origins and Birth of a Europe of Football*, 28–29 September 2012, Besançon, France.

Sonntag, A. (2008) 'The Unbearable Lightness of Belonging: The World Cup as Producer of Virtual Emotion and Postmodern Sociability' in T. Pavlin (ed.), *Sport, Nation, Nationalism* (Univerza v Ljubljana, Fakulteta za sport: Zavod Ekvilib), pp. 259–69.

Sonntag, A. (2013) 'The Tempting Parallels', *The FREE Blog*, 3 May 2013, at: www.free-project.eu/Blog/post/the-tempting-parallels-1250.htm (accessed 10 September 2014).

Triandafyllidou, A. (2002) *Negotiating Nationhood in a Changing Europe – Views from the Press* (Lewiston/Queenston/Lampeter: The Edwin Mellen Press).

Wæver, O. (1996) 'European Security Identities', *Journal of Common Market Studies*, Vol. 34, Issue 1, pp. 103–32.

5
Up to the Expectations?

Perceptions of Ethnic Diversity in the French and German National Team

Albrecht Sonntag

National football teams are more than simple line-ups for sports competitions. Especially during international tournaments they are heavily charged with symbolic meaning and serve as powerful projection screen for the national community.

Twenty-five years ago, in the apparently post-national zeitgeist of Western Europe, this statement would have made many observers smile. But then, the very idea of football as an object of serious academic research would have provoked the same smiles...

Attitudes have changed since then. The 1998 World Cup in France and all following major international competitions have repeatedly demonstrated to what extent the theatre of international football and the national teams it stages are capable of reaching very large parts of the public and of triggering emotional reactions that go way beyond the sports scene. There is every reason to believe that the nation, this extremely abstract community that only ever seems to exist as an 'imagined' one, to quote the seminal phrase of Benedict Anderson (1983), has found in the line-up of eleven young men or women who measure themselves against others in a popular game a particularly efficient emblematic incarnation.

In his history of *Nations and Nationalism*, the great historian Eric Hobsbawm identified precisely this emblematic character of national football teams as a constant all throughout the 20th century. According to him, what made them 'so uniquely effective a medium for inculcating national feelings' is their capacity to provide virtually everybody – 'even the least political or public individuals' – an offer for identification with the nation 'as symbolized by young persons excelling at what practically every man wants, or at one time in his life has wanted, to be good at' (Hobsbawm, 1990, p. 143). He concludes by stating that these teams help the 'individual, even the one who only cheers', to become 'a symbol of the nation himself'.

This identification offer, however, only fully functions if the team is perceived to be representative of the nation concerned. A national team, whatever its success on the pitch, will have much less resonance among the national public if there is a widespread perception that the players themselves are hardly concerned by their role as representatives of the nation but are only interested in the extra money or the added market value to be made from participating in a World Cup (the 'mercenary' syndrome). Likewise, identification suffers significantly if the players do not respond to 'expectations of representativeness' among the national public. Such expectations relate to behaviour patterns that are commensurate with dominant norms and values of the national culture concerned, often reflected in auto-stereotypical narratives. 'Expectations of representativeness' are built up and consolidated over decades, sometimes unconsciously, sometimes voiced explicitly, whether in the media or in the private sphere.

In an age of increasingly multicultural societies in Europe another layer of 'expectations of representativeness' has appeared. It concerns the different ethnic origins of the players selected for the national team. What went without saying for the largest part of the 20th century – the fact that a national team was supposed to represent the ethnic group the nation had been built upon in the first place – has become an increasingly complex and controversial question in societies where a large number of ethnic minorities have become more and more visible, and more or less integrated. Of course, rather than mirror the ethnic diversity of a given society, a national team mainly reflects the rules and practices governing citizenship and access to nationality that are currently in place in the nation-state concerned. As a result, some European national teams, such as France, England, Belgium, the Netherlands, Switzerland or Germany, have become multi-ethnic to various degrees over recent decades, while others, such as Italy or Spain, appear to be rather mono-ethnic.

This chapter will deal with expectations of ethnic representativeness in two countries that may both be considered major footballing nations: France and Germany. At Euro 2012, both featured multiethnic squads made up by players with a large variety of migration backgrounds. And in both national public spheres the ethnic composition of the national team has become a major issue of public debate and political implication over the last fifteen years, both internally and in comparative perspective, especially with regard to their neighbour. After an analysis of the historical link between the concept of the nation and modern football since its inception in the last third of the 19th century, the chapter will provide an overview of the evolution of perceptions and self-perceptions of French and German national teams since their first encounter in the 1930s, and attempt to show how these perceptions and self-perceptions have interacted and mutually influenced each other over time. It will conclude with the respective debates on representativeness around Euro 2012 and an appreciation of football as mediator of perception in a cross-cultural perspective.

Football and the nation – for better or worse

For better or worse, football and the nation form 'an old couple'. Contemporary football is a child of modernity, born in England in 1863 with the first codification of its rules. Its institutionalisation, development and international dissemination over the following decades were thus contemporary to a period marked by a strong political and cultural nationalism across the entire European continent. In the wake of the Franco-Prussian war of 1870–71 this nationalism, with its exacerbated revanchist and jingoist undertones, was particularly strong in the France of the Third Republic and the German *Kaiserreich*.

Against this backdrop, it is not surprising that from the beginning of the 20th century, when the first international matches were played on the continent, football was, due to its intrinsic territorial layout and battlefield terminology ('attack', 'defence', 'wings', 'shots', 'captain', and so on), understood everywhere as a mock confrontation of nations – 'war minus the shooting', as George Orwell famously called it half a century and two world wars later (Orwell, 1945). At a moment where 'social Darwinism underwent considerable vulgarisation' and where the principle of 'struggle' – between animal species, social classes, capitalistic enterprises – started to be conceived as the main 'motor of life' (Ehrenberg, 1984), the organisers of international football fixtures very quickly saw the extraordinary identification potential that this sport held for crowds already prepared by nationalistic brainwash.

They were not alone in their discovery. Throughout its history football has been the object of countless attempts by political regimes of all sorts to exploit and instrumentalise it for their purposes. But even though some of these attempts were rather successful, it would be a mistake to draw the conclusion that football is nationalistic 'by essence'. It is not. Its link with the concept of nation and the idea of nationalism is much more complex than such a shortcut would suggest. Ethnic considerations, and the relative importance attached to them in different contexts, which will be at the core of this chapter, are a good illustration of this complexity.

A look at the chronological tables of the first international matches on the continent – putting aside the so-called 'international' matches between the British home nations, the first one of which was played as early as 1872 – is revealing: it is striking to see the speed with which encounters between national teams became a regular fixture in the football calendar during the first decade of the 20th century. France played its first international match in 1904 in Belgium, but by the outbreak of the Great War only ten years later, it had already played thirty-four against a total of eight national teams! For Germany, the figures are comparable: its first match took place in 1908 in Switzerland; six years later thirty matches against nine different opponents had already been played (Sonntag, 2008, p. 101)

Given the means of transport available at the time and the lack of genuine professionalism in these two countries, the impressive number of matches that were still complicated to organise illustrates well to what extent the nationalist spirit of the period favoured the popularisation of football, just like it illustrates this game's propensity to become 'nationalised'. In France, according to Alfred Wahl (1989, p. 73), football was very quickly absorbed by the nationalist thinking that pervaded French society at the turn of the century:

Conceived in Great Britain by the upper class in the framework of liberal educational projects, association football underwent, as soon as it had been introduced to France, the influence of the militarist and authoritarian spirit that impregnated the gymnast movement. The ideals of upper class sportsmen were very quickly thwarted by the other dominant currents in 19th-century French society, and soon the national association football team was equated with a miniature army.

These observations from the left side of the Rhine correspond well to the description that Christiane Eisenberg (1997, p. 94) provides of football in the Kaiser's Germany. From its beginnings, the German federation (DFB), created in 1900,

> was much less interested in clubs and local identifications than in the national team and *'Deutschland'*. The DFB's most prestigious trophy, the Cup of the Crown Prince, [...] was played by selections from regional member federations and had as prime function to identify an elite with the sole purpose of setting up a national team.

In such an overheated environment it is only logical that in August 1914, when the real war broke out, the bellicose discourse blurred the metaphorical boundaries between football and war even more, revealing 'a structural affinity between sport and war', which, according to the French school of Marxist sports sociology, has remained a constant until today (Caillat, 1995, p. 33).

But it is probably during the inter-war years that football nationalism reached its paroxysm (Dietschy, 2010, pp. 196–246). While there is every reason to believe that it would have been much easier to set up a European competition for professional club teams, it turned out that there was a stronger motivation to create a World Cup for national teams right away, despite the huge logistic and organisational challenge.

And with the surge of fascist regimes the national teams were exploited without restriction for ideological purposes. In Mussolini's Italy, the game was 'systematically penetrated by references to a nationalist politics rather than only national symbolism, (...) reflecting the nationalist "culture" of the 1930s' (Vigarello, 1990).

It is interesting to compare the football of these times with the one played in the Europe of the 1970s and 1980s. As attested by both empirical evidence from the World Values Survey and the political support for the continuing process of European integration, this latter period is marked by a significant weakening of national or nationalist values and attitudes, at least in the Western part of the continent, in the countries that had been strongly impacted by the different movements of May 1968. Simultaneously, attendance figures in football stadiums stagnated or decreased in all major European championships, indicating a decline of football's popularity, to the benefit of new sporting activities such as the fitness wave (jogging, aerobics and the like) or other individual sports. Many observers imputed the presumably irreversible decline of football to the overall trend of individualisation of lifestyles. In Germany, for instance, the journalist Helmut Böttiger (1989) was not alone in announcing the forthcoming death of football:

> Football has abandoned its identity. Tennis represents the new paradigm, which, in case there are no further German winners at Wimbledon, may also be applied without problem to other sports like boxing or car racing: everything turns around the individual fighter.

We now know that he was completely wrong in his prediction: football has undergone a spectacular renewal since the 1990s and today dominates more than ever the sporting landscape. Curiously, this renewal in interest and perceived attractiveness is perfectly parallel to the resurgence in the attractiveness of 'national' values not only in the reconstituted nations of Central and Eastern Europe, but across the entire continent.

There is of course no direct interdependence between the degree of public interest in football and the attractiveness of nationalist attitudes in a given geopolitical configuration. Nationalism, in all its forms, does not need football to thrive. What the study of the different periods described above suggests, however, is that football may not have become what it is today if it had not benefited, at certain key periods of its development, from the fact that it offers national sentiments an incomparable, easily accessible and widely visible stage.

Football, with its regular and dense calendar of international events, provides a unique 'identity fair' to national communities

(Sonntag, 2014). There is even every reason to believe that neither football federations nor fans can get enough of them: as announced in March 2014 UEFA will add yet another competition to the calendar, the so-called 'Nations League', whose finals will take place every odd year and which as a side-effect will phase out friendly matches on the European continent almost entirely. The decision seems to meet with approval at grassroots level: in a flash survey run by *L'Equipe* two thirds of the 28,000 respondents declared themselves in favour of introducing such an extra tournament (*L'Equipe*, 2014).

As a result, as of 2018 there will be no summer any more without a 'vanity fair' of 'representations and identities', to quote the title of this volume again. There is little likelihood that the intensity of public display of national sentiments and symbols will decrease with the inflation of the number of competitions. In a period of destabilisation and loss of certainties, in which individuals seem to be in need of reassuring themselves in public about their collective belonging, the appeal of these 'fairs' will remain unchanged. But it can only remain as strong as it is if the communities in question feel appropriately represented in the spectacle they are following. In other words: if they consider the team that represents them compatible with their dominant 'vanity', that is, the collective self-perception of the community.

The family metaphor

What kind of community are people looking for when they celebrate their national belongings through football? With reference to the seminal conceptual dichotomy of *Gemeinschaft* and *Gesellschaft* framed by Ferdinand Tönnies at the end of the 19th century, discourses and behaviour patterns that may be observed at international football events suggest that there is, at the beginning of the 21st century, a strong desire for the expression of a pre-modern *Gemeinschaft*, a family-type solidarity, felt to be 'natural' and innate rather than constructed and acquired (Tönnies, 1944). In one of his later works, Norbert Elias described this communitarian nostalgia as 'the fossilization of habitus': a 'constellation in which the dynamic of unplanned social processes is tending to advance beyond a given stage towards another while the people affected by this change cling to the earlier stage in their personality structure' (Elias 1997, p. 274).

According to Edgar Morin, what contemporary individuals are expressing when they celebrate the national community as embodied in a national football team is the 'fundamental psycho-affective component' of the national sentiment, which is nothing else but a child's feeling towards the family extended to the nation as a kind of mega-family (Morin, 1984, p. 131). For Anthony Smith, such an extension of the family metaphor from an original community based on blood to the abstract and imagined community of the nation is 'indispensable to nationalism' and inseparable from the myth of fraternity that responds to the need for *Gemeinschaft* in the modern nation-state (Smith, 1991, p. 71). The history of nationalism provides ample evidence for the fact that the national community as imagined and promoted by nationalist elites could never be solely based on abstract reasoning and community of interest, but always needed an emotional underpinning, a *philia* in the Aristotelian sense, in order to create strong bonds across a linguistically diverse and socially fragmented society. The myth of fraternity transforms the nation into one large, extended community of destiny – a family – and thus provides exactly this underpinning. Even in presumably 'civic', 'political' or 'occidental' nations – as opposed to 'ethnic', 'romantic' or 'oriental' nations in the classical, though perfectly misleading typology – individuals are 'linked to their nation by a sentiment that comes close to the one that links them to their family', as Sophie Duchesne concluded, rather perplexed, at the end of a significant field study on French citizenship (Duchesne, 1997, p. 173):

> In reality, even if in its 'Republican' variant the nation is supposed to depend effectively on the political will of the citizens to consent to act according to the subjective sentiment of national belonging that motivates them, it appears that this sentiment, just like the nation itself, is perceived as natural, a given.

National football teams provide an accessible, humanly understandable sample of the 'national family'. As Eric Hobsbawm famously formulated, 'the imagined community of millions seems more real as a team of eleven named people' (Hobsbawm, 1990, p. 143). It takes, however, a good deal of abstraction to perceive a football team as 'representative' sample of a national community. First, the members of the team belong all to one single age group. Second, male or female, they exclude by definition half of the population from their 'sample'. Third, the teams are not put together according to principles of geographic representation. Still, a very large number of people seem to be ready to make this leap of abstraction in attributing their team a representative character, which is of course facilitated by the (already abstract) national symbols such as colours and hymns that accompany and identify the teams wherever they appear.

At an age of increasing migration flows and dual citizenships, however, the question arises whether criteria of ethnicity, that are very clearly a powerful component of nationality and underpin at least unconsciously the family metaphor, interfere with the perceived representativeness of the national teams. What discursive strategies of inclusion or exclusion are devised by spectators and commentators to adapt explicit or subliminal expectations of ethnic representativeness to the reality of multicultural squads? How are other national teams perceived with regard to their 'representativeness'?

The following sections will address these questions in a comparative historical approach, studying evolving perceptions of oneself and the other between France and Germany. The two nations have traditionally been considered to embody two presumably opposed conceptions of nationality and citizenship, often framed in ideal-types such as 'political' nation' vs. 'cultural nation', or 'contractual nation' vs. 'ethnic nation' etc. (Cabanel, 1997, p. 10).

This fundamental dichotomy, introduced by the German historian Friedrich Meinecke at the beginning of the 20th century, quickly turned into an *idée reçue*, a paradigm whose artificial, constructed character and inherent contradictions went mostly unnoticed, probably because it fitted dominant ideological discourses on both sides of the Rhine:

> The fact that the evocation of this opposition most of the time served purposes of domestic politics shows at the same time that the respective perception of the (own and foreign) nation is itself a historical construct (Kallscheuer and Leggewie, 1994, p. 113).

Despite numerous attempts at deconstructing this paradigm (Schnapper, 1995; Dieckhoff, 2000; Schulze, 1996, Woehrling, 2001, to name but a few examples), it has remained a powerful frame of academic and public discourse between the two nations. Against this backdrop of discursive inertia, the study of how the representativeness of national football teams is perceived and described and how this description evolves over time provides particularly revealing evidence for the dynamic character of national patterns of perception and self-perception in contemporary Europe.

Not really French

From the very beginning of international matches, the desire to project collective perceptions and self-perceptions on national football teams appears almost irrepressible. The invention of supposedly 'national football styles' by discursive construction and repetition is a wonderful illustration of this need to link football to the 'mentalities' or 'characters' of nations, including one's own. 'The patriotic valorisation of the national team forces the commentators to find a national playing style for it, dissimilar from others' – what Stéphane Beaud and Gérard Noiriel described for France could be applied across the entire continent (Beaud and Noiriel, 1990). Great semantic effort is made to find in football the 'people's game', 'a fundamental link to the national or racial characteristics' that would reflect and reinforce the 'soul of the people' and for facility's sake, parallels are drawn between the teams and pre-existing stereotypes and auto-stereotypes (Lanfranchi and Taylor, 2001, p. 35).

This essentialist narrative, repeated and reinforced with each new international match, was of course framed by journalists. By drawing on a large stock of perception patterns accumulated and consolidated over generations, it has however been easily interiorised by the actors themselves (players, coaches, federations) and confirmed and legitimated by the 'expert' interpreters of the game. As countless examples over the decades show very clearly, this discourse has generated expectations with spectators, which in turn have produced a self-fulfilling selective perception (Sonntag, 2008, pp. 147–68). Even today, in the age of globalised football, some of these beliefs seem to be upheld despite better evidence, an observation that brought the German sport philosopher Gunter Gebauer to conclude, not without a good dose of despair, that 'the link between national myths and playing styles seems indestructible' (Gebauer, 2002).

Against this backdrop, it is only logical that the ethnic origins of players attracted the attention of journalists and was integrated into the analysis within the framework of playing styles. A comparative study between two nations like France and Germany, which until 1999 had very divergent citizenship laws, is particularly revealing. In unravelling the history of French–German football encounters since their first official match in 1931, it appears that for a long time the issue is almost exclusively salient to German commentators, who were often intrigued by the pluriethnic character of the French team. Which is not surprising, as the French national team has always included in its ranks players of diverse origins, mainly in line with its long and significant immigration history (Braun, 1986; Noiriel, 1988, pp. 320–21) and the *ius soli*, which was introduced in 1889 and which conferred French citizenship to each individual born on French soil, whatever the origins of his/her parents. It also greatly facilitated access to full citizenship for immigrants (Noiriel, 2000). On the German side, the *ius sanguinis*, formulated in the *Kaiserreich* in 1913, remained virtually unchanged until the end of the 20th century, all across the Weimar Republic, the Third Reich and the Federal Republic, making it rather difficult for immigrants to obtain German nationality. As a consequence, despite the significant migration flows towards Germany since the 'economic miracle' of the 1960s, there was not a single player from a 'visible minority' in the German team until the 1970s. This did not appear to be an issue worth discussing for French media: before the mid-1990s no French match report or analysis mentions or questions the absence of players of foreign origin in the German team.

It is striking to see that until the 1998 World Cup and the wave of euphoria surrounding the winning French team described as '*black-blanc-beur*', every single German football commentator revealed a total absence of knowledge with regard to the French citizenship law that was at the origin of the ethnic plurality of the national team over almost a century. Not a single newspaper article found it necessary or relevant to seize the opportunity of one of these football matches to provide an explanation or simply compare the two different nationality codes. Quite the contrary: what becomes evident in numerous comments is the outright condemnation of this dubious manner of obtaining a competitive advantage by naturalising foreign players by the dozen. In 1935, for instance, when France played Germany for the third time – a 1–3 home defeat in the Parisian Parc des Princes – the German radio reporter, Paul Laven, asked himself the rhetorical question, 'Was this team really France?', regretting that several players had obviously 'been naturalised for the glory of French football' (Laven, 1950).

In 1952, at the first encounter after the war – played in Colombes, and ending with the same score as in 1935 but in favour of the French team – the tone of the match analyses was very similar. Among the German press, the reporter for the *Frankfurter Allgemeine Zeitung* was not alone in observing that 'even with a better physical condition and more agility on the side of the German players, the French professionals – among whom there were also naturalised Hungarians and Poles – would have won the match' (*Frankfurter Allgemeine Zeitung*, 1952). His colleague from the *Stuttgarter Zeitung* insisted on referring to the French right winger Ujlaki consistently as 'the Hungarian', pointing out that this player had 'obtained French nationality only three weeks ago' (Appel, 1952).

Given the depth and outreach of French–German reconciliation and rapprochement since the 1960s, it is surprising to see, as late as the 1980s, the astonishment in the German comments with regard to the ethnic composition of the French team and the persistence with which the expression '*waschechte Franzosen*' is used. Although there is good reason to believe that the adjective *waschecht* – 'waterproof' – was being used in a rather naive manner, the profoundly racist connotation of its application to human beings can by no means be denied.

Even Francophile journalists with an excellent knowledge of French society like Hans Blickensdörfer, long-standing correspondent of *L'Equipe* and *France Football*, jury member of the Ballon d'Or and author of several novels on France, were prone to distinguish between players that were more or less French. As he wrote right before the semi-final of the 1982 World Cup which was to become the legendary 'night of Sevilla', 'the composition of this group based on Spanish, Italian, African or Carribean elements is striking. [. . .] Among the first line-up, there are only three waterproof Frenchmen: Bossis, Rocheteau, and Six' (Blickensdörfer, 1982). Similarly, when the 1986 World Cup had France and Germany again opposed in the semi-finals, the major German news agency simply enumerated the different origins of the players, without providing its readers with a single explanation: 'The French national football team: a colourful mix of peoples. [. . .] It counts only four players whose cradle stood in France. Four others descend from Spanish parents, two from Italian ancestors, and two were born in Algeria. But the most exotic members of the French team come from the paradisiac islands in the Caribbean like Guadeloupe and Martinique' (dpa, 1986).

How are such superficial descriptions to be interpreted? Were they written by negligent journalists who are too lazy to dig deeper, understand and explain the concept of French nationality and its attribution to immigrants? Or were they motivated by the desire to deprecate, even unconsciously, a rival team that is suspected to have 'hired' foreign 'mercenaries'? Whatever the motivations, the discourse about the French players who are not really French remained remarkably stable over almost seven decades.

The French team as role model

Things changed dramatically in 1998. The winning French team, with its ostentatious ethnic plurality, was celebrated in unison by the German media. In an editorial for the *Frankfurter Allgemeine Zeitung*, entitled *'Equipes multiculturelles'* (in French!), Michael Eder insisted on the way in which the *Bleus* of 1998 were representative for French society:

> The *équipe tricolore* is a copy of French society. [...] It is an honest team; it was not 'bought'. It represents French reality, and promotes it. Its message is: only as a multicultural team will France stand international competition (Eder, 1998).

In a rare consensus across the media spectrum, all other daily newspapers agreed. Some of them even went further, providing, like for instance the *Süddeutsche Zeitung*, more detailed explanations:

> This is one the major differences between France and Germany: Zinedine Zidane, the French midfielder, is automatically French thanks to the *ius soli*, even if his parents were foreigners. In Germany each child born from foreign parents first needs to deserve its integration. But can a society function like this? [...] Wouldn't it be encouraging for integration if young people of Turkish origin had the opportunity to celebrate football players of Turkish origin in the German team? In any case, it would have for sure been useful for the German team... (*Süddeutsche Zeitung*, 1998).

In *Die Welt*, yet another editorial with a French title – *'Vive la différence !'* – explained that 'the French triumph at the World Cup is also a victory of integration' (Hehn, 1998). And the *Stuttgarter Zeitung* openly asked 'if something similar could not be possible in Germany, too', admitting that 'France has given us a lesson' (Zielcke, 1998). Very similar statements could be heard across audio-visual media, too. In a formidable, exhaustive French–German discourse analysis on the 1998 World Cup, Jochen Müller concluded that German media, as a whole, demonstrated 'profound and differentiated' journalistic work, expressing 'enthusiasm, respect, and even a certain admiration for the multicultural French team' (Müller, 2004, p. 285).

This radical change in media attitude with regard to the multiethnic character of the French national team was caused by two simultaneous, mutually reinforcing trends.

One the one hand, the integration into German society of second and third-generation immigrants had become a pressing and vividly discussed issue in the 1990s, and the question of reform of the citizenship law had already been a prominent one in the public debate for several years (Kastoryano, 1996). In July 1998, only two months before the legislative elections, the joint programme of the Social Democratic Party (SPD) led by the future chancellor Gerhard Schröder and its coalition partner, *Bündnis 90/Die Grünen*, clearly announced the contours of such a reform, including the facilitation of access to citizenship for foreign residents born in Germany or having spent a significant number of years in the country, as well as the introduction of simplified accession to double citizenship.

On the other hand, German football was rightly perceived to have entered a phase of decline, and the French world champions were regarded as a role model. This 'French model' that was unanimously praised was in fact an amalgamation of two distinct phenomena. The 'multicultural model' celebrated by the German media was actually underpinned by a 'training model' for young footballers that had been introduced by the French federation on a large scale two decades before and was now bearing fruit. While there is obviously a link between citizenship law and the size of the national pool of homegrown talents available for a highly developed elite training system, it is of course totally absurd to draw the conclusion of any sort of intrinsic superiority of pluriethnic national teams on monoethnic ones.

After all, the World Cup winners of 2006 and 2010, Italy and Spain respectively, did not display a great deal of ethnic diversity.

The question that deserves to be asked, however, is whether the sympathetic character of the French team of 1998, the deeply moving manner in which it was celebrated by the French public across all social, generational and ethnic divides, as well as certain individual biographies like Zinedine Zidane's did actually have a significant impact on German self-perception and, consequently, on the debate on the overdue change in the very concept of German nationality and its enactment in a new citizenship law.

Football as mediator of change

At first sight, one might be tempted to give a negative answer to this question. After all, the reform had already figured as a promise in the electoral programme of the future government coalition. Moreover, the reform was received by the population in a very ambiguous manner, to say the least. This was highlighted in spring 1999, when the Christian-Democratic Party of the *land* of Hessen, in a desperate attempt to instrumentalise this symbolic reform of the new federal government in their regional election campaign, started to collect signatures against double citizenship provisions in the new law. Although this political manoeuvre was easily identified as highly populist and both intellectually and morally debatable, the response to it revealed that a good part of the German population was 'clearly not mature yet to accept such an ambitious reform that was to switch Germany from the right of blood to the right of soil' (*Le Monde*, 1999).

In other words: when it comes to societal issues that are as heavily loaded with meaning and consequences, football does not seem important enough to play a role, not even a secondary one.

This being said, football did actually enter the debate through the back door. The press not only repeatedly expressed regrets with regard to the large number of talented young players born, socialised and trained in Germany, but who were, as things stood, not qualified for the national team. It also started to connote 'multiculturalism' as a positive value, especially with regard to the French national team, which was attributed a model character. What was radically new in this context was the unprecedented coalition across the entire media spectrum on this specific topic. While there was nothing essentially novel in the fact that quality media of liberal left-wing obedience started to refer to football in order to give a concrete illustration of the benefits of multiculturalism (which they had always supported anyway), the fact that a tabloid known for its conservative populism like the *Bild-Zeitung* started to use the adjective *'multi-kulti'* in a positive manner came close to a rhetorical revolution. It is important to understand that *'multi-kulti'*, an abbreviation for *'multikulturell'* with a diminutive connotation, had emerged in the 'alternative' leftist circles of the 1970s, and had always been used by conservative politicians and media in order to depreciate and ridicule presumably 'utopian' ideological postures. Its repeated use by the *Bild-Zeitung* in an entirely non-ironical manner was revealing. The 'multi-kulti heroes' of the French team were even hailed as 'the perfect blend at this World Cup' (*Bild-Zeitung*, 1998).

Given this semantic shift, it is not surprising that a publication with the intellectual reputation of *Die Zeit*, the quality broadsheet weekly whose level, style and political positions are in diametrical opposition to those of the *Bild-Zeitung*, also started to refer to football in order to illustrate its plea for the reform of German nationality. In February 1999, when the public debate on the new law entered a decisive phase with the above-mentioned regional elections in Hessen, it displayed a large picture of the French national team across its entire cover page, openly demanding a law *'A la française!'*, as the title read, and stressing, in the caption of the photo, that 'if the colourful team of the French have become football World Champions in 1998, it is also because of the citizenship law' (Leicht, 1999).

It is of course not football that has opened the eyes of German policy-makers and citizens to the relative anachronism of their citizenship law. But football may well be considered a mediator of change in this specific case. At a crucial moment in recent German cultural history, it gave an abstract and complex issue a concrete and understandable face.

A white, old and tired Germany

It is, however, not only the German vision of the French national team that changed in 1998. The French also started to cast a different look on the German squad. At the moment when they began to celebrate their *'black-blanc-beur'* heroes, the French media, who had never shown any interest in the ethnic composition of the German team, started to insist in a very explicit manner on the absence of visible minorities in the German team. The rhetoric deployed pursued mainly one objective: from the comparison between the compositions of the two teams it was possible to draw the conclusion that the French model of society was inherently superior to the German one. There were numerous references to 'the poor performances of a *Mannschaft'* that appeared 'white, old, and tired, without racial minority', as Henri Haget put it in an article for *L'Express* that was actually dedicated to the impact of the French team's victory on the nation (Haget, 1998). Others were even more explicit, like Claude Droussent in his editorial for *L'Equipe Magazine*, who proclaimed that 'the law of the soil' was 'the law of football' (Droussent, 1998). As *Libération* speculated, 'the colourful team lined up by the French' must have 'inspired some healthy reflexions in Germany. [...] Perhaps the German team would have performed better if it had integrated a number of Turks' (Millot, 1998).

In the follow-up to the World Cup, this comparative discourse in generalist and sports media was corroborated by the pseudo-scientific underpinning provided by many intellectuals from the Parisian *rive gauche* microcosm who all of a sudden developed a strong interest in a game they had for decades disdainfully ignored or, at best, condemned as 'opium of the masses'. Numerous hastily written op-ed pieces and interviews praised 'the French melting pot that undoubtedly exists, very unlike the German situation where you find no young player of Turkish origin' (Vigarello, 1998). The renowned demographer Michelle Tribalat described a 'magic day that incarnated the French ideal of the melting pot', drawing an explicit comparison with 'a German team with white skin and blond hair [*sic!*] that does not count a single player of Turkish origin' (Simonnot, 1998).

Very clearly, as sociologist Charles Suaud once remarked with a good deal of sarcasm, France had 'not only become World Champions of football, but also World Champions of popular partying, and of course World Champions of Republication integration ... '

In the 'vigorous torrent of prose' (Rioux, 1999) provoked by the success of the French team, only very few voices were raised in order to point out the over-simplification of this rather superficial interpretation of a football event. To start with, not a single article or op-ed piece highlighted the fact that the exclusive fixation on the Turkish minority in Germany did no justice to the large diversity of migrant flows towards Germany since the 1960s. Just like the eagerly repeated slogan of *'black-blanc-beur'* occulted the fact that with the exception of Zinedine Zidane, the largest migrant group was not present among the 23 players that had been selected for the World Cup (despite the fact that football is without any doubt the most popular and the most practised sport in the migrant community of North African origin).

Moreover, not a single commentator put into question the very fragile and in fact absurd link between a specific conception of nationality and footballing success, although the latter is obviously always subject to the hazards of sports competitions. If the French citizenship law was to be considered the reason for success of the French team, and if this success in turn proved the superiority of the French model of society, did this mean that over decades the German model had been superior because Germany had accumulated international football titles such as, rather recently, the World Cup of 1990 and the European Championship of 1996?

One of the very rare exceptions to the dominant discourse was the vehemently polemical diatribe signed five weeks after the World Cup by philosopher Alain Finkielkraut under the title 'French Vanity'. In his article he condemned the use of Germany as 'antithesis to French pride' and the widely shared view according to which 'the glorious *Mannschaft* was punished through a painful defeat for its xenophobia' and France had 'won because she was morally superior' (Finkielkraut, 1998).

In the massive outpour of self-celebration Finkielkraut's polemical 'throw-in' remained perfectly unnoticed. It was only three years and one European Championship victory later that the euphoric rhetoric was dampened by a series of events that put the narrative of national integration through football into question.

The first one occurred in October 2001, when France played for the first time a friendly against Algeria, almost forty years after the Evian treaty through which de Gaulle signed the independence of the former colony. Everything was set for a politically correct display of fraternity, when a significant part of the crowd, mainly composed of young, second or third-generation migrants from Algeria, ostentatiously whistled the Marseillaise before the match. And with twenty minutes to play, some of them invaded the pitch with Algerian flags, forcing the security staff to interrupt the match, which was never finished. Although it turned out, over the days that followed, that this incident had not even had a clearly articulated political meaning and that the 'protesters' on the pitch were not even quite sure themselves what exactly they had protested against, the event was unanimously considered a sign of integration *malaise*, the expression of a diffuse feeling of non-belonging and (self-)exclusion, putting strongly into question the function of the symbolic bridge across the ethnic divide that had been, somewhat hastily, ascribed to football.

Only half a year later, on 21 April 2002, the French were shocked to discover that Jean-Marie Le Pen, founder-president of the Front National, obtained over 17 per cent of the vote in the first round of the presidential election, eliminating the Socialist prime minister Lionel Jospin and qualifying for the second round against Jacques Chirac. Over years Le Pen had repeatedly claimed publicly that he did not consider the French national team, because of its ethnic composition, representative of the French nation as he understood it. It was therefore not surprising that in 1998 a large number of commentators saw in the popular *black-blanc-beur* euphoria a slap in the face to Le Pen and the Front National. Editorial cartoonist Plantu summed up the collective feeling very nicely in a drawing on the title page of *Le Monde* that showed Le Pen sulking in rage and disgust behind some players of *les Bleus* who were joyfully singing the Marseillaise. Similar cartoons appeared in 2000 after the French team had won the European Championship in the Netherlands and Belgium. Le Pen's electoral success only two years later therefore came as a painful reminder of the fact that football, even if it had created in 1998 a precedent of national union across ethnic groups and thus produced some unforgettable 'souvenir photos for the national family album' (Sonntag, 2007), was of course perfectly unable to provide a sustainable solution to France's problem of residual racism, persistent stereotyping and urban ghettoisation.

This was confirmed during the suburban youth riots of 2005 and 2007 which, while mostly blown out of proportion by Anglo-American media, pointed out to the French that something had gone wrong with their presumably meritocratic education system and workplace. While it would be wrong to consider these riots as driven by ethnic or religious motives – in fact, they were mainly fuelled by economic frustration and a widely shared perception of unequal access to the labour market – the above-mentioned ghettoisation inevitably adds diffuse elements of ethnic self-consciousness to such displays of indignation.

Finally, even the national football team itself has in the meantime contributed to demolishing the beautiful myth of successful multicultural co-existence on the pitch. Towards the end of the first decade of the new century, the French team was still pluriethnic, but much less successful and, most of all, no longer presentable as a 'role model'. As pointed out in the introduction to this chapter, there is a sharp decline in identification with the national team if the manner in which players represent the nation abroad is no longer perceived to be in line with the expected behaviour patterns and dominant values of the society concerned. With the French team under Raymond Domenech at Euro 2008 and, even more so, at the 2010 World Cup, this was definitely the case. The behaviour, language and, eventually, strike of the players during the South African World Cup were considered a national shame, to the extent that Nicolas Sarkozy sent his sports minister, Roselyne Bachelot, on an urgent diplomatic mission to South Africa! The name of the town that hosted the French headquarters during the World Cup, Knysna, has since entered the French vocabulary as a metaphor for a brand-image disaster. If the public indignation with the national team was based on both poor performance and behaviour that was deemed immature and unacceptable, ethnic considerations were not totally absent, as sociologist Stéphane Beaud pointed out in a polemical book (Beaud, 2011). By establishing the link between the massive media discourse triggered by the events in South Africa and the socialisation trajectories of those of the players that were most blamed as leaders of the mutiny, Beaud revealed not only an almost classical process of scapegoating, in which public opinion was all too ready to stigmatise the social ghettoes of the *banlieue* for everything that was going wrong in French society. He also managed to show rather convincingly that the entire scandal was underpinned by a both generational and social gap between the journalists and the players – the former establishing the expectations against which the latter's behaviour was assessed – and that ethnic causalities were subliminally constructed in the aftermath of the events.

And as if the Knysna outrage was not enough, the newly appointed national coach, Laurent Blanc, himself a member of the brilliant *black-blanc-beur* squad of 1998, very awkwardly poured further oil into the fire in October 2010. In a regular internal meeting of the technical staff of the football federation, he complained about the selection criteria in the French youth training system, which according to him favoured physically strong players over weaker though technically more gifted ones. Stupidly, he illustrated his case with references to the *'blacks'* when referring to physical strength, which provoked a heated debate about alleged racism among the national coaches when the recordings of the meeting had been published by the investigative news website Mediapart. Yet again, the accusation of racism was not supported by any evidence. Anyone who bothered to read the protocols in detail soon found out that the discussion focused on concerns about the increasing tendency of home-grown young players – born, socialised, educated and trained in France – to make use of their double citizenship and favour the national team of their country of 'origin' (that some of them had never even visited) over the French. This was a perfectly legitimate concern that raised justified questions about the perceived attractiveness of the French team among young footballers. What the debate did confirm, however, was on the one hand how sensitive the issue of ethnic origins in the national team had become following the series of events described above, and on the other hand how carelessly unaware, not so say stupid, some football officials were as to the sensitivity of certain terms and issues (Sonntag, 2011).

Against this backdrop of a decade of self-doubt, French media, intellectuals and public opinion are understandably much less likely to highlight the ethnic plurality of their national football team as an illustration of society. What remains in the discourse, however, is a certain interest in the manner in which other teams have over the years increasingly integrated players of migrant origin. The most spectacular development is the one of the German team, and given the comments from 1998 on a 'white, old and tired' Germany, it is not surprising that the metamorphosis of the *Nationalmannschaft* has not gone unnoticed in France.

'United Colors of Germany'

It is at the 2010 World Cup that the change in German legislation became visible to all. Even if, needless to say, the new law of 1999 had started to have a major impact on the German youth selections (U17/U19/U21) all over the previous decade. Still, given the much lower media presence of these youth teams, only specialists had taken note of this 'silent revolution'. At the World Cup, the ethnic composition of the *'Allemagne New Look'* (France Football, 2010a) became a major topic across the entire media spectrum. Taken by surprise, the French public discovered the presence of coloured players like Jérôme Boateng, son of a German mother and a Ghanaian father; or Cacao, a Brazilian immigrant who had – without ever hoping to be selected for the national team – successfully passed all stages of acquisition of German nationality for himself and his family. Wondering at the not very German-sounding names in the line-up like Mesut Özil, born in Gelsenkirchen of Turkish origins, or Sami Khedira, born in Stuttgart of a Tunisian father and German mother, the French public suddenly also realised that even Miroslav Klose and Lukas Podolski, albeit pillars of the German team since 2002 and 2004 respectively, were Polish-born.

Journalists started to count and point out that eleven of the twenty-three players of the German squad had some kind of migrant background. With astonishment the different countries of origin were enumerated and commented upon (*France Football*, 2010b). Particular attention was given to the case of the Boateng brothers, both born and raised in Berlin, one of whom, Jérôme, wore the German jersey, while the other, Kevin-Prince, had opted for his father's home country, Ghana. Since Germany and Ghana were to meet at the group stage, this case was of course much commented upon in the media (Menuge, 2010).

However, just like in 1998, the same (illogical) shortcut was made between, on the one hand, the 'surprising' ethnic diversity of the young German team and, on the other hand, its relative success (it finished third) and its playing style, perceived as an attractive and enthusiastic exception in a tournament that was judged 'globally disappointing', with too many 'boring and technically weak matches' (*France Football*, 2010c). The most significant error was to attribute the remarkable technical quality of the German team not so much to the youth training system that had been entirely modernised and professionalised on a large scale since the end of the 1990s (not without inspiration from France!), but to the ethnic origins of this new *'Inter-Nationalmannschaft'* as it was re-named by *L'Equipe* (Champel,

2010). The old stereotypes of the German team endowed mainly with physical power and defensive rigour (AFP, 2010) were opposed to the technical virtuosity imported from elsewhere. According to *France Football*, the new 'United Colors of Germany' revealed that Germany had 'become multiracial in order to better fulfil its ambitions' (*France Football*, 2010d). Knowing that the vast majority of the players concerned had been entirely socialised and trained in a German environment, such essentialist theories appear problematic at best, if not outright racist. Even if they seek to appreciate, with a good dose of naiveté, the added value of exogenous cultures, they are no less founded on ethnocentric or even racist presuppositions than those that propagate a supposed inferiority of these same cultures or ethnic origins.

If at the South African World Cup the new face of the German team was thus unanimously, if sometimes awkwardly, praised by the media, in internet forums and during casual workplace conversations the positive perception of the *Nationalmannschaft* as a reflection of the German model of integration of minorities has been somewhat relativised since.

To start with, in October 2010 there was a good deal of transnational indignation in the social networks following a speech by Angela Merkel at the national congress of the *Junge Union*, the youth organisation of the CDU/CSU. The context of this speech was quite a delicate one. For weeks Germany had been discussing the highly polemical anti-immigration bestseller by the former central banker Thilo Sarrazin (Sarrazin, 2010). Underpinning his anti-Islamic discourse with pseudo-scientific figures and rather crude eugenicist theses, Sarrazin had put the alleged failure of decades of integration policies high on the agenda again, provoking a heated, partly hysterical, public debate. For Merkel who, since her accession to power in 2005, had deployed significant efforts to calm down the integration debate by successfully establishing a regular, well-publicised 'integration dialogue' with civil society, the situation was complicated. On the one hand, it was clearly essential for her to condemn firmly the theses of Sarrazin as well as the statements of Horst Seehofer, president of the Bavarian coalition partner CSU, who had repeatedly and heavily criticised immigrants of Turkish and Arabic origin for their alleged lack of will to integrate. On the other hand, she was also under pressure to rally the right-wing members of her own party behind her rather liberal and progressive immigration policy. It is in this context that she delivered a kind of 'tightrope' speech, in which she declared at the same time that Islam was definitely 'a part of Germany' (quoting and confirming a recent statement by the Federal President Wulff), but that the *'multi-kulti'* approach had 'failed, utterly failed' (Connolly, 2010; Smee, 2010; Schnee, 2010).

In the German context, this pejorative allusion to the leftist origins of the adjective *'multi-kulti'* – which, as described above, had shown a surprising semantic shift around the 1998 World Cup – and reference to an ideological posture that refuses to demand an integration effort from immigrants, was perfectly understandable and considered a rhetorical feature in a very secondary public speech that was not worth paying attention to. Taken out of context, however, as short video or text extract and without linguistic decoding, this sentence created an immediate global buzz on the social networks. Ignoring the semantic subtleties and taking *'multi-kulti'* for a fully positively connoted adjective, as in football, internet users worldwide interpreted the Chancellor's statement as a strict refusal to integrate migrant populations, in other words: as a revelation of blunt racism.

They were even more scandalised as just one week before another picture of Chancellor Merkel had been circulated widely across the media spectrum. Thanks to the hazards of the sporting calendar the German national team had played Turkey in a Euro qualifier on 8 October. The match took place in the Olympiastadion in Berlin, whose large Turkish community occupied two thirds of the seats, turning the match into an away game for Germany, and continuously booed Mesut Özil for having become a 'traitor' to the land of his forefathers by opting to play for the country he was born and raised in. It was one of those moments where football becomes a highly politicised affair.

Özil himself, who since the World Cup had been made, without having asked for it, a symbol of integration by the media, reacted with remarkable stoicism, not only during the interview marathon that was imposed on him prior to the match but also on the pitch, delivering an excellent performance and scoring the second goal of what ended in a 3–0 victory for Germany.

After the final whistle, the Chancellor, who had attended the match, asked to be received in the team's changing room in order to congratulate the players, most of whom she knew already personally from previous occasions. A photo was taken – not by the sports journalists or the football federation, but the chancellery's communication service! – that showed Merkel shaking hands with a half-naked Özil who donned his usual shy smile. This was a photo which could only become an instant icon, such was its obviously huge symbolic potential.

One might wonder if the communication experts in the German chancellery had an idea about the extent to which the international image of Merkel was damaged, at least among the generation that informs itself mainly through online channels and social networks, by the juxtaposition of the changing room photo and her speech only some days later. In virtually hundreds (probably thousands) of posted messages she appeared as the archetype of the cynical politician, exploiting a gifted footballer from migrant origins for image reasons, while revealing her 'real face' one week later. Similar to the incidents around the France–Algeria match in 2001, the symbolic impact of the national football team could only reach its limits when confronted with political reality.

Due to its current playing style, infused since 2006 by Jürgen Klinsmann and Joachim Löw, and a generation of rather outstanding players, the German team continues to enjoy an overall positive reputation – quite a change from the previous three decades – but there are increasing doubts, both in Germany and in France, about its capacity of reflecting, in an emblematic manner, the alleged success of integration of migrants in German society. If at the 2010 World Cup, Germany was hailed as 'champion of integration' (AFP, 2010), two years later, on the occasion of a France–Germany friendly in Bremen (29 February 2012), a question mark made its appearance: 'The *Mannschaft*, a model of integration?', as *Le Monde* prudently wrote with a dose of healthy scepticism in a rather differentiated and well-documented piece that – for once! – highlighted the absurd link between the popular celebration of a pluriethnic team and its success on the pitch (Versace, 2012). The article quoted several sceptical voices from Germany, emphasising the rather fragile 'communitarian equilibrium' of the team that could easily be damaged (Wolfram Pyta) or the risk of a German 'Knysna' in case of repeated failures to win (Diethelm Blecking).

The reactions within Germany to the defeat to Italy in the semi-final of Euro 2012 suggest that the popularity of the current team is more closely linked to its attractive playing style and implicit promise of success than to its ethnic composition or symbolic role. When Felix Magath, former German international and a renowned coach since the 1990s, suggested in the press that the German players had been less engaged and willing to fight than their Italian opponents because they did not identify enough with the nation they represented (as proven by the failure to wholeheartedly sing the national anthem), he was firmly dismissed by many (including Joachim Löw and players like Sami Khedira), but he also earned a large amount of applause, mainly from conservative politicians and, surprisingly, from Franz Beckenbauer who had hardly ever sung the anthem himself during his long career as captain of the German team. The debate was easy to dismiss – and its ridiculousness probably definitely revealed with the World Cup triumph of these same players two years later – but it also showed that players of migrant origin have to prove over and over again how 'German' they really are.

Up to the expectations

What does this cross-comparative approach to discourse on the ethnic plurality of national football teams teach us? First of all, it is a good reminder of the fact that in the analysis of the impact of football on society, a good dose of humility becomes the researcher, who is well advised not to over-interpret his/her discursive data. One needs to keep in mind that this game, which is omnipresent in the media and whose terminology even penetrates political discourse, certainly has an impact on contemporary identity dynamics, but at the same time still remains a playful pastime and rather simple entertainment.

The cross-cultural Franco-German perspectives that were analysed in this chapter also confirm two other lessons about football. On the one hand, football has proven over more than a century that it possesses an amazing capacity to integrate individuals from very different migration waves through a social practice that is widely shared across socio-economic categories and ethnic groups. On the other hand, it cannot possibly be used as a 'symbolic showcase' meant to reflect the success of different kinds of immigration policy. In this respect again, it is wise to be humble, however tempting some conclusions may be.

What can be asserted beyond any doubt, though, is the fact that football, thanks to its universality, its great popularity and its permanent coverage by all types of media, is definitely not without influence on the manner in which national communities look at themselves and each other. In the Franco-German sphere, it has thus contributed, among other factors, to a paradigm change in German social history, by conveniently providing promoters of a reform of the German nationality act with a meaningful model (which happened to be French). This paradigm change would no doubt have occurred sooner or later without any interference from football. But it is not an exaggeration to assert that football has facilitated its acceptance and continues to contribute today to connote its consequences positively.

Likewise, it is possible to claim that for several years now the German national team has contributed – perhaps even more so than numerous other initiatives of cultural politics reserved to the small circle of Goethe Institute visitors – to raising awareness worldwide of the new cultural diversity of contemporary German society. The fact that (for the time being) it does so with generosity, enthusiasm and style is of course beneficial in this respect, even if the spontaneous sympathy it has attracted due to its performances remains a very shaky, easily reversible element of this positive image.

At the beginning of this chapter the concept of 'expectations of representativeness' was introduced. While these refer first and foremost to projections of collective identity on a national football team supposed to represent the national community, the above cross-cultural comparison between France and Germany has shown that these expectations may be applied not only to oneself but also to 'the other'.

Football thus appears as a mediator of perceptions. As has been highlighted countless times and as this text has recalled in detail, football has been, since its very beginnings, a carrier of a large number of stereotypical images. Yet it is essential to recognise that at the same time it contributes to move, put into perspective, and sometimes even undermine these very stereotypes. It helps updating perceptions – even the most selective ones – that we have of ourselves, and it unfolds the ways in which nations coexist, look at each other and meet with each other. It, finally, reveals significant, often unconscious aspects of the difficult transformation of national identities – shaken, weakened and undermined by the cumulative effects of the globalisation process – that European society experiences today.

References

Non-academic sources

AFP (2010) 'L'Allemagne, enfin championne de l'intégration', 19 June.

Appel, R. (1952) '3:1– Sieg Frankreichs über Deutschland noch schmeichelhaft', *Stuttgarter Zeitung*, 6 October.

Bild-Zeitung (1998) 'Die Multi-Kulti-Helden', 14 July.

Blickensdörfer, H. (1982) 'Was die Franzosen stört', *Stuttgarter Zeitung*, 7 July.

Braun, D. (1986) 'Français ... comme vous et moi'; 'Au temps des Polaks'; 'Un filon épuisé'; 'Nous, Marocains de Dreux'; 'Demain, les Beurs?'; series of articles published in *L'Equipe*, 28 January to 1 February.

Champel, E. (2010) 'L'Inter-Nationalmannschaft', *L'Equipe*, 18 June.

Connolly, K. (2010) 'Angela Merkel declares death of German multiculturalism', *The Guardian*, 17 October.

dpa (1986), untitled dispatch, 24 June.

Droussent, C. (1998) 'Droit du sol, droit du foot', *L'Equipe Magazine*, 18 July.

Eder, M. (1998) 'Equipes multiculturelles', *Frankfurter Allgemeine Zeitung*, 3 July.

Frankfurter Allgemeine Zeitung (1952) 'Herberger ist nicht zu beneiden', 8 October.

Finkielkraut, A. (1998) 'Vanité française', *Le Monde*, 21 August.

France Football (2010a) untitled article, 29 June.

France Football (2010b) 'Huit origines différentes', 22 June.

France Football (2010c) untitled article, 13 July.

France Football (2010d) 'United Colors of Germany', 22 June.

Haget, H. (1998) 'Ce Mondial qui a change la France', *L'Express*, 16 July.

Hehn, J. (1998) 'Vive la différence!', *Die Welt*, 14 July.

Laven, P. (1950) *Fair Play. Meister des Sports im Kampf* (Bad Homburg: Limpert).

L'Equipe (2014) 'Une Ligue des nations dès 2018–2019?', *L'Equipe*, 26 March.

Le Monde (1999) 'Nouvelle identité allemande', 18 March.

Leicht, R. (1999) 'A la française!', *Die Zeit*, 11 February.

Menuge, A. (2010) 'L'affiche Allemagne–Ghana va ressembler à une querelle de famille entre les Boateng', *France Football*, 22 June.

Millot, L. (1998) 'Les grands déçus moitié bleus, moitié jaunes', *Libération*, 13 July.

Orwell, G. (1945) 'The Sporting Spirit', *Tribune*, 14 December 1945.

Sarrazin, T. (2010) *Deutschland schafft sich ab* (Munich: DVA).

Schnee, T. (2010) 'Immigration: Merkel vire sa "multi-kulti"', *Libération*, 20 October.

Simonnot, D. (1998) 'Ce jour est magique, il incarne l'idéal du creuset français' (interview with Michèle Tribalat), *Libération*, 10 July.

Smee, J. (2010) 'Merkel's Rhetoric in Integration Debate is "Inexcusable"', *Spiegel Online International*, 18 October.

Süddeutsche Zeitung (1998) 'Black-blanc-beur', 11 July.

Versace, E. (2012) 'Allemagne-France: la Mannschaft, un modèle d'intégration?', *Le Monde*, 29 February.

Vigarello, G. (1998) 'Quand le foot fait la France', *Le Nouvel Observateur*, 16 July.

Zielcke, A. (1998) 'Frankreichs multikulturelles Nationalteam', *Stuttgarter Zeitung*, 18 July 1998.

Academic publications

Anderson, B. (1983) *Imagined Communities* (London: Verso).

Böttiger, H. (1989) 'Verdrossen vor den Toren: Fußball ist nicht mehr die Leitsportart', *Die Zeit*, 17 February.

Beaud, S. (2011) *Traîtres à la nation? Un autre regard sur la grève des Bleus en Afrique du Sud* (Paris: La Découverte).

Beaud, S. and Noiriel, G. (1990) 'L'immigration dans le football', *Vingtième siècle*, No. 26, April–June, pp. 83–96.

Cabanel, P. (1997) *La question nationale au XIXe siècle* (Paris: La Découverte).

Caillat, M. (1995) *L'idéologie du sport en France* (Paris: Editions de la Passion).

Dieckhoff, A. (2000) *La nation dans tous ses Etats* (Paris: Flammarion).

Dietschy, P. (2010) *Histoire du football* (Paris: Perrin).

Duchesne, S. (1997) *Citoyenneté à la française* (Paris: Presses de Sciences Po).

Ehrenberg, A. (1984) 'Le football et ses imaginaires', *Les Temps Modernes*, No. 460, November, pp. 841–84.

Eisenberg, C. (1997) *Fußball, soccer, calcio. Ein englischer Sport auf seinem Weg um die Welt* (Munich: dtv).

Elias, N. (1997) *La société des individus* (Paris: Fayard).

Gebauer, G. (2002) 'Nationale Repräsentation durch Körperinszenierungen', *Sport in der Gesellschaft des Spektakels* (Sankt Augustin: Academia), pp. 172–8.

Hobsbawm, E. (1990) *Nations and Nationalism since 1780* (Cambridge: Cambridge University Press).

Kallscheuer, O. and Leggewie, C. (1994) 'Deutsche Kulturnation vs. französische Staatsnation?', in H. Berding (ed.), *Nationales Bewußtsein und kollektive Identität* (Frankfurt: Suhrkamp) pp. 112–62.

Kastoryano, R. (1996) *La France, l'Allemagne et leurs immigrés. Négocier l'identité* (Paris: Armand Colin).

Lanfranchi, P. and Taylor, M. (2001) *Moving with the Ball, the Migration of Professional Footballers* (Oxford: Berg).

Morin, E. (1984) *Sociologie* (Paris: Fayard).

Müller, J. (2004) *Von Kampfmaschinen und Ballkünstlern* (Saarbrücken: Röhrig Universitätsverlag).

Noiriel, G. (1988) *Le creuset français. Histoire de l'immigration XIXe–XXe siècle* (Paris: Seuil).

Noiriel, G. (2000) 'La construction historique de la nation', in Y. Michaud (ed.), *Qu'est-ce que la société? (Université de tous les savoirs, Volume III)* (Paris: Odile Jacob), pp. 739–48.

Rioux, J.-P. (1999) '1998 – L'échappée bleue', in J.-P. Rioux and J.-F. Sirinelli (eds), *La France d'un siècle à l'autre 1914–2000* (Paris: Hachette), pp. 118–22.

Schnapper, D. (1995) *La communauté des citoyens* (Paris: Gallimard).

Schulze, H. (1996) *Etat et nation dans l'histoire de l'Europe* (Paris: Seuil).

Smith, A. (1991) *National Identities* (Harmondsworth: Penguin).

Sonntag, A. (2007) 'Un été noir-rouge-or', in C. Demesmay and H. Stark (eds), *Radioscopies de l'Allemagne 2007* (Paris: IFRI Travaux et Recherches), pp. 19–39.

Sonntag, A. (2008) *Les identités du football européen* (Grenoble: Presses Universitaires de Grenoble).

Sonntag, A. (2011) 'Ein Kreuz', *Der tödliche Pass*, No. 61, June, pp. 48–53.

Sonntag, A. (2014) 'La grande foire aux identités', *Revue Internationale et Stratégique*, No. 94, May, pp. 135–42.

Tönnies, F. (1944), *Communauté et société: catégories fondamentales de la sociologie pure* [1887] (Paris: Presses Universitaires de France).

Vigarello, G. (1990) 'Les premières Coupes du monde', *Vingtième siècle*, No. 26, June, pp. 5–10.

Wahl, A. (1989) *Les archives du football. Sport et société en France (1880–1980)* (Paris: Gallimard).

Woehrling, J.-M. (2001) 'Le concept de citoyenneté à la lumière d'une comparaison franco-allemande', *Revue d'Allemagne et des pays de langue allemande*, Vol. 33, Issue 1, pp. 13–32.

6
Mediating Turkishness through Language in Transnational Football

Yağmur Nuhrat

Citizenship has conventionally been defined through two distinct yet sometimes overlapping principles: belonging on the basis of territory (*jus soli*) versus right of blood (*jus sanguinis*). Social scientists focusing on Turkey have long argued that while the case of Turkey is ostensibly closer to territorial citizenship, historical and current state policies and practices point to the prevalence of an ethno-religious basis as well (İçduygu and Kaygusuz, 2004; Maksudyan, 2005; Parla and Davison, 2004; Yeğen, 2004). How then, do these definitions of Turkish citizenship translate to the imaginations of citizens, and how do they construe and experience Turkishness in everyday life? Football (soccer), both at the level of national teams and professional clubs, offers fertile ground for exploring this question.

Besnier and Brownell (2012, p. 452) argue that, 'Athletes and trainers form an increasingly mobile category of migrant labour facilitated by a transnational network of agents in multiple locations...' Intense transnational movement and boundary crossing in the current state of global football have tangible effects on re-imagining nation-state sovereignty as well as the concepts of citizenship, belonging and identity. In Turkey, the migratory movements of football labourers in the global flexible sports market allow one to explore the dynamics of shifting and cementing notions of citizenship. As such, this chapter sets out to explore how various agents in the site of football construct and mediate 'Turkishness', drawing attention to the motifs and tropes that are mobilised to claim or assign nationality to migrant footballers. I specifically demonstrate how 'language ideology' (cf. Cameron, 2003) is employed as a tool to prescribe or deny Turkishness to groups such as third-generation 'Turkish' migrants in Western Europe and non-Turkish footballers playing in Turkey.

As Ginsburg et al. (2002) explain, anthropologists have often considered media to be a rich site through which to observe the construction of regional, national and transnational identification. Thus, a number of anthropologists have engaged in ethnographies of various media to trace how 'imagined communities' (cf. Anderson, 1983) or national 'imaginaries' (cf. Lacan, 1967) are created, circulated and negotiated in mediation (Dávila, 2002; Mankekar, 2002; Spitulnik, 2001; Wilk, 2002). Following this ethnographic attention to mediated national identities, I have found that football media in Turkey (in the form of printed, televised and online sports news, blogs, fan forums and commentaries) offers blunt expressions of what counts as Turkish and what does not. As footballers' multi-directional migratory movements and shifting citizenship affiliations intensify, sports-media actors in Turkey appear in a position to not only report identity claims but also to assign national identifications (also see Alpan and Şenyuva, Chapter 4 in this volume, for an exploration of how Turkish national identity is formulated in relation to imagining Europe).

The following provides an account of how football actors in Turkey manage transnational trends in global football by demarcating what is essentially Turkish. At the same time, the reader must be aware that sports media are significant actors in this demarcation process. Therefore, the goal of this chapter is twofold: first, I set out to explore what football in Turkey may teach us about dynamics of national identification. Second, I highlight the centrality of media in this process since this identification is continually mediated. Specifically, I concentrate on the example of Mesut Özil, a German-Turkish footballer who plays for the German national team. Using his case as one example among others, I describe how the football media in Turkey engaged in a negotiation of Özil's identity as the national football teams of Turkey and Germany got ready to play against each other for the Euro 2012 qualifiers. Ultimately, I argue that despite intensifying transnationalism and the presence of multiple, transient national identities, the dogma of singular national identity survives in various social sites in Turkey, one of which is football.

Transnationalism, regionalism and citizenship in football

For the last decade, social scientists have been stressing that citizenship debates take on a new meaning with the advent of globalisation and transnational migration (Ehrkamp and Leitner, 2003; Joppke, 1999; Schiller et al., 2004; Vertovec, 2001). The post-Westphalia era allows us to question the assumption that singular nations map tidily onto states and produce distinct nation-states with mutually exclusive citizenry. As Yeğen (2004, p. 52) explains, '... despite its evident contingency, nation state society has been... assumed for the most part to be the ultimate form of political community and, accordingly, citizenship has been identified with it'. While one may argue that this assumption was faulty at inception, transnationalism both in terms of substantial supranational organisations or regional integration and in relation to intensifying practices of migration surely makes it even harder to sustain. The social-scientific question then becomes one that deals with multiplicity – of nation-states, citizenships, identities and ultimately of belonging. Evidently involving various challenges, this sort of multiplicity is, today, relatively easier to conjure. There are various accounts of migrant belongings that delve into this issue, theoretically exploring how personal and political manoeuvres manage multiple national loyalties (Çağlar, 1998; Fortier, 2000; Kaya, 2007).

Global professional football, on the other hand, presents us with a situation where such multiplicity is less recognised. In other words, there are no 'dual citizenships' in football; a player with dual citizenship must declare a national team to pledge allegiance to and thereon represent that team's nation-state alone.[1] Besnier and Brownell (2012, p. 451) argue that anthropology must observe how sport travels across national boundaries and use sport to understand the dynamics of global society. On the other hand, they also acknowledge, 'Because these are transnational actors in a world system of sovereign nation-states, sport provides insight into the national structures that still limit transnational action'. In fact, this strenuous relationship between levels of identification is present already in the self-descriptions of international governing bodies like UEFA (Union of European Football Associations).

UEFA, organiser of the Euro 2012 tournament, is a pan-European organisation; it describes itself as a 'European body' and showcases football on this regional scale (UEFA, 2013). In accordance with the Bosman Ruling of 1995, UEFA recognises the lifting of nationality quotas on European footballer labour migrants in Europe. In other words, the boundaries of native versus foreign are drawn based on the status of Europeanness and not in terms of specific nation-states. On the other hand, UEFA (2013) repeatedly stresses that it is committed to including national football associations in decision-making processes. It declares that 'national team and club football are vital' for them and that 'FIFA [Fédération Internationale de Football Association], UEFA and national associations work hand in hand... respecting the principle of subsidiarity'. Moreover, while FIFA may intervene in national associations' internal affairs when the 'laws of the game' are in question, neither FIFA nor UEFA may take decisions that bind national football associations. In fact, this is how some national associations in Europe are able to move beyond the Bosman Ruling and choose not to apply foreign quotas at all in club football. Therefore sport, and in the present case football, both cause and provide insight into the complex relationship between singular national affiliation and multiple transnational identities. International governing bodies of football simultaneously erase and reaffirm national structures. In Turkey, this tension crystallised in the process leading up to the Euro 2012 championship, which pitted the Turkish and German national teams against each other during the qualifying group stage matches.

The case of Mesut Özil

In 1961, Turkey and Germany signed the 'Recruitment Agreement', which allowed Turkish citizens to travel to Germany as 'guest work-ers'. In five decades, the programme produced three generations of Turkish migrants in Germany who currently compose a population of nearly three million. One member of this community is Mesut Özil, a third-generation 'migrant' from Gelsenkirchen whose grand-father migrated to Germany from Zonguldak. Özil is an exceptional footballer, much adulated for his technique and skills. After playing for Germany's Schalke 04 and Werder Bremen, he was recruited by Real Madrid in 2010 where he stayed for three seasons until moving to play for Arsenal in 2013. In 2009, right before the UEFA European Under-21 championship, he declared that he would play for the German national team.

These choices on the part of migrant footballers like Özil are cast as major decision-making moments by the football media in Turkey. Sensationalist news along the lines of 'Is Mesut German or Turkish?' (Vatan, 2012) or 'Which goalpost should Mesut aim for?' (Sol Haber Portalı, 2010) are followed by speculations about and negotiations of athletes' origins, nationalities and loyalties. Reports along similar lines are published upon migrant footballers choosing to play for Turkey as well, more recent examples of which include Mannheim-born Hakan Çalhanoğlu and Kaan Ayhan from Gelsenkirchen. When in 2013, Hakan Çalhanoğlu declared that he would play for the Turkish national team, Turkish sports media reported the decision with the headline: 'The Germans Pressured Him but He Still Chose Turkey' (Eurosport Türkiye, 2013). In fact a simple Google search with the phrase 'he chose Turkey' (*'Türkiye'yi seçti'*) is enough to yield thousands of results with numerous footballers who have throughout the years experienced the same decision-making process and chose to play for Turkey over their 'host' nations. As these decisions pit footballers for or against the Turkish national team, the reports and debates about their identities intensify.

The conversation about Özil got especially heated in October 2010, as Germany got ready to play against Turkey in Berlin, a city highly populated with migrants from Turkey and their German-born families, for the Euro 2012 qualifiers with Özil in the squad. Printed, televised and online media in Turkey, including news portals, football blogs and forums, were filled with journalist and fan commentary on how Özil would play given this predicament of being stuck between two nations. Outright discussions about whether he would be able to score or not were complemented by descriptions of Özil's hometown and family in Zonguldak, thus reminding the readers of his 'roots' and creating ground for further discussion about his 'true' nationality (*Hürriyet*, 2010). One day before the game, two sports commentators in Turkey, Sergen Yalçın (also a former footballer and current manager in the Turkish Super League) and Mehmet Demirkol discussed the situation:[2]

Yalçın: I don't think Mesut will be able to play well tomorrow. Why? Because for a whole week, for 10 days, he has been under immense psychological pressure. This must have affected him. [...] He will definitely be crushed under this pressure... After all, this man is Turkish. He is playing against Turkey. OK fine, it's not that big of a problem. But the events of the last 10 days will surely grip him psychologically.[3]

At this point, the program host reminded the commentators about what Özil had said earlier: 'I will be concentrating intensely during the recital of the national anthems and therefore no one will be able to see my lips move.'

Demirkol: It wouldn't be okay if he sang the Turkish national anthem and neither would it be okay if he sang for Germany. Of course he will sing neither. It's a tough situation for him. I also think that they'll play him hard tomorrow. Our team – they'll push him.

Özil did play well during that game where Germany beat Turkey 3–0 the second goal of which was scored by Özil himself. After scoring, he briefly hugged his teammates while they congratulated him for the goal but refrained from displaying any overt celebration of his goal. His quarter of a smile and wink were the only gestures that indicated he had just changed the scoreboard in a highly significant international game. He later explained his lack of visible rejoicing with these words: 'Of course I was very happy to score. But my decision was spontaneous where I chose not to scream in joy, out of respect for my ancestors and roots...' (*Radikal*, 2010a) By referencing his 'roots' as opposed to his 'routes', Özil is able to recall a primordial sense of belonging to Turkey which is in fact the very criterion mobilised by Yalçın to assert, 'After all, this man is Turkish'. Demirkol indicates that Özil is in a 'tough situation' in regard to the recital of national anthems since his singing of one would attest to his affiliation with the respective nation. Yalçın and Demirkol share the same ethnicist basis to define Özil's belonging to Turkey.

The commentators above were not alone in their classification of Özil's belonging. The Germany versus Turkey match in Berlin saw thousands of Turkish fans booing Özil, whistling loudly each time he touched the ball. Turkish newspapers went as far as to claim that Germany won without any Germans scoring a goal since the team's three goals were scored by 'Turkish' Özil and 'Polish' Miroslav Klose (*Sabah Spor*, 2010). While this is the case, Özil's repeated public declarations about his national team choice point to a different apprehension of his own subjectivity. Özil has repeatedly said that he 'feels German', that 'he is a third generation migrant in Germany, born and raised [there], is proud to wear the German jersey and has never considered to play for an alternate national team' (NTVSpor, 2010a). In response to how he felt as other German-Turks protested against him in the Turkey game in Berlin, he stated:

> Some people feel sad that I don't play for Turkey; I understand this. But I have repeatedly said it: I feel German. I was born in Germany and I never considered playing anywhere else but in the country where I was born and raised... (*Radikal*, 2010b).

In this quote, as in his speech after he refrained from celebrating his goal against Turkey, Özil concedes that it is understandable for him to hear that some people situate him within the national community of Turkey. As such, he is able to make sense of how the ethnicist component in defining Turkish citizenship works. At the same time, he lays territorial claims to German citizenship by referring to where he was born and raised. However, he complements this territorial claim by stating that 'he feels German' which works to invoke a sense of 'Germanness' that is situated more in his essence than in his relationship to the polity. Therefore, Özil's presentation of his subjective national belonging is much more complex than Yalçın's depiction of 'after all this man is Turkish'. Özil's subjectivity lies at the entanglement of territorial and ethnicist bases of citizenship and his discourse allows us to observe how nation-state configurations of citizenship are appropriated and transformed by individual and community imaginations of belonging. It is also worth noting here that, finding himself under the spotlight as often as he does, Özil demonstrates a remarkable level of diplomacy as he is asked to navigate contradictory expectations and this complexity.

The ethnicist component of Turkish citizenship, language and football

As Yeğen (2004, p. 54) describes it, 'While it is sometimes suggested that Turkish citizenship, especially at the time of its original constitution, signifies a political–territorial definition of Turkishness instead of an ethnic one, many works have acknowledged the traces of both a political and an ethnicist logic in the very definition of Turkishness.' Moreover, both Yeğen and Maksudyan (2005) argue that these 'ethnicisms' or the presentations of ethnic, religious or racial bases as criteria for citizenship in Turkey are not mere 'accidental', 'exceptional' or 'deviational' practices; they are indeed systematic theoretical components of how citizenship in Turkey is officially described in legal and academic texts. As such, even though dominant discourse about Turkish citizenship may be that it is 'expansionist and inclusive' on the basis of *jus soli*, in fact it is also characterised by 'exclusivism and differentialism' on the basis of *jus sanguinis*. This exclusivism has especially been salient in describing Turkey's relationship with its Muslim and non-Muslim minority communities including but not limited to Kurds, Armenians, Greeks and Jews.

In fact, both Yeğen and Gülalp (2006) argue that exclusivism is based on religion in the Turkish case where being Muslim constitutes the major criterion of inclusion and assimilability. In other words, there are boundaries around who can and must 'achieve Turkishness' and these boundaries include Turkey's Muslim minorities (mainly Kurds), not its non-Muslim minorities (Greeks, Armenians and Jews). Gülalp (2006) contends that based on this classification of citizenship, Kurds are considered suitable for assimilation whereas non-Muslim populations of Turkey, even though they have citizenship based on the pillar of *jus soli*, are deemed forever foreign and unsuitable for assimilation (see Zeydanlıoğlu, 2008 for more on Kurdish assimilation in Turkey).

Bora (2013) traces how the ethno-religious basis of Turkish citizenship is found and reinforced in and through club football in Turkey. There are numerous foreign players in Turkish football leagues but according to the Turkish Football Federation's ruling, one team can sign up to ten foreign players where at most six of them can be included in the match line-up or on the pitch at any given time. These foreign player quotas have generated a practice on the part of football teams in Turkey where they sponsor foreign players who have spent enough time in Turkey to receive Turkish citizenship. As long-term migrant footballers thus gain Turkish citizenship, teams are able to recruit more foreign footballers. These naturalisation procedures, which are all too common through football in Turkey, point to the very clash between the bounded logic of the nation-state and the growing flexibility of the global sports labour market. It is through these formal procedures of 'naturalising' that we see the kind of tension between the transnational and the national explored by Besnier and Brownell (2012) above. The manoeuvres to manage nationally in an ever-expanding transnational market go hand in hand with such complex imaginations of subjectivity and belonging, as in the case of Özil.

As numerous examples demonstrate and as Bora continues to explain, one practical imposition on people who receive Turkish citizenship after birth is for them to acquire new Turkish first names. Some examples include former Brazilians Marco Aurélio taking on the name Mehmet and Marcio Nobre becoming Mert Nobre or previously Nigerian Uche Okechukwu playing as Deniz Uygar. Bora (2013, p. 497) wrote:

> ... the rule to assign Muslim-Turkish names to foreign footballers who are given Turkish citizenship ... is a clear demonstration of ethno-culturalism. Nowhere else in the world do you find migrant sportsmen being forced to change their authentic names – forced maybe not explicitly but in terms of expectations.

The ethnicist basis for defining Turkishness includes a significant religious component whereby Islam is posited as a precondition to 'achieve Turkishness' in Turkey. Furthermore, Bora's insights allow us to identify a 'language ideology' within Turkish ethnicism. Through naming examples in football, we clearly see that the Turkish language that is supposed to identify Turkishness is in fact a Muslim-Turkish language. Therefore language becomes a tool to delineate the religious in the ethnicism of Turkish national belonging. The 'language ideology' or the 'sets of representations through which language is imbued with cultural meaning for a certain community' that are in play here is one which equates Muslim-Turkish language, and that alone, with essential Turkishness (Cameron, 2003, p. 447).

Bora continues to explain how renaming instances in football in Turkey provide discursive spaces to question and contest the claims of renamed footballers on Turkishness:

> Moreover, Brazilian Marco/Mehmet Aurélio's inclusion in the [Turkish] national team constituted a chronic subject of debate for the media ... And during the time when he played for [the Istanbul team] Fenerbahçe, one rival fan group displayed a banner saying

'You cannot become a Mehmet, you have to be born a Mehmet' (Bora, 2013, p. 497).

'Mehmet', a derivate of the name Mohammed and the generic name used to refer to Turkish soldiers, is thus essentialised in this discourse whereby it is assumed to naturally index Turkishness by birth, dismissing all claims to Mehmetness that may arise based on political-territorial unity. Indeed, Brink-Danan (2012) has written on how naming and names are significant indexes of Turkishness as signs of inclusion or exclusion in everyday life. By tracing the performative functions of Jewish names in Turkey, she argues that even though Turkish Jews may be completely fluent in the Turkish language, their conspicuously 'foreign' (that is, non-Muslim)-sounding names will always index their ultimate foreignness and lead to their reclassification as strangers in the public space in Turkey. Once again, we are able to see that the Turkish language indexes Turkishness so long as it is coupled with Islam.

Silverstein (1992) defines second-order indexicality as occurring when speakers find social rationalisations or justifications to link linguistic form to specific social categories and reach conclusions about the users of those linguistic forms. The way in which someone speaks ends up indirectly, or secondarily, indexing their social status, class, politics, education level and, in this case, their nationality. An indexical bundle, in turn, is when a mental schema or map is formed about the social attributes of a person based on the way in which they use language. In relation to Özil, numerous reader comments for online sports news articles interject that he should take on a German name if he so wishes to play for Germany. Below are two examples from football daily *Fanatik* (2009):

> ...I think that this guy should change his name. A Turkish name does not suit him well. He should call himself Mattheus or something like that.

> People who do not carry a love of Allah, homeland, nation or the flag should not be wearing this jersey. Live like a German Mesut. Change your name too. Become a Hans.

Özil's Muslim-Turkish name exists in an indexical bundle with his unquestionable Turkishness similarly to how the language ideology about his Muslim-Turkish name and speech make him Turkish. Therefore his declared Germanness upsets this indexical bundle and causes people to desire that he simply fix his name to reflect his non-Turkishness.[4]

Language is a device to define, calibrate, allocate or to deprive peoples of national belonging (cf. Anderson, 1983). The history of the Turkish Republic is abundant with instances of Turkish linguistic domination from the early republican 'Citizen Speak Turkish!'[5] Campaign to present-day democracy debates that revolve around rights to education in the mother tongue mainly in relation to Turkey's Kurdish minority. Turkish nationalism is interwoven tightly with the Turkish language, which explains the reign of the specific language ideology described above. Therefore it is no surprise that in relation to Özil it was again the criterion of language that football media in Turkey employed to negotiate a true identity. Besides his name, his potential recital of national anthems and the language in which he swears were frequently drawn on to establish his accurate nationality.

The Turkish daily *Radikal* (2009) interpreted Özil's choice of national football teams as his declaration of '*Deutschland Über Alles*', referencing the former German national anthem.[6] And as Yalçın and Demirkol's exchange indicates, Özil's use of language through the recital of the national anthem was a concrete point of deliberation in the negotiation of his identity. Following a question in a press conference, Özil was made to declare that he would refrain from singing either anthem during the opening ceremony of the game and would instead recite silently verses from the Koran to better concentrate on his match performance. With this declaration, Özil dissociates from Turkishness through a denial of the national anthem which both in its form and content index Turkish national belonging. At the same time, however, he latches on to Islam as a marker of identity, one that is repeatedly used to assign his Turkishness.

Another genre of language that is invoked when deliberating nationality or belonging is swearing. Özil has been caught on camera multiple times swearing in Turkish during a match as he played in various European leagues. For some members of the Turkish football community this is proof enough to show that 'this kid is Turkish'. Here is a quote from the most popular online forum/community[7] in Turkey:

[Özil is] without a doubt the best Turkish footballer there ever was. How am I able to call him a Turk so easily? Because I think *'siktir'* [fuck] or a man who swears like *'hassiktir'* [oh fuck] is more Turkish than Emre Belözoğlu [a Turkish-born Turkish footballer] who swears in English when he is angry on the pitch with words like 'fuck off...' (Ekşi Sözlük, 2012)

J. L. Austin (1962) put forth the theory that language has a function alternative to referencing or describing objects in the world, namely that it can also effect change in the world; uttering something, in effect, 'does' something. I argue that in the case of Özil the performative function of his speaking Turkish, whether in terms of singing (or not singing) the national anthem or swearing, continually establishes him as Turkish or deprives him of Turkish nationality. His everyday linguistic practices as well as his name systematically either *make* him Turkish in the eyes of the football community in Turkey or exclude him from Turkishness whose ethnicist precondition is locked in with Muslim-Turkish language.

As I explained earlier, there are numerous athletes in the same position as Özil and they too actively take part in negotiating Özil's identity. A few days before the Germany versus Turkey Euro 2012 qualifier game in Berlin, another Turkish-German migrant footballer, Hamit Altıntop, also born in Gelsenkirchen, was probed in a press conference for comments on Özil's national team choice. Altıntop had faced a similar decision-making process a few years earlier and, unlike Özil, he had chosen to play for Turkey. Upon a journalist's question, he said:

Mesut is my brother. I love him very much. I don't understand Mesut's decision and I do not support it. But what's important is his own happiness. The bottom line is, there is a word called 'roots' in the literature. A person will always go back to his roots. I respect him and I wish him all the best (NTVSpor, 2010b).

Similarly in 2012, Nürnberg-born Servet Tazegül, an Olympic and European champion taekwondo practitioner, commented on Özil's national team choice during a Turkish Sports Writers Foundation panel. He was asked to compare amateur sports in Germany and Turkey and he responded:

> They practice taekwondo professionally in Germany. Germany is also very successful in taekwondo. I started taekwondo in Germany. I was offered to fight for Germany but I did not accept. Just like Halil and Hamit Altıntop and just like Nuri Şahin,[8] I preferred Turkey. I did not sell out Turkey like Mesut Özil did. I chose Turkey. After all, we will fight for our nation. In Germany, we spoke Turkish at home, not German (NTVSpor, 2012).

When Gelsenkirchen-born İlkay Gündoğan was asked to explain why he chose to play for the German national football team rather than the Turkish team he said:

> I was born in Gelsenkirchen. I speak German better than I speak Turkish. When I had to decide whether to play for Turkey or for Germany, I chose Germany. Because I am from Germany. I always played football here and I grew up here (Spor X, 2012).

On a different occasion, he declared:

> Let me say this. Even though I play for Germany, I represent all Turkish people, with brother Mesut. We love Turkey. Basically, we are representing Turkey with the German national team jersey. We represent Turkish people living in Germany and those Turkish people in Turkey who support us. Obviously, some people criticise us but we are not in a position to respond to those critiques. I believe that most people understand us (*Fotospor*, 2012).

One may note here the parallels between Gündoğan's discourse and Özil's navigation of national identity described above. Gündoğan also establishes himself as 'German' with reference to language as well as territorial groundedness. Moreover, he too recognises critiques against his choice of national teams. By stating that he is 'representing Turkey in the German national team', he is struggling to open up conceptual space to accommodate all of the mediations of his identity. This struggle is perhaps best demonstrated in the photo Özil posted on his Instagram account after Germany won the World Cup in 2014, where he displayed a German flag with the Turkish crescent and the star occupying the middle, red section (*Turkish Football*, 2014). The growing fragility of national identification puts both these athletes in a position to defend national boundaries and also allocates to them a role of mediating each other's national belongings. In this prolific discourse about identity, we repeatedly see the invocation of the Turkish language as tying one down to their 'roots' or distancing one from them, decisively configuring inclusion and exclusion.

On the one hand Özil recalls a Muslim identity, invokes his 'roots' and engages in linguistic practice that establish him as Turkish in the eyes of the football community in Turkey. When he visited his grandparents' hometown, Zonguldak, in 2011, he gave an interview in Turkish and expressed that he had come to visit 'his land' and that 'he had not forgotten his village' (YouTube, 2011). On the other hand, he stresses that he feels German; he plays for the German national team and he scores against Turkey. Even though Özil seems to navigate well his multiple belongings, the football community and media in Turkey seem less at ease with his classification. His every linguistic performance is mobilised as a criterion for or against his Turkishness. His every action thus ends up constituting the precise dynamics of negotiating his identity. It is through these negotiations that we are able to confirm the everyday existence and utilisation of the ethnicist face of Turkish national belonging and citizenship. The more Özil and other players like him threaten the dominating views about the boundaries of Turkishness, the clearer we are able to see the circulation and prevalence of exclusionary Turkishness shaped as a part of national imaginaries in everyday life.

Jiwani (2008) wrote about Zinedine Zidane and his infamous head butt against Marco Materrazi during the final of the 2006 FIFA World Cup by tracing media discourse on the incident. She showed that while numerous orientalists' portrayals of Zidane were put forth to explain his behaviour, he was also quickly redeemed by the French President. She argued that Zidane's redemption could be explained by the French state's insistence on sustaining the image of a well-integrated and unitary France. Zidane had, for years, been the poster child for the successful integration of suburban North African communities and the state could not afford to lose their 'emblematic ambassador of the new France *pluriel*'[9] (Jiwani, 2008,

p. 16). Therefore, the question one must ask in relation to attempts to confirm or dismiss claims to nationality is: which and whose stakes are involved? In France, according to Jiwani, casting Zidane as the 'Muslim other' would challenge France's claims to have established inclusive, territorial citizenship.

In this section, I have shown which stakes are involved in negotiating the identities of footballers like Özil. In describing the Turkification of Kurds during the first few decades of the Turkish Republic, Zeydanlıoğlu (2008, p. 5) argues that 'The ethnic, religious and linguistic diversity of the society were constructed as a source of instability and a barrier to progress'. The Turkish Republic was built on theories and practices that go absolutely against those that allow Özil to claim Germanness. As such, Özil's denial of Turkishness and Marco Aurélio's Mehmetness challenge the ethnicist component of Turkish citizenship, visible through language ideology, indexicality and the performative function of language. Migrant identities of footballers expose the building blocks of Turkish nationalism and citizenship configuration and, more importantly, identify the tensions between those structures and today's transnational labour flows. The threat to Turkish ethnicism caused by Turkey's presence in the global football market leads football actors to work hard to negotiate notions of Turkishness (please see Sonntag, Chapter 5 in this volume, for the exploration of the reverse side of this question where the notion of Germanness is under focus).

Conclusion

The way in which football relates to nationalism has been a fertile topic for social scientists (for example, Alegi, 2008; Archetti, 2003; Bairner, 2008; Magazine, 2007; Tuastad, 1997). Some of these examples point to how already cemented notions of nationalism are manifested in football; others explain how national myths are created through the practice of football itself. In this chapter, I showed that these two dynamics enmesh in Turkey. First, we are able to see the manifestation of Turkish ethnicist nationalism in football through the case of renaming policies discussed by Bora. Also, football supplies us with discourses and practices that extend, cement and thus sustain such conceptualisations of Turkishness. It is through football that these calibrations and definitions of identity get such wide circulation and such explicit, blunt formulation. Various forms of media make these negotiations available in everyday life and the football community in Turkey gains access to furthering identity debates by using media channels such as online news commentaries or fan forums.

In this chapter, I have argued that one can clearly observe the exclusionist, ethno-religious components of defining Turkishness in the social site of football in Turkey. I have also stated that despite the globalising trends in professional football, transnational organizations and competitions such as UEFA's Euro 2012 can in fact create discursive spaces for the solidification of singularity in national identification, belonging and ultimately citizenship. Third, this account demonstrates the frustration of the football community in Turkey as they grapple with the negotiation of migrant identities. Multiplicity in loyalties caused by migration makes it crucial to engage in a campaign to delimit Turkishness, pull certain people and types of behaviour inside these boundaries and push others out. As it becomes harder to demarcate singular national identities for footballers, we find intense and intensely mediated efforts of negotiation and deliberation of nationalities and citizenship. Achieving Turkishness is played out and mediated through football. Finally, we find religion-imbued language at the centre of these debates where one's engagement with the Turkish language either makes or breaks claims to national identity.

Notes

1. According to the FIFA Statute on 'Eligibility to play for representative teams' (FIFA, 2013), a player may only play for one national association at the senior level. If they desire to change their national team affiliation, they can only do so if they have not previously played for another national team in an official competition at 'A' international level. This means that players may change national team affiliation as they move from youth football associations to senior football associations, that is if they request this change before their 21st birthday. They may only request this change once in their careers. Even in cases where players may qualify to play for multiple national teams, FIFA has requirements that they must fulfil in order to be considered eligible. Please consult the referenced statute for these. The additional requirements have been set in place to avoid excessive naturalisations (see Sepp Blatter's declaration, BBC, 2007). Please also note that there have been several instances in the mid-20th century where footballers played for more than one national team throughout their professional careers but this practice was later banned by FIFA. The most drastic change to eligibility rules came in 2004.

2. Find the video link here: www.sinirsizvideoizle.net/sergen-yalcindan-milli-takima-mesut-ozil-taktigi-izle-41266.html.
3. All translations are by the author.
4. Also, Özil's accent when he speaks Turkish has occupied agendas in fan commentaries in Turkey where on the one hand his speaking Turkish attests to his Turkishness and on the other hand he is ridiculed and othered for his combined Anatolian and German accent.
5. 'Citizen Speak Turkish!' (*Vatandaş Türkçe Konuş!*) was a government-sponsored campaign that dates back to 1928 and continued throughout the 1930s in Turkey. As a part of the nation and nation-state-building efforts of the Republican era, its main goal was to stop minority populations from speaking their own languages in public as well as private space. See Brink-Danan (2012) for more.
6. Even though this stanza has been banned in Germany since World War Two and the national anthem has been called 'Einigkeit und Recht und Freiheit' since 1952, the Turkish newspaper cited here still referred to the former national anthem, perhaps unaware of the current-day connotations of this phrase in Germany.
7. *Ekşi Sözlük* (Sour Dictionary) is a collaborative online dictionary or forum with approximately 400,000 registered users. Besides other topics, there is a topical strand for nearly every football game (national and international) where fans are able to discuss issues pertaining to that game in their entries.
8. Halil Altıntop (Hamit Altıntop's brother) and Nuri Şahin are two other German-Turkish footballers. They both chose to play for the Turkish national team.
9. The spelling of the word '*pluriel*' here is taken from the original quotation as is.

References

Non-academic sources

BBC (2007) 'Blatter wants EU to allow quotas', at: http://news.bbc.co.uk/sport2/hi/football/7112767.stm, accessed 20 July 2014.
Ekşi Sözlük (2012) 'Mesut Özil', at: https://eksisozluk.com/mesut-ozil–1566775?focusto=28551898, accessed 6 June 2012.
Eurosport Türkiye (2013) 'Almanlar Baskı Yaptı, Yine de Türkiye'yi Seçti' ('The Germans Pressured Him But He Still Chose Turkey'), at: http://tr.eurosport.com/futbol/hazirlik-maclari-milli-takimlar/2013/almanlar-baski-yapti-yine-de-turkiye-yi-secti_sto3909171/story.shtml, accessed 2 January 2014.
Fanatik (2009) 'Mesut Özil'e Şok Haber' ('Shocking News for Mesut Özil'), at: www.fanatik.com.tr/default.aspx?aType=HaberTumYorumlar&ArticleID=128348&TotalItems=39&Page=2, accessed 2 January 2014.
FIFA (2013) *FIFA Statutes, July 2013 Edition*, at: www.fifa.com/mm/document/affederation/generic/02/14/97/88/fifastatuten2013_e_neutral.pdf, accessed 20 July 2014.

Fotospor (2012) Neden Alman Milli Takımını Seçti?' ('Why Did He Choose the German National Team?'), at: www.fotospor.com/haber_neden-alman-milli-takimini-secti_63814, accessed 20 July 2014.

Hürriyet (2010) 'Mesut Özil'in Babaannesi Toprağa Verildi' ('Mesut Özil's Grandmother Was Buried'), at: www.hurriyet.com.tr/gundem/15145908. asp, accessed 6 June 2012.

NTVSpor (2010a) 'Özil: Türkiye'yi Hiç Düşünmedim' ('Özil: I Never Considered Turkey'), at: www.ntvspor.net/haber/futbol/24631/ozil-turkiyeyi-hic-dusunmedim, accessed 6 June 2012.

NTVSpor (2010b) 'Mesut'un kararını desteklemiyorum' ('I Do Not Support Mesut's Decision'), at: www.ntvspor.net/haber/futbol/24655/mesutun-kararini-desteklemiyorum, accessed 6 June 2012.

NTVSpor (2012) 'Mesut Özil gibi Türkiye'yi Satmadım' ('I Did Not Sell Turkey Out Like Mesut Özil Did'), at: www.ntvspor.net/haber/diger-sporlar/56845/mesut-ozil-gibi-turkiyeyi-satmadim, accessed 6 June 2012.

Radikal (2009) 'Mesut "Deutschland über alles" dedi' ('Mesut Said "Deutschland über alles"'), at: www.radikal.com.tr/spor/mesut_deutschland_uber_alles_dedi-920402, accessed 6 June 2012.

Radikal (2010a) 'Özil: Gol Attıktan Sonra Tabii ki Çok Sevindim' ('Özil: Of Course I Was Very Happy to Score'), at: www.radikal.com.tr/spor/ozil_gol_attiktan_sonra_tabii_ki_cok_sevindim-1023032, accessed 6 June 2012.

Radikal (2010b) 'Özil: Islıklayanları Anlayabiliyorum' ('Özil: I Can See Why They Would Whistle'), at: www.radikal.com.tr/spor/ozil_isliklayanlari_anlayabiliyorum-1024244, accessed 6 June 2012.

Sabah Spor (2010) 'Atmadan Kazandilar' ('They Won without Scoring'), at: www.sabah.com.tr/Spor/Futbol/2010/10/09/atmadan_kazandilar? fuvqepezynhfkluf, accessed 29 November 2013.

Sol Haber Portali (2010) 'Mesut Hangi Kaleye Atsın?' ('Which Goalpost Should Mesut Aim For?'), at: http://haber.sol.org.tr/postal/mesut-hangi-kaleye-atsin-34752, accessed 30 November 2013.

Spor X (2012) 'Almanya'yı seçtim, çünkü...' ('I chose Germany because...'), at: www.sporx.com/futbol/dunya/almanya/almanyayi-sectim-cunkuSXHBQ295128SXQ?utm_source=Google, accessed 20 July 2014.

Turkish Football (2014) 'Mesut Ozil Marks World Cup Victory by Sharing Turkish-German Hybrid Flag', at: www.turkish-football.com/news_read. php?id=6143, accessed 20 July 2014.

UEFA (2013) 'About UEFA: 11 Values', at: www.uefa.org/aboutuefa/elevenvalues/index.html, accessed 2 January 2014.

Vatan (2012) Mesut Alman mı, Türk mü?' ('Is Mesut German or Turkish?'), at: http://haber.gazetevatan.com/mesut-alman-mi-turk-mu/458959/30/dunya, accessed 30 November 2013.

YouTube (2011) 'Mesut Özil Özel Uçakla Memleketi Zonguldak'ta' ('Mesut Özil on a Private Plane and in His Homeland Zonguldak'), at: www.youtube. com/watch?v=Sm2BmGDBAtQ, accessed 2 January 2014.

Academic publications

Alegi, P. (2008) '"A Nation To Be Reckoned With": The Politics of World Cup Stadium Construction in Cape Town and Durban, South Africa', *African Studies*, Vol. 67, Issue 3, pp. 397–422.

Alpan, B. and Şenyuva, Ö. (2015) 'Does Qualifying Really Qualify? Comparing the Representations of the Euro 2008 and Euro 2012 in the Turkish Media' (Chapter 4 in this volume).

Archetti, E. (2003) 'Playing Football and Dancing Tango: Embodying Argentina in Movement, Style and Identity', in N. Dyck and E. Archetti (2003) (eds), *Sport, Dance and Embodied Identities* (Oxford: Berg).

Anderson, B. (1983) *Imagined Communities* (London: Verso).

Austin, J. L. (1962) *How To Do Things with Words* (Cambridge, MA: Harvard University Press).

Bairner, A. (2008) 'The Cultural Politics of Remembrance: Sport, Place and Memory in Belfast and Berlin', *International Journal of Cultural Policy*, Vol. 14, Issue 4, pp. 417–30.

Besnier, N. and Brownell, S. (2012) 'Sport, Modernity and the Body', *Annual Review of Anthropology*, Vol. 41, pp. 443–59.

Bora, T. (2013) 'Futbolda Erkeklik, Militarizm, Milliyetçilik' ('Masculinity, Militarism and Nationalism in Football'), in Y. N. Sümbüloğlu (ed.), *Erkek Millet Asker Millet (Manly Nation, Military Nation)* (İstanbul: İletişim).

Brink-Danan, M. (2012) *Jewish Life in 21st Century Turkey* (Bloomington: Indiana University Press).

Çağlar, A. S. (1998) 'Popular Culture, Marginality and Institutional Incorporation: German-Turkish Rap and Turkish Pop in Berlin', *Cultural Dynamics*, Vol. 10, Issue 3, pp. 243–61.

Cameron, D. (2003) 'Gender and Language Ideologies', in J. Holmes and M. Meyerhoff (eds), *The Handbook of Language and Gender* (Malden, MA: Blackwell).

Dávila, A. (2002) 'Culture in the Ad World: Producing the Latin Look', in F. D. Ginsburg, L. Abu-Lughod and B. Larkin (eds), *Media Worlds* (Berkeley: University of California Press).

Ehrkamp, P. and Leitner, H. (2003) 'Beyond National Citizenship: Turkish Immigrants and the (Re)Construction of Citizenship in Germany', *Urban Geography*, Vol. 24, Issue 2, pp. 127–46.

Fortier, A. (2000) *Migrant Belongings: Memory, Space, Identity* (London: Bloomsbury Academic).

Ginsburg, F. D., Abu-Lughod, L. and Larkin, B. (2002) 'Introduction', in F. D. Ginsburg, L. Abu-Lughod and B. Larkin (eds), *Media Worlds* (Berkeley: University of California Press).

Gülalp, H. (2006) 'Introduction: Citizenship versus Nationality?', in H. Gülalp (ed.), *Citizenship and Ethnic Conflict* (London: Routledge).

İçduygu, A. and Kaygusuz, Ö. (2004) 'The Politics of Citizenship by Drawing Borders: Foreign Policy and the Construction of National Citizenship in Turkey', *Middle Eastern Studies*, Vol. 40, Issue 6, pp. 26–50.

Jiwani, Y. (2008) 'Sports as a Civilizing Mission: Zinedine Zidane and the Infamous Head-Butt', *Topia: Canadian Journal of Cultural Studies*, Vol. 19, pp. 11–33.

Joppke, C. (1999) 'How Immigration Is Changing Citizenship: A Comparative View', *Ethnic and Racial Studies*, Vol. 22, Issue 4, pp. 629–52.

Kaya, A. (2007) 'German-Turkish Transnational Space: A Separate Space of Their Own', *German Studies Review*, Vol. 30, Issue 3, pp. 1–20.

Lacan, J. (1982) *Ecrits* [1967]. Translated by Alan Sheridan (New York: Norton).

Magazine, R. (2007) *Golden and Blue like My Heart: Masculinity, Youth and Power among Soccer Fans in Mexico City* (Tucson: University of Arizona Press).

Maksudyan, N. (2005) 'The *Turkish Review of Anthropology* and the Racist Face of Turkish Nationalism', *Cultural Dynamics*, Vol. 17, Issue 3, pp. 291–322.

Mankekar, P. (2002) 'Epic Contests: Television and Religious Identity in India', in F. D. Ginsburg, L. Abu-Lughod and B. Larkin (eds), *Media Worlds* (Berkeley: University of California Press).

Parla, T. and Davison, A. (2004) *Corporatist Ideology in Kemalist Turkey: Progress or Order?* (Syracuse: Syracuse University Press).

Schiller, N. G., Basch, L. and Blanc-Szanton, C. (2004) 'Transnationalism: A New Analytic Framework for Understanding Migration', in M. Mobasher and M. Sadri (eds), *Migration, Globalization, and Ethnic Relations* (Upper Saddle River: Prentice Hall).

Silverstein, M. (1992) 'The Uses and Utility of Ideology: Some Reflections', *Pragmatics*, Vol. 2, Issue 3, pp. 311–23.

Sonntag, A. (2015) 'Up to Expectations? Perceptions of Ethnic Diversity in the French and German National Team' (Chapter 5 in this volume).

Spitulnik, D. (2002) 'Mobile Machines and Fluid Audiences: Rethinking Reception through Zambian Radio Culture', in F. D. Ginsburg, L. Abu-Lughod and B. Larkin (eds), *Media Worlds* (Berkeley: University of California Press).

Tuastad, D. (1997) 'The Political Role of Football for Palestinians in Jordan', in G. Armstrong and R. Giulianotti (eds), *Entering the Field: New Perspectives on World Football* (Oxford: Berg).

Vertovec, S. (2001) 'Transnationalism and Identity', *Journal of Ethnic and Migration Studies*, Vol. 27, Issue 4, pp. 573–82.

Yeğen, M. (2004) 'Citizenship and Ethnicity in Turkey', *Middle Eastern Studies*, Vol. 40, Issue 6, pp. 51–66.

Wilk, R. R. (2002) 'Television, Time, and the National Imaginary in Belize', in F. D. Ginsburg, L. Abu-Lughod and B. Larkin (eds), *Media Worlds* (Berkeley: University of California Press).

Zeydanlioğlu, W. (2008) '"The White Turkish Man's Burden". Orientalism, Kemalism and the Kurds in Turkey', in G. Rings and A. Ife (eds), *Neo-colonial Mentalities in Contemporary Europe? Language and Discourse in the Construction of Identities* (Newcastle upon Tyne: Cambridge Scholars Publishing).

7
Doing Ethnography and Writing Anthropology
A Single-site-multiple-ethnography of a Protest Event against the 2012 UEFA European Championship in Poznań

Michał Buchowski and Małgorzata Zofia Kowalska

The 2012 UEFA European Championship in football (Euro 2012) was the first to be held in former socialist countries, Poland and Ukraine. Poznań, a medium-sized city with a population of over half a million and with its immediate suburbs close to one million, was one of the four Polish cities which hosted the Championship. Three first-round matches were played here between 10 and 18 June 2012. Five years of preparations culminated in three weeks of festivity lasting from 8 June to 1 July. The event drew tens of thousands of citizens and sport-tourists both from Poland and abroad – the latter comprising mainly Irish, Croatian and Italian visitors, whose national teams played their group stage matches in Poznań – as well as volunteers engaged to help them to navigate their ways in the city. They all attended several games and hundreds of events organised in and outside the fan-zones. Both UEFA and the national and Poznań city authorities presented the event as a carnival of football and, later, as a great promotional success. However, the idea of hosting the Championship in Poland and in the city of Poznań also raised certain objections among (relatively small) groups of people who perceived it as an unnecessary expenditure. In Poznań, they protested against the fête in several public events, most interestingly, by organising a football tournament called *'Euro za jeden euro'* ('Euro for one euro') at a dilapidated old stadium located close to the city centre, and by staging a nationwide demonstration, 'Chleba Zamiast Igrzysk' ('Bread instead of Games'). In this chapter, we will focus on the second event.

We have three major and interrelated objectives. First, we want to describe the event; second, we intend to present the way in which an ethnographic account of it was generated; and third, we propose an anthropological interpretation of the event. In other words, while analysing the protest, we also hope to shed light on some aspects related to doing ethnography and writing anthropology.

Ethnography and anthropology

In this chapter we take up a rarely discussed issue, which is, in our opinion, of crucial importance for social, and especially anthropological, research on football. Each singular aspect of the topic raised here has been discussed separately and thoroughly in anthropological literature. However, various threads we put together have hardly ever been raised explicitly in literature on football. Here we want to explore the theoretical and practical questions emerging from doing participant ethnography of a singular event, which is just a part of a much larger football-related mega-event. In our attempt we are driven by Joan Vincent's astute opinion that 'what gives political anthropology its vitality is the complex interaction of field research with ethnography, and ethnography with theory and theory with critique' (Vincent, 2001, p. 1; see also Demossier, 2012, p. 2).

One may wonder, why write about anthropological cultural critique, which we discuss closer below, in a book on football? We do so because in our particular research we insist on seeing football in the broad perspective of modern capitalism encroaching upon the post-socialist context. Of course, in a short book chapter only very few aspects can be discussed, so in order to introduce ethnography properly, and at the same time give a taste of the critical insights that one can arrive at on the basis of fieldwork, we will focus on a single event, an event developing on one site within the larger field, and which, as previously mentioned, took place during the European Championship in Poznań.

Field research can be conducted with the help of ethnographic methods, but ethnography itself is not synonymous with anthropology. The latter is a discipline which uses ethnographic field methods but cannot be reduced to them. In other words, recourse to ethnographic fieldwork methods in itself does not make an enterprise anthropological. Fieldwork is, as Vincent indicates, just a starting point, or rather an element of a spiral cycle, of the whole anthropological endeavour. Data gathered in an ethnographic way are put into a dynamic relationship with theoretical insights. Such dialectical interactions should result in a critical reassessment of social life and the existing relations of power which govern these relations and are most often not clearly identified by people engaged in the social practice. Only this complete process enables us to see anthropological practice as one of the forms of cultural critique. This critique can be understood as a desire 'to disturb [the readers'] cultural self-satisfaction' (Marcus and Fischer, 1986, p. 111), and as an attempt to de-familiarise something that appears as obvious or natural to social actors.

Just like the celebrated thinkers of the 19th and 20th centuries – it is enough to mention Karl Marx, Emile Durkheim and Max Weber – who proposed a critique of their own societies undergoing the industrial capitalist transformations, many anthropologists today, such as Jean and John Comaroff (2011), James Ferguson (2006), Michael Burawoy et al. (2000), Gordon Matthews et al. (2012) or Richard H. Robbins (2005), are writing in reaction to the neoliberal capitalism that operates on a global scale. What differentiates anthropologists from the classic authors and from several contemporary commentators – such as Anthony Giddens, Ulrich Beck and Zygmunt Bauman who preferred and continue to prefer writing in a grand-narrative style and very often in abstract terms – is their devotion to ethnographic detail and locality. For modern anthropologists, a thorough description of singular, apparently piecemeal or disconnected events is the starting point for an intellectual endeavour that leads to findings which may be valid globally. Thanks to this devotion to ethnographic detail, general conclusions are grounded in empirical material.

Fieldwork based on ethnographic methods still appears as a *sine qua non* of genuinely anthropological work. However, a lot has changed in the understanding of how fieldwork should be conducted since the method was pioneered by Bronisław Malinowski (1922) in the 1920s, who gave detailed descriptions and interpretations of the Trobriand Islanders' social, economic and cultural practices. Stationary fieldwork lasting several months or a couple of years has become a rarity in the peripatetic contemporary world. George E. Marcus (1998) tried to systematise the ways of collecting this increasingly erratic data. These changing fieldwork practices are aimed at grasping increasingly complex phenomena in an economically globalised, socially mobile and culturally hybridised world. Marcus gives testimony to the growing importance of 'multi-sited research [which] is designed around chains, paths, threads, conjunctions, or juxtapositions of locations in which the ethnographer establishes some form of literal, physical presence...' (Marcus, 1998, p. 90). Researchers can therefore follow people, things, metaphors, plots, stories or allegories, as well as lives or biographies (ibid., pp. 90–94).

In our attempt to give an ethnographic account of the aforementioned protest, which was part of a larger event (mega-event), we encountered problems with multifariousness, multivocality and multiconnectedness of the data somewhat similar to those addressed by Marcus: we found ourselves at the intersection of global capital flows and local needs, but we also faced other methodological and theoretical challenges. First, we were doing something that has become known as 'anthropology at home' (Jackson, 1987). (For continental ethnologists, by the way, anthropology at home sounds like the reinvention of the wheel, as they had been practising ethnography in their home countries since the second half of the 19th century, whenever they ventured to study their own folk.) Doing ethnography at home implies that various things are evident or easier to grasp by the sole fact of knowing them from long-lasting and daily experience. Second, we did not have to search for anything, since the event 'came to us' and it was enough to go where it was about to take place. In this sense, we dealt with the inverse situation to that tackled by Marcus, since we did not trace any leads – we 'simply' went where the social actors gathered. Therefore, our field-site can be defined as a bounded one, as an 'arbitrary location' (Candea, 2007), 'the symmetrical inversion of the [Weber's] "ideal type"... [and] explicitly partial and incomplete window onto complexity' (Candea, 2007, pp. 167, 179–80).

Nonetheless, it did not make our work child's play. Being embedded in one's own culture has its flipside: it creates a risk of becoming blind to behaviours and issues which appear obvious or self-explanatory, but which are not such for the external observer. More importantly, such phenomena that might possibly be over-looked can be highly significant for the critical analysis of the subject in question. (It is worth mentioning here that, to some extent, the protest was not a purely 'domestic affair', as many actors arrived from outside the city and country. This fact added an international component to the happening and signalled a more than local dimension of social attitudes to the complex phenomenon called Euro 2012.) Moreover, doing ethnography of a mass event asks for new tools. A single ethnographer is unable to register as many facts as several trained people can. An individual account is not only one-sided or subjective, but can distort the actual action and its multiple forms. The researcher cannot be in various places and observe them from different vantage points simultaneously. Hence, s/he can potentially omit something crucial for the analysis.

For all these reasons, we opted for a team fieldwork of the event. Five people participated independently in the protest and delivered their written reports immediately after it.[1] One can therefore say that we practised a *single-site-multiple-ethnography*. This kind of collective ethnography has been carried out in the past. Marcel Griaule's (1957) documentary system 'governed by images of collection, documentation, and interrogation' (Clifford, 1988, p. 65) is a classic example, although it was a different sort of enterprise implemented among the Dogons in Africa in the first half of the 20th century. Before the Second World War, a Romanian sociologist, Dimitre Gusti (1934), employed collective ethnographic research. As Călin Cotoi emphasised, the Bucharest School of Sociology founded by Gusti 'had a strong focus on peasants and carried out exhaustive village monographies with big, interdisciplinary groups of researchers...' (Cotoi, 2011, p. 139). Sending groups of students to investigate a given community for a certain period of time was a common practice among Central European ethnographers until the end of the last century (both authors had previously partaken in such endeavours). However, these efforts were usually coordinated in the sense that each researcher had a distinctive function in the team or was meant to study a defined aspect of community life. In our case, each member of the team performed regular participant observation without being ascribed to any specific task. We do not claim originality, but we are convinced that using this one-site-multiple-ethnography appeared to be the most adequate method to describe the protest we wanted to scrutinise anthropologically. It took the form of a collective ethnography of an event, and opened the possibility of making Clifford Geertz's 'thick description' even thicker – a problem to which we return in the last section of this chapter.

A short explanation of what 'thick description' means seems unavoidable here. The celebrated American anthropologist borrowed the term from Gilbert Ryle whose aim was to show how many different meanings a simple eye blinking can have, and how the same gesture can be interpreted by different actors guided by their own cultural norms of interpretation and by their social competencies. In a hermeneutic fashion, Geertz argues that Ryle's example of eye-wink 'presents an image...of piled-up structures of inference and implications through which the ethnographer is continually trying to pick up his way' (Geertz, 1973, p. 7). All data found in the field should be interpreted as socially established codes which actors use and – sometimes – bend or misinterpret. 'Analysis, then, is sorting out the structures of signification...' (Geertz, 1973, p. 9). However, the description is thick only 'if it conveys the layers of meaning that may be read into an action' (Kuper, 1999, p. 110). Meanwhile, in his leading example of sheep stealing in Morocco, Geertz does not make it clear who is the author of the story, if it is a compilation of various narratives delivered by different people or his own account of various stories. Therefore, it is rather a 'straightforward action narrative' and description that is 'anything but "thick"' (ibid.). We want to avoid Geertz's mistakes here.

Our 'event ethnography' consists of written accounts of what our team had observed during the protest, as well as short, often fleeting interviews with the participants and photo documentation. The on-site ethnography is supported by other data collected around the event, such as media reports, blog posts and opinions voiced on internet forums. Such field and mass media data cannot 'hang in the air' and needs to be put in the context of the debates on the legacy of the European Championship in Poland and Ukraine, that is, its social readings and consequences as well as cultural connotations. This is the moment when the ethnographic enterprise transmutes into anthropology.

The socio-economic context

The city of Poznań spent 24.8 million zloty (approximately €6 million) on the preparation and promotion of the event (Deloitte, 2012), and approximately 750 million zloty (€180 million) on renovating the city's stadium with a capacity of over 44,000.[2] These figures exclude loans taken out for the city's own contribution to infrastructural projects co-funded by the EU, such as road construction, the modernisation of the railway station and the expansion of the airport. The main benefits claimed for Euro 2012 were the promotion of the city and the acceleration of infrastructural modernisation (Deloitte, 2012; see also the report by the Ministry of Sport and Tourism, 2012). On the national level, the impact of Euro 2012 has been labelled 'the Polish Effect', and the Ministry of Sport and Tourism claimed that 'its influence on the economy, image and national development is greater than in [the] case of [the] Barcelona Effect'[3] (Ministry of Sport and Tourism, 2012).

The event brought hundreds of thousands of visitors to Poznań and the three matches played at the city's stadium were watched by more than a 130,000 spectators. Afterwards, the city authorities announced that the Advertising Value Equivalency (AVE)[4] in Poznań was estimated at a total of 231 million zloty (€57 million).[5] For the city authorities the supposed promotional effect has become the main benefit of Euro 2012. One has to admit that the number of tourists who visited Poznań was impressive, and they usually expressed a very positive opinion about the event and the city (Report 2, 2012).

Those who contested this positive story, members of more or less radical social groups and political activists, but also quite a few 'ordinary citizens', have dismissed the purported profits from organising the championship and claimed that it diverted public money from welfare to business. Arguments about the public good and priorities were raised: according to the opponents, the money wasted on one event should have been devoted to housing, kindergartens, schools, public transportation and the improvement of basic infrastructure. As one of the arguments went: 'For the amount of money spent on the stadium ... it would have been possible to pay for the placement of six thousand babies in public nurseries for 10 years' (Chleba Zamiast Igrzysk, 2012). More concrete data were provided: 'Preparing the EURO means special expenditures which will not be compensated by foreign tourists or investors. Economists... calculated that thanks to the organisation of the EURO, the total accumulated increase of GNP could reach the level of 27.9 billion zloty. This is merely 1/3 of the total expense of the event – what about those remaining billions?' (Chleba Zamiast Igrzysk, 2012). The opponents' conclusion is devastating for the authorities: 'UEFA will make the biggest profits from the Euro. According to the agreement with the Polish government, it was exempted from all taxes, among them VAT and CIT, as well as local taxes and customs duties! It appears that the championship generates profit for elites – a profit to which we all have to contribute' (Chleba Zamiast Igrzysk, 2012).

In this milieu, critical to neoliberal capitalism and to the idea of hosting the Championship, several groups organised a protest; the number of associations participating in the event amounted to fifteen and included, among others, the Anarchist Federation, Feminist Think Tank, Nationwide Trade Union Workers Initiative, Socialist Alternative, Leftist Alternative, and Food, Not Bombs.[6] Posters and leaflets were distributed in print and via the internet. On 10 June, on the very same day that the first Euro match between Ireland and Croatia took place in Poznań, the nationwide demonstration called 'Bread instead of Games' was held in the city.

The event

Posters inviting people to the demonstration were hung all over the city (Jakub, Małgorzata, Michał[7]), and the organisers tried to promote it as widely as possible in the media and via social networks. About a month before the event, in a leftist and socially engaged theatre in the city centre, a discussion was held on the reasons for and consequences of organising sports mega-events not only in Poland and Poznań, but also elsewhere (Michał, Małgorzata). However, the mainstream media hardly noticed any of these actions and impatiently counted the days left to the opening of the tournament.

On the day of the demonstration, one of us (Paweł) started a conversation about the event on the train from the neighbouring city of Gniezno (c. 50km northeast of Poznań). He talked to a group of Irish football fans and introduced the topic of the rally. They showed full understanding of the idea of the protest and agreed that authorities everywhere tend to make decisions without asking people their opinion. According to them, the Euro championships are only UEFA's business and therefore 'it is not all about sport'. Strikingly enough, this view strongly coincided with the reasoning behind the demonstration. However, this standpoint did not prevent them from having great fun in Poland, and they did not intend to join the protesters. Agreeing on how dirty a business UEFA events are, the group continued their earlier conversations about the similarities between the historical fate of the Polish and the Irish nations, the excellent taste of the Polish vodka 'Żubrówka' and plans of not returning home and having even more fun in Poland after the matches are over. They arrived at Poznań not in order to study and solve local problems, but to enjoy their free time and take advantage of a unique celebration of leisure.

The meeting point for the demonstration was located by the Opera House in the city centre. The whole march's winding route included Poznań's main streets and significant administrative buildings. It was scheduled to start at 2pm and was to last for about two hours.

The day was hot and humid. A colourful crowd gathered at the stairs of the Opera House and, for a while, it looked like a usual 'leftist' meet and greet, with people talking and cheerfully welcoming the latecomers. Paweł remarked that 'the march was not very big'. Most of the demonstrators seemed to be, and in many cases actually were, a group of old friends who knew each other from various activities in the city and elsewhere. (We too spotted a few colleagues from the university and the department, who were not doing research, but demonstrating.) But they were joined by a number of other participants and comprised a total number of more than 500 demonstrators. Małgorzata, in contrast to Paweł, was surprised by the relatively large number of participants of what was, after all, to an extent an anti-government protest, and spotted representatives of teacher and nursery' worker groups, as well as two or three elderly women sitting in a van with a megaphone mounted on top – not a usual sight during leftist protests.[8]

The march was delayed by half an hour. Participants assembled and took off to the rhythm of samba pummelled on drums. The familiar get-together atmosphere changed into that of a serious protest. 'Slogans broadcast over loudspeakers were scrupulously copied and chanted. It was difficult not to follow the pace of the march' (Jakub). Carrying out interviews during the march turned out to be a virtual impossibility, since people were engaged in lively and noisy protest.

When, at some point, Jakub started to engage with two girls who were apparently keen to start a conversation, it turned out 'they too were doing research and were looking for someone to interview. We all burst into laughter, wished each other good luck and went away in different directions'.

Despite the common cause, different groups taking part in the protest could be distinguished according to their dress code and involvement. 'At the peak, there were the organisers escorting a car with a megaphone on top of it. Many of them had orange vests and some were blowing whistles. They were closely followed by those most devoted to the protest – mostly highly vocal, young people, often dressed in black and holding banners with different messages; among them were banners written in German (but at least partly held by Polish protesters). They were followed by a large group of quieter and less engaged participants of different age and affiliations. Some of them were walking with or piggybacking children, some were taking pictures. They were not chanting or shouting, some were silent, others were talking to friends and laughing while walking. There was also a group of black-and-pink samba dancers; and at the end, the stragglers and bicyclists slowly driving or wheeling their bikes' (Jakub). For a while, an Irishman dressed in national colours and communicating in broken Polish was spotted at the head of the column; Paweł reported that 'he said that he understood the problem and showed his support by participating in the march'.

There were several other foreigners spotted during the march, mostly Irish fans who were going to the Old Market and who joined the protest for a while, at least some of them eagerly discussing the problem with the participants (Małgorzata). Some 'Irish men misunderstood one of the slogans about *zyski* ['profits' in Polish] and started chanting *cycki, cycki, cycki* ['tits' in Polish] in joy' (Kamila). Many foreigners passing by seemed to be lost in translation and joined the march thinking that this was yet another Euro event. Jakub and Małgorzata described 'a group of Irish fans with at least one *bodhrán* [an Irish frame drum] who played on it for a while, probably not having a clue as to what it was all about and simply having great fun'. Indeed, fun they had.

This international dimension acquired yet another, humourless form. On the tenth day of each month, radical rightist groups would commemorate the crash of the Polish President's aircraft near Smolensk (Russia), which occurred on 10 April 2010. They also did so on the day of the event, with about ninety people gathering around the Katyn Monument[9] in a small park near the march's route. On hearing the noise from the street, they decided to greet the Irish visitors. A man started his speech in rather broken English, and one of us managed to catch the phrase 'killed our president', and at the end: 'good luck and have a nice time in Poland' (Paweł). For a while, among the many banners held by the protesters, there was also one saying 'this was an assassination', a clear indication of an anti-government position and rightist political sympathies of at least one participant of the march – or a provocative joke.

There were several stops and speeches on the way of the march. The representatives of kindergartens and nursery school teachers described their difficult financial situation. They pointed at the ludicrous spending on organising Euro 2012 as a reason for budgetary cuts in education. In front of Neobank, a bank recently become famous (or notorious) for its malicious policy of buying tenement houses and then forcefully evicting the tenants, the representatives of the Greater Poland Tenants' Association introduced the ladies travelling in the van as the victims of the gentrification process taking place in the city. Some of them gave short speeches and linked their stories to the general problem: the city has taken care of big business and the rich, and left its poorer citizens on their own. Feminist groups discussed sexism and aggressive male behaviours that are ubiquitous during football events. In Jakub's eyes, in general, women were more active with respect to speeches.

Making sense of the speeches, the banners held by the protesters and the chants sung by them was much easier for those of us who knew the context. This is an unquestionable advantage of doing anthropology at home. Nevertheless, we noticed that it was not only the foreigners who needed more explanation about the protest, as many local observers or passers-by seemed to have problems in deciphering the meaning of the slogans written on the banners as well as the overall sense of the march.

The reactions of the general public were very diverse. Some people told us that they understood the reasons for the protest and agreed with them: 'we will have to pay the bills for Euro 2012 and the rich'. Some were quietly observing the protest from their balconies or sidewalks, while some talked to the participants. Others questioned the expense borne by the city, because 'all the money came from the outside'. A middle-aged woman was indignant and expressed her disbelief in 'people wasting their time on protesting rather than working, like everyone else' (Małgorzata). At one point, a thin man in his fifties or sixties, wearing a white-and-red scarf in Polish national colours, expressed an unusual attitude to the protest. He tried to block the crowds' way, shouting and waving his scarf in national colours: '"What are you doing? You should not do this!" He kneeled down and made gestures in Rejtan style'[10] (Paweł). In Jakub's view, this man was trying to convince the protesters that their march was a 'disgrace to Poland'. A fan painted in the Polish national colours protested against the march even more expressively: 'He stood "frozen" with his middle finger pointed at the protesters' (Paweł). Meanwhile, however, Małgorzata talked to two thirty-year-old men who described themselves both as Lech Poznań fans and as sympathisers of the protest: they said that the Euro is a 'rich boys' game', which had no significance for Polish football.

In most windows on the route of the march, national and sometimes other European flags and banners were visible. Not randomly, one could hear offensive comments of those watching the march from their balconies. 'In their eyes I see hate,' one of us wrote when the protest was passing a tenement house with bare-chested young-style men drinking their beers and shouting 'you should all be fucked, slobs' to the crowd (Jakub). In response, some of the protesters responded aggressively, but in general the demonstration proceeded peacefully. It was escorted by a number of policemen, some of them dressed in blue vests marked 'Anti-Conflict Team'.

According to all reports, the general atmosphere deteriorated with time. The air was getting more and more sticky, people were becoming increasingly tired and some of them got irritated. Eventually, the march arrived at its final destination, that is, the regional (voivodship[11]) governmental building. The organisers made only a few final remarks, and 'sensing that everyone is exhausted, invited the protest for a free meal and finished the manifestation' (Jakub).

Ethnography in perspective and anthropological interpretation

We hope that our summarised ethnographic account showed some aspects of conducting participant observation of an event, in this case related to a sports mega-event. A festival of football was accompanied by a two-hour protest that became the focus of our attention. Our aim was to evidence the proceedings and to convey the general atmosphere of the march. Only a few common points can be found in our accounts. We cannot cite all the descriptions, but they also differ significantly. We found ourselves in various spots during the march and, therefore, we were able to see diverse occurrences. Furthermore, the same events were seen in dissimilar ways. Team members paid attention to and emphasised divergent aspects of the story, and we can even associate this with the ethnographers' varying interests and political views. Finally, our chapter is the result of a subjective selection of different accounts.

This story, based on multi-layered, subjective perceptions is, in our opinion, more complex than individual accounts would have been. This does not mean that it is more objective, but rather more comprehensive and open to interpretation. This is the advantage of such collective single-site-multiple-ethnography, which we recommend for doing the anthropology of an event. Now, however, it is time 'to tramp the moody boots of experience across the patterned carpet of system' (Smith, 1999, pp. 14–15), and propose an interpretation of the event while making reference to its broad context.

Victor W. Turner made a classical distinction between the various levels of interpretation of symbols pertinent to a given ritual or culture. He distinguished between exegetical meaning, which 'represents the interpretation of indigenous informants'; operational meaning, which 'results from equating a symbol's meaning with its *use*'; and positional meaning, which is 'found in examining a symbol's relationship to others belonging to the same complex' (Turner, 1962, p. 125). All three levels are at work in our account. As a matter of fact, we did not conduct interviews, which are the usual tool for re-constructing the 'native's point of view' (Geertz, 1974). In our position, we were unable to realise the ideal of an ethnographic method 'that focuses on the perspectives of living individuals as they understand themselves in actual life' (Ouroussoff, 2010, p. 1). However, our intimate knowledge of the cultural context, doing anthropology at home, have enabled us to decipher the symbols of the protest. By conducting a sort of phenomenology of the march, based on multiple-single-site-ethnography, we have hopefully been able to see how various symbols have been used and interpreted. Finally, all symbols and practices which appeared during the protest and around it can be confronted and mutually related. All these levels of use and interpretation are dynamically entangled. As the march proceeded and subsequent actors with their symbols appeared, new meanings were evoked and put into dialogue. They represented different values and worldviews for various individuals and groups.

To some extent, the march proved to be a typical leftist circle event. In comparison to previous socially motivated protests held in Poznań, however, it was exceptionally big. The nationwide status of the demonstration contributed to its size. Only a few state protests organised by trade unions in Poznań drew comparable or larger crowds.[12] The event was a social meeting of the anti-neoliberal circles from the city and outside, ranging from anarchists to leftist trade unionists to journalists. Euro 2012 provided an opportunity to express their opposition to neoliberal capitalism, in particular to its extraordinary form of a popular sports event organised to make profit.

Leftist groups are usually aware that they are a negligible minority, but feel obliged to undermine the mainstream opinion and the dominant rhetoric about the assumed profits for local communities, the city and the whole country. For them, the Championship was just another occasion for big business to multiply its capital, which was 'sold' to the public as beneficial to society as a whole. Meanwhile, certain business groups, UEFA and the local authorities involved in the event were the only real economic or political beneficiaries of the whole undertaking. Ultimately, it is ordinary people who pay for the mega-event, since investments in Euro 2012 were made at the expense of ventures in more down-to-earth infrastructure or at a higher cost than they would have been if they had been better planned. To the leftist groups, *panem et circenses*, bread and circuses, appear as an opiate for the masses, who are unable to see the leftist-minded people's argument. The protest was a means for demonstrating the disagreement with neoliberalism and its sports-industry branch, and it was aimed at raising the consciousness of its catastrophic effects on society. A closer look reveals the festival 'as a signifier [meant] to obscure an uncomfortable reality' (Kalb, 2009, p. 217) of post-socialist transformation. The elites had a political and economic interest in organising Euro 2012. The discourses produced about it legitimised the business-oriented undertaking. The man in the street was duped by the elites and became an active participant and supporter of the costly event. The cultural hegemony exercised by neoliberal forces proved its effectiveness.

According to many external local observers, these protesting groups are, in general, considered to be a strange youth alternative at best, and rowdy troublemakers or even louts at worst. They are easily recognised by their appearance: pierced noses, lips and ears, dread-locks and informal, either black or colourful outfits. The majority of citizens are aware that the protesters do not comprise mainstream society. Of still greater importance, however, are their political views and activity: they openly criticise the neoliberal politics of the city and national governments, and the way capitalism and international business have been introduced in post-communist Poland. Moreover, they often refer explicitly to socialist, Marxist or anarchist traditions, which in Poland remain, especially for older generations, rhetorical tools of the communist regime. The mainstream press and politi-cians, as well as presumably most citizens, do not recall these times with fondness. In public debates before Euro 2012, there was very little or even no discussion of the costs and downsides of the event. In such a political and cultural milieu, friendly to Euro 2012 and hos-tile to the protesters, greeting the march with booing and often vulgar and discouraging shouts and gestures becomes more comprehensible.

Politicians and the media virtually unanimously presented the Championship as a chance for the country's 'gargantuan civilisa-tional jump' (see, for instance, the interview with the Minister of Sport and Tourism, 'Euro to boost economy', 2012). For 'Poles as a nation', it provided an opportunity to present themselves as 'true Europeans'. 'Joining Europe' or 'catching up with the West' was prob-ably the most popular slogan in the first years after 1989, a desire strongly embedded in the national mythology of Poland as a bulwark of Western civilisation (cf. Davies, 1981, p. 159; Buchowski, 2001). Euro 2012 appeared as the culmination of this process of reunifica-tion with Europe, and a proof that Poland has become recognised as a truly European country. This kind of publicising was also per-petuated after the event. As Tomasz Kayser, the deputy mayor of the city of Poznań said, 'promotional success can be really accounted for only after several years, but we have already shown that Poland is a modern European Union country, and Poles are open, joyful and can have fun. We hosted a lot of fans who became our ambassadors and will tell the others what they saw here'.[13] No wonder that for most people subjected to such discursive bombardment, the demonstration was an unnecessary or harmful extravaganza which could spoil the image of the nation, and in particular Poznań's image in the eyes of the international public. Rejtan's gesture and shouts like 'People, what the hell are you doing?' express the standpoint of those who were convinced that organising Euro 2012 was a risk worth the gamble. Most Poles eagerly joined the festival of pleasure and fetishised consumption. In the vein of emulating the West, they wanted to demonstrate their Europeanness by exercising popular culture the way they think Western Europeans do. In their own eyes, they succeeded. No wonder that in such a context there was little room for any contestation. Protesting against something that most people desire, that is, cultural membership of the Western world, where football-related consumerism plays a conspicuous, even spectacular part, would have been self-contradictory. The rally did not fit in with the perception of Euro 2012 – at least not in the context of the hegemonic discourses in which modern sports-entertainment consumption, proud patriotism (but not nationalism) and civilisational Europeanism were fused.[14]

The disproportion between the number of those who attended the Euro 2012 Championship in Poznań and those who participated in the protest is striking. Official data for the Fan Zone and stadium as well as other visitors show attendance of close to one million.[15] The number of protesters was estimated at between 500 and 1000 participants (not surprisingly, the latter data were provided by the organisers). Those crude figures indicate that each dissenter was outnumbered by 1000 to 2000 people eagerly celebrating the games. As Deputy Mayor Kayser proudly announced, according to the opinion polls, 94 per cent of Poznań citizens admitted 'that the atmosphere [during Euro 2012] was very good or good'.[16] These proportions mirror the attitudes of the general public to this mega-event. Euro 2012 was a chance for self-presentation to the world and, simultaneously, a festival not only for football fans, but the majority of the population in the country and beyond. It was a holy period for festive and merry popular culture consumption, during which people preferred to forget about their daily problems and did not bother about the structural problems addressed by the protesters. This was, for instance, explicitly expressed during the debate between two journalists from *Gazeta*

Wyborcza (Michał Wybieralski and Marcin Wesołek, 2012). One of them admitted that there are many urgent social issues in Poland like poverty, but 'we can afford some luxury' and that he was going 'to have good fun, and I encourage the anarchists to do the same'. Only a minority, which perceives itself as ideologically vigilant and aware of dangers created by global capitalism, managed to resist dominant discourses and dared to go against the grain. We can assume that not all protesters were absolutely against the tournament being held in Poland (as they saw certain advantages of hosting it in the city) and some were later seen on the streets enjoying the event, but they felt obliged to show solidarity with their group of identification and to protest against the system as a matter of principle.

For the 'patriots' who wanted to commemorate the national tragedy in Smolensk, the presence of the international public was not an obstacle for holding their own event. They simply used the occasion to internationalise their case by the simplest means available, that is, giving a short speech and presenting their views.

With very few exceptions (some participants from neighbouring Germany, and a few Irish showing interest in what was going on), foreigners did not know about the protest at all, misinterpreted it, ridiculed it or showed utter lack of interest in it. Even if they could identify with some of the ideas of the protest, such as the fact that, in their view, elites all over the world tend to do things without caring about the people or the people's opinion ('they make decisions over people's heads'), they travelled to Poland to watch games and have fun, and not to protest against the Championship. They took advantage of the mega-event in order to satisfy their own cultural-recreational needs.

All these social actors met during one event. Some of them joined in on purpose, while others found themselves in it by sheer coincidence. Those who protested intentionally had divergent ideas in mind. This is why anti-neoliberal anarchists and radical leftists marched hand-in-hand, not only with rightist nationalists represented by the believers in the assassination in Smolensk, but also with the local Lech Poznań football club supporters (presumably sympathising with the ideas of Against Modern Football). The believers in the Smolensk assassination fear cosmopolitanism, which in their opinion endangers their tradition; the local football fans oppose Europeanisation and globalisation, which uproots them from local football and national loyalties. Dwellers evicted from their tenement houses, as well as those with no interest in football at all, in an act of solidarity actively joined the protest of their allies, who had supported them in their struggles against displacement by Neobank. This was a fleeting and, at first glance, strange amalgamation of divergent interests and interpretations.

There were also groups who were professionally related to the protest. Journalists and other people working in the media were looking for rare material they could use in their reports on Euro 2012. The number of persons shooting films and taking pictures was overwhelming. Policemen and other security personnel had to protect the march, although it proceeded peacefully. Finally, several researchers, including our team, joined the event in a craving for (ethnographic) material. Sometimes, they even ran into each other in attempts to conduct their study. All these actors contributed to the character and meaning of the protest.

In a self-reflective enterprise, the role of the observers remains to be addressed. The phenomenology of the protest does not imply that the events appeared to us as they were. 'There is no direct experience of naked reality independent of classifications' (Rottenburg, 2000, p. 99). Each fieldworker described the phenomena as they appeared to her or him. However, assuming their transparency would be wrong. When at the site of the event, all of us conceptualised the experiences according to our own cultural competences. Our concepts have immediately become a part of the 'reality' we were describing, because 'of the two, reality and classification, one does not come before the other' (Rottenburg, 2000, p. 99). Therefore, 'the essay deliberately eschews the trappings of an ethnographic panopiticism . . . [and] thus admits to its own partiality' (Bunzl, 2000, p. 78; see also Rosaldo, 1986; Clifford, 1986). Nevertheless, there is hope that confronting various groups' readings of the whole situation, putting all of them in the cultural context, and confronting our reports has made this account of a single event not only multivocal, but also in some sense akin to Geertz's ideal of thick description (Geertz, 1973, pp. 5–6, 9–10). In our procedure, which differed from Geertz's original meaning, we aimed to explain not only the same behaviour of the actors, but also what it meant to various people, and how the event and the participants' actions were interpreted by other participants as well as by ethnographers and, eventually, to apply these images interactively in the interpretation of what happened in Poznań on 10 June 2012. One should not forget that these collective images are shaped in socially and economically conditioned discursive practices, in which cultural hegemony plays a significant role. We hope that this chapter comprised a complex and vivid picture of ethnographic fieldwork, which may be considered 'a control for a broader abstract object of study... [allowing one] to reflect on and rethink conceptual entities, to challenge their coherence and totalising aspirations' (Candea, 2007, p. 180), and therefore paved the way for further anthropological analysis and interpretation.

Notes

1. We would like to thank Jakub Alejski, Paweł Bąkowski and Kamila Grześkowiak for their work during the protest event.
2. In 2012 total city spending amounted to over 2,296 million zloty (approximately €400 million). See Załącznik nr 2 do uchwały Nr XXV/341/VI/2012 Rady Miasta Poznania z dnia 24 stycznia 2012r, at: http://bip.poznan.pl/bip/budzet-2012,doc,1003,2719/budzet-2012-r-budzet-miasta,52739.html, accessed 19 February 2014. Even considering the central government's subsidy for the (re-)construction of the city stadium (88.5 million zloty; see www.msport.gov.pl/stadiony/2690-Program-Wieloletni-Przygotowanie-i-Wykonanie-Przedsiewziec-Euro-2-12, accessed 19 February 2014), it is evident that it was a heavy burden for the city's finances.
3. By the 'Barcelona Effect' the Polish authorities understood all the positive influence that an organisation of a mega-event can have on local development. The expression refers to the Olympic Games organised in Barcelona in 1992. The 'effect' combines the material profits (improvement of infrastructure, tourist boom, revenue profits, enhancement of transportation) and the intangible ones (favourable perception of the host city and other kinds of so-called projective profits) (cf. Davis, 2012).
4. AVE is the amount of money one would have to pay for editorial, internet, radio or TV coverage if it was an advertisement. This index is used to measure PR efficiency, although it is strongly criticised even within the PR sector worldwide as irrelevant and misleading.
5. Report 1 (2012) Ekonomiczne efekty..., compare Delloite (2012) and www.gloswielkopolski.pl/artykul/633671,wiemy-ile-poznan-wydal-i-zarobil-na-euro-2012,id,t.html, accessed 19 February 2014.
6. See: http://chlebazamiastigrzysk.wordpress.com/komitet-organizacyjny, accessed 19 February 2014.
7. In this section, we refer to the field notes of the different members of our team by their first names.

8. For reasons of space, we are not able to describe the contextual meaning of the term 'leftist' we use in this paper. Suffice to say that in the public discourse most anti-systemic and contesting groups in Poznań are commonly referred to as leftist or anarchist. For an ethnographic account of the anti-systemic groups in Poznań see Schwell, 2005.

9. During the Second World War, in 1940, approximately 22,000 Polish officers and prisoners of war were murdered by the Soviets in Katyn in today's Russia. The plane crash in 2010 with President Lech Kaczyński and several other top Polish officials on board occurred when they were on route to Katyn to attend an event marking the 70th anniversary of this massacre. It is believed by certain right-wing circles that the plane crash was not an accident, but an assassination.

10. Tadeusz Rejtan was a Polish noble who tried to prevent the legalisation of the first partition of Poland at the Parliament gathering (Sejm) in September 1773. He was immortalised in Jan Matejko's painting as a deputy who bared his chest and laid himself down. This was a dramatic attempt to stop the other members from leaving the chamber where the debate was being held. According to the law, leaving the chamber signified the end of the discussion, and the acceptance of the motion.

11. Poland is administratively divided into 16 regions called voivodships. Poznań is the capital of the second largest of them – Wielkopolska (Greater Poland).

12. For instance, see the protest by policemen, firemen and border guards, at: www.mmpoznan.pl/399650/2012/1/12/protest-sluzb-mundurowych-w-poznaniu-zdjecia?category=news.

13. See http://wielkopolskie.naszemiasto.pl/artykul/galeria/1464467,podsumowanie-euro-2012-poznan-700-tysiecy-osob-w-strefie,id,t.html, accessed 19 February 2014.

14. Compare this with the disapproving accounts of fights between Polish and Russian fans in Warsaw during the match between the two national teams.

15. '700,000 people in the Fan's Zone, 106,000 spectators at the City's Stadium and more than 125,000 foreign supporters were hosted in Poznań during Euro 2012', according to the City-Voivodship Operation Headquarters. Poznań was visited by 70,000 Irish fans, 40,000 Croats and 15,000 Italians. 'On City's Stadium games were watched by 106400 spectators, among them 42,000 Irish, 26,000 Croats and 10,000 Italians. Others were the UEFA guests (12,000) and fans from other countries than those playing at the Poznań arena,' declared Tomasz Kayser, the deputy mayor of the city. (http://wielkopolskie.naszemiasto.pl/artykul/galeria/1464467,podsumowanie-euro-2012-poznan-700-tysiecy-osob-w-strefie,id,t.html, accessed 19 February 2014).

'The Poznań Fan Zone functioned for 260 hours in 24 days. The record attendance was reached on the day when Poland played against Russia (12 June). On this day 60,500 people passed through the gates.

A record (39,000) on the day without any game was established during 'Poznań Alternative Energy' Festival (26 June), where the band *Die Antwoord* was the headline act' (www.europoznan2012.pl/aktualnosci/ 336, accessed 19 February 2014).

16. See: http://wielkopolskie.naszemiasto.pl/artykul/galeria/1464467,podsum-owanie-euro-2012-poznan-700-tysiecy-osob-w-strefie,id,t.html, accessed 19 February 2014.

References

Buchowski, M. (2001) *Rethinking Transformation: An Anthropological Perspective on Postsocialism* (Poznań: Humaniora).

Bunzl, M. (2000) 'The Prague Experience: Gay Male Sex Tourism and the Neocolonial Invention of an Embodied Border', in D. Berdhal, M. Bunzl and M. Lampland (eds), *Altering States: Ethnographies of Transition in Eastern Europe and the Former Soviet Union* (Ann Arbor: The University of Michigan Press), pp. 70–95.

Burawoy, M., Blum, J. A., George, S., Thayer, M., Gille, Z., Gowan, T., Haney, L., Klawiter, M., Lopez, S. H. and Riain S. Ó. (eds) (2000) *Global Ethnography: Forces, Connections and Imaginations in a Postmodern World* (Berkeley: University of California Press).

Candea, M. (2007) 'Arbitrary Locations: In Defence of the Bounded Field-site', *Journal of the Royal Anthropological Institute*, Vol. 13, Issue 1, pp. 167–84.

Chleba Zamiast Igrzysk (2012) 'Oficjalne stanowisko w sprawie Euro 2012', at: http://chlebazamiastigrzysk.wordpress.com/2012/04/20/stanowisko-en, accessed 19 February 2014.

Clifford, J. (1986) 'Introduction: Partial Truth', in J. Clifford and G. Marcus (eds), *Writing Culture: The Poetics and Politics of Ethnography* (Berkeley: University of California Press), pp. 1–26.

Clifford, J. (1988) *The Predicament of Culture: Twentieth Century Ethnography, Literature, and Art* (Cambridge, MA: Harvard University Press).

Comaroff, J. and Comaroff, J. (2011) *Theory from the South: Or, How Euro-America Is Evolving Toward Africa* (Boulder: Paradigm Press).

Cotoi, C. (2011) 'Sociology and Ethnology in Romania: The Avatars of Social Sciences in Socialist Romania', in U. Brunnbauer, C. Kraft and M. S. Wessel (eds), *Sociology and Ethnography in East-Central Europe: Scientific Self-description is State Socialist Countries* (München: Oldenbourg Verlag), pp. 133–46.

Davis, J. A. (2012) *The Olympic Effect: How Sports Marketing Builds Strong Brands* (Singapore: John Wiley and Sons).

Davies, N. (1981) *God's Playground: A History of Poland* (Oxford: Oxford University Press).

Euro to boost economy (2012) 'Poland will use Euro 2012 to boost economy and global image', at: www.insideworldfootball.com/

world-tournaments/european-championship/10286-poland-will-use-euro-2012-to-boost-economy-and-global-image-says-sports-minister, accessed 19 February 2014.

Deloitte (2012) 'Raport: Podsumowanie kosztów i oszacowanie korzyści z organizacji turnieju UEFA EURO 2012', at: www.deloitte.com/view/pl_PL/pl/branze/sport/24b45edccc8db310VgnVCM3000003456f70aRCRD.htm, accessed 19 February 2014.

Demossier, M. (2012) 'What Can Anthropology Bring to the Debate on Identity?', *FREE – Football Research in an Enlarged Europe Working Papers*, at: www.free-project.eu/documents-free/Working%20Papers/Anthropology%20and%20the%20debate%20on%20identity%20%28M%20Demossier%29.pdf, accessed 19 February 2014.

Ferguson, J. (2006) *Global Shadows: Africa in a Neoliberal World Order* (Chapel Hill: Duke University Press).

Geertz, C. (1973) *The Interpretation of Cultures* (New York: Basic Books).

Geertz, C. (1974) '"From the Native's Point of View": On the Nature of Anthropological Understanding', *Bulletin of the American Academy of Arts and Sciences*, Vol. 28, Issue 1, pp. 26–45.

Jackson, A. (1987) (ed.) *Anthropology at Home* (London: Tavistock).

Gusti, D. (1934) *Sociologia militans. Introducere in sociologia politică* (Bucureşti: Editura Institutului Social Român).

Griaule, M. (1957) *Méthode de l'ethnographie* (Paris: Presses Universitaires de France).

Kalb, D. (2009) 'Conversations with the Polish Populist: Tracing Hidden Histories of Globalization, Class, Dispossession in Postsocialism (and Beyond)', *American Ethnologist*, Vol. 36, Issue 2, pp. 207–23.

Kuper, A. (1999) *Culture: The Anthropologists' Account* (Cambridge, MA: Harvard University Press).

Malinowski, B. K. (1922) *Argonauts of the Western Pacific: An Account of Native Enterprise and Adventure in the Archipelagoes of Melanesian New Guinea* (London: Routledge).

Marcus, G. E. (1998) *Ethnography through Thick and Thin* (Princeton: Princeton University Press).

Marcus, G. E. and Fischer, M. J. (1986) *Anthropology as a Cultural Critique: An Experimental Moment in the Human Sciences* (Chicago: Chicago University Press).

Matthews, G., Ribeiro, G. L. and Vega, C. V. (eds) (2012) *Globalization from Below: The World's Other Economy* (London: Routledge).

Ministry of Sport and Tourism (2012) 'The Polish Effect: The Success of Euro 2012 Beyond Expectations', at: http://en.msport.gov.pl/article/the-polish-effect-the-success-of-euro-2012-beyond-expectations, accessed 19 February 2014.

Ouroussoff, A. (2010) *Wall Street at War: The Secret Struggle for the Global Economy* (Cambridge and Malden: Polity Press).

Report 1 (2012) 'Ekonomiczne efekty bezpośrednio związane z turniejem UEFA Euro 2012', Official report by Euro Poznań 2012.

Report 2 (2012) 'Podsumowanie UEFA Euro 2012 w Poznaniu', Official report by Euro Poznań 2012.

Robbins, R. H. (2005) *Global Problems and the Culture of Capitalism* (Boston: Pearson Publishers).

Rosaldo, R. (1986) 'From the Door of His Tent: The Fieldworker and the Inquisitor', in J. Clifford and G. Marcus (eds), *Writing Culture: The Poetics and Politics of Ethnography* (Berkeley: University of California Press), pp. 77–97.

Rottenburg, R. (2000) 'Sitting in a Bar', *Studies in Cultures, Organisations and Societies*, Vol. 6, Issue 1, pp. 87–100.

Schwell, A. (2005) *Anarchie ist die Mutter der Ordnung. Alternativkultur und Tradition in Polen* (Münster: LiT Verlag).

Smith, G. (1999) *Confronting the Present. Towards a Politically Engaged Anthropology* (Oxford and New York: Berg).

Turner, V. W. (1962) 'Three Symbols of *Passage* in Ndembu Circumcision Ritual', in M. Gluckman (ed.), *Essays on Ritual and Social Relations* (Manchester: Manchester University Press), pp. 124–73.

Vincent, J. (2002) 'Introduction', in J. Vincent (ed.), *The Anthropology of Politics: A Reader in Ethnography, Theory and Critique* (London: Blackwell), pp. 1–12.

Wybieralski, M. and Wesołek, M. (2012) 'Co będziesz robić na Euro? Bawić się czy demonstrować?', at: http://poznan.gazeta.pl/poznan/1,36001,115 49440,Co_bedziesz_robic_na_Euro__Bawic_sie_czy_demonstrowac_.html, accessed 19 February 2014.

8
Afterword

Albrecht Sonntag

Ah! Vanitas Vanitatum!
Which of us is happy in this world?
Which of us has his desire? or, having it, is satisfied?

William Makepeace Thackeray,
Vanity Fair, Chapter LXVII

As emerges from the chapters of this volume, the contemporary Vanity Fair of European Football measures up to the complexity and multifariousness of the 19th-century fair described by Thackeray in his great novel: whatever perspective you may adopt in your participant observation, you will inevitably be confronted with 'the strangest contrasts', with 'gentle and pathetic' behaviour patterns, with 'savage and cynical' strategies of action. It is not surprising that the exceptional and excessive character of an event that provides a point of convergence of so many different stakes, claims, interests and concerns is encapsulated and reflected in metaphors. A variety of such metaphors, depending on the respective authors' angles of vision, has been used throughout the book, where Euro 2012 is alternatively referred to as 'football carnival' (Schwell), 'loyalty jungle' (Szogs) or 'festival of consumption' (Buchowski and Kowalska). All these sub-metaphors are encompassed in the big picture of the 'Fair', an event which is the stage for carnivalesque self-exhibition and serious politics, for cheerful entertainment and opportunistic business, for the production of singularity and the consumption of community.

First and foremost, the Vanity Fair of European Football appears as a place of constant negotiation, where narratives and stereotypes are put to the test, where identities and alterities are balanced out in a complex process of selfing and othering, where expectations and interpretations of outcomes are assessed against each other, where loyalties and hostilities are built and rebuilt. There is nothing static, everything is open to change.

A striking characteristic of all these negotiations and re-negotiations is their asymmetry.

Given the host of Euro 2012, the most conspicuous asymmetry is the one between West and East, which is analysed in detail by Alexandra Schwell in her chapter and which continues to be dominated by narratives and strategies of 'Orientalism'. But there are other asymmetric divides or fault lines across Europe, beyond the well-known antagonisms like 'big vs. small', 'North vs. South' or 'rich vs. poor', that are laid bare by such a mass event and that become visible in the different contributions to this volume. Buchowski and Kowalska show, for instance, how the event may provoke asymmetric relations not only between spontaneously formed 'catholic' coalitions (Poles+Irish+Spanish+Croats) and the 'secular' mainstream of 'postmodern' Europe, but also between alternative leftist critique as defended by a minority of vigilant citizens and hegemonic neoliberal ideology as embodied by corporate actors and policy-makers. Szogs provides evidence for the persistence of exclusive nationalism despite the visible dominance of light and actually 'flexible' patriotic loyalties. Alpan and Şenyuva problematise the decreasing asymmetry between 'non-Europeans' and members of the EU as observed in media discourse, while both Nuhrat and Sonntag deal extensively with the particularly asymmetric negotiations between migrant and native communities, including linguistic rites and strategies of inclusion and exclusion.

All these negotiations require mediation, and football, disguised as a simple game and source of pleasure with popular appeal, provides an event where such mediation can take place in a reassuring environment. For it is important to realise that the 'flexibility', 'liquidity' and 'fluidity' of representations and identities are deeply destabilising and unsettling for many. 'Flexibility' may be a term with mostly positive connotations, especially as opposed to 'rigidity' or 'intransigence', but flexibility always comes at the price of effort, physical or mental. As Nina Szogs so appropriately puts it in her chapter, 'it's a loyalty jungle out there', and despite the apparent playfulness and cheerful mood in and around the stadia, identity negotiation is a rather stressful exercise.

It is not an exaggeration to say that the processes of Europeanisation and globalisation have imposed new stresses on individuals and groups in their construction of identities. One of the most stringent and powerful sources of identity – national belonging – has been strongly impacted by the new demand for flexibility. In some social groups this destabilisation by 'liquid modernity' is more visible than in others who seem to remain more firmly anchored in traditional patterns of identification. Is there a better place to study individual and collective reactions to these processes than a football mega-event like Euro 2012? In any case, it is difficult to imagine one. A championship like the Euro or the World Cup not only penetrates society in a manner that hardly any other event does, but also condensates, at one specific moment in time, major issues of identity construction in a period of transition that started towards the end of the 20th century and which seems to be patently open-ended. For a football researcher who has been following very closely over the last twenty years the evolution of what is very aptly named 'the people's game', the difference between the mid-1990s and the second decade of the 21st century is striking. Not only have the size and scope of these events dramatically increased, but so have the stakes of the identity negotiations carried out by the huge mass of people that are concerned by them, in all senses of the word. There is no doubt that there is a causal link between the increasing acuity of these concerns and the ever-increasing scope of international football events. And there is no doubt either that forthcoming football events of European outreach like Euro 2016 in France or Euro 2020 spread across the continent will again provide fertile ground for the observation of how collective identity is constructed in increasing complexity. If the Vanity Fair of European Football did not exist, it would deserve to be invented if only for the sake of the social sciences!

It is certainly a place that William Makepeace Thackeray would have very much appreciated visiting. As the regretful sigh placed as epigram above these concluding remarks clearly shows, he had, behind his sarcastic description of the manifold weaknesses and follies of the human species that he examined like a biologist examines insects under his magnifying glass, a great compassion for their vain pursuits. With such interest for detail, capacity for empathy, and sense of humour, he would most certainly have made an excellent football anthropologist.

Index

Printed and bound by CPI Group (UK) Ltd, Croydon, CR0 4YY